POSTCULTURAL THEORY

Postcultural Theory

Critical Theory after the Marxist Paradigm

Eve Tavor Bannet

PARAGON HOUSE
New York

First U.S. edition, 1993

Published in the United States by
PARAGON HOUSE PUBLISHERS
90 Fifth Avenue
New York, NY 10011

Copyright © 1993 by Eve Tavor Bannet

All rights reserved. No part of this book may be
reproduced, in any form, without written permission from
the publishers, unless by a reviewer who wishes
to quote brief passages.

First published in Great Britain by
THE MACMILLAN PRESS LTD
Houndmills, Basingstoke, Hampshire RG21 2XS
and London
ISBN 0-333-53949-4 hardcover
ISBN 0-333-58456-2 paperback

Library of Congress Cataloging-in-Publication Data
Tavor Bannet, Eve, 1947–
Postcultural theory : critical theory after the Marxist paradigm /
Eve Tavor Bannet. — 1st U.S. ed.
p. cm.
Includes bibliographical references and index.
ISBN 1-55778-611-9 : $41.95. — ISBN 1-55778-612-7 (pbk.) : $15.95
1. Culture. 2. Critical theory. 3. Postmodernism. I. Title.
HM101.T37 1993
306—dc20   92-33910
                                                             CIP

Printed in Hong Kong

In Memory of
Wylie Sypher
Dorothea Krook
Zerubavel Gilead

Contents

Preface		ix
1	**Critical Theory and the Marxist Paradigm**	**1**
	Society as a Whole	5
	The Collective and the Individual	9
	The Literary Text	14
	History: Utopian and Scientific	18
	The Critic and the Party	26
2	**Limits of the Marxist Paradigm**	**29**
	Febvre, Foucault, Greenblatt	35
	The Quest for Likeness	44
3	**The Other Body of Man in Derrida, Levinas, Lacoue-Labarthe, Nancy and Borch-Jakobsen**	**50**
	Man the Producer and the Poet	54
	Man's Spectral Double	59
	Psychology and Psyche-ology	68
	(En)gendering the Law	73
	Double-Speak and Undecidability	80
4	**The Logic of Both/And**	**88**
	Both/And in some Anglo-American Feminisms	90
	Both/And in Irigaray	95
	Theorizing Both/And	100
5	**Factitive Fictions and Possible Worlds**	**113**
	Accessible Worlds	117
	Compossible Worlds	132
	Simulated Worlds	140
	World-Making	151

6	**The Critic as Translator**	**158**
	On Babel and Ivory Towers	158
	Some Questions of Translation	164
	The Other in Translation	172
	Intertranslation	180
	The Times of Translation	189

Notes 195

Bibliography 209

Index 223

Preface

During the late '70s and 1980s – while much of the academy was absorbing and institutionalizing that unstable mixture of poststructuralism, deconstruction, political critique and materialist historicism which is variously known as Cultural Materialism, the New Historicism and Cultural Studies – some people were working up other theories. These other theories take us beyond the boundaries of current Cultural Theory, even as they tackle some of the most intractable questions it has been found to raise. This book is about some of the less familiar theories of the '80s, and about the ways in which they challenge current thinking and open other, affirmative and constructive, possibilities for thought and research in the '90s.

The relative neglect or marginalization in the '80s of French (De)construction, of a far-reaching Feminist Logic common to Anglo-American and French Feminisms, of Possible Worlds Theory and of the radical redefinition of the Critic as Translator, can be attributed to a number of factors. In some cases, recent work is still incompletely translated or not yet translated at all. In some cases, much of the writing has been done in fields which theorists in the humanities are not yet in the habit of following with any degree of attention. In some cases, institutional and ideological factors have clearly been at work. The most avant-garde theorists can sometimes be as unwilling to rethink the premises and approaches in which they are heavily invested as those who *a priori* reject the theoretical project itself. In other cases, one can only suppose that theorists, literary and cultural critics, and historians have been looking the other way, in the mistaken belief that there was nothing there which could have any bearing on what they were doing.

The other theories of the '80s do, however, deserve our attention. Compendious, suggestive, and diverse from one another, they give us different ways of speaking the singularity, agency or spirituality of subjects and the diversity of texts despite, or sometimes within, social subjectivation, education, and immersion in the common languages of collective con-texts. They also give us access to other, more complex and less deterministic, concepts of materiality; to other, non-linear, concepts of historicity; and to a logic which obviates the traditional formal logic, the binary oppositions and the subsuming, exclusionary dialectic which have dominated Western thinking since the Enlightenment.

The other theories of the '80s make breaches in the epistemological impasse which arose from the collapse of traditional distinctions between subject and object, and from the fictionalization of languages and theories which could no longer be said to correspond to any 'objective reality'. They give us other concepts of knowledge and truth or, indicating how fictions can speak the real, they show us how we may approach fictional worlds – past and future – in promising new ways. They also charge us in the academy with other missions and other tongues.

I have been interested in opening possibilities, and have tried to avoid premature closure. Issues recur throughout the book, but there are relatively few repetitions. And apart from the paragraphs you have just read, which are to marketing what invocations once were to poesie, no attempt has been made to reduce the diverse possibilities in different chapters to each other or to subsume them under any single overarching meta-theory. Most of the theories I discuss are still in process. This book participates in the process, and it would be as artificial to fix it by pretending to any last word, as it was to label the more unfamiliar theories discussed in this book 'the other theories of the '80s'. As will become apparent, the temporalities involved are much more complex than that.

I have, on the whole, written *with* the theorists I discuss, both as one writes *with* a pencil, and as one walks *with* the help of an other. One or two exceptions apart, where it seemed necessary to clear a space so that something other could begin to be heard, I have avoided critique, preferring to pass over what I found unhelpful and to build on what seemed to me interesting, important or promising.

No-one writes without, to one extent or another, refashioning the matter they are writing about. As will become evident, my part in the theories I evoke varies considerably from chapter to chapter. In some chapters, it consists largely in the manner of exposition or in the construction of what Milton would have called the Argument. In some chapters, it has fallen to my part to foreground and theorize what others have done without taking note of the pattern in their doings. As Nietzche pointed out, 'deeds require time even after they are done, before they can be seen and heard . . . though they have done it themselves.' And in some chapters, my part consists of weaving the work of others into

Preface

theoretical discourses which are not to be found, as such, in any one.

There has also been interesting new work in the '80s which I have not attempted to touch on. This has not been prompted by any desire to exclude any theory or any group, but is due to a perhaps outdated sense of propriety and to a strong sense of my own limitations. I use the old sexist terms 'man' and 'he' when it seems to me that the theorists I am discussing have either subsumed women under 'Man' or not given them any particular thought. I do this because it seems to me that no useful purpose is served by pretending that there was any real question of women in their work, and that speaking of s/he or humankind oneself in such cases either preempts discussion of whether/how their work also applies to women, or makes it sound as though that question no longer needs to be raised.

I am using the term 'postcultural' in the title of this book to indicate that I am discussing theories which take us beyond the boundaries and limitations of the current paradigm of Cultural Studies, not to suggest that Cultural Studies are, or should be, abandoned. Questions of Cultural Theory recur in different ways throughout this book, and for my part, I think that Cultural Theory can and should be allied to the 'other theories' I discuss. But these other Postcultural theories also prevent Cultural Theory from closing into the premature totalization to which it continues to be prone despite the introduction of plurality and difference. They substantially change the profile, the premises and the roles of Cultural theory, and prevent the culture of a particular time and place from continuing to figure as the all-encompassing, all-determining horizon of our thinking and being. In some respects, the relation of Postcultural theories to Cultural theory therefore resembles that of Poststructuralism to Structuralism.

I have done my own translations when working closely with texts, including in the relatively few cases where translations have already been made, partly because translations inevitably transmit the translator's understanding of the source text and differ accordingly, and partly because the play of meaning in many of the source texts I am using is not readily translatable into any single English version.

I would like to thank Greg Jay, Peter Jaszi, David Miller, Phil Rollinson, Sue Rosser, Andrew Wernick, and Martha Woodmansee for giving me opportunities to present some of the material in this book to colleagues in a variety of disciplines, as well as the participants in those forums for their support and absolutely invaluable feed-back. I am grateful to Art Berman, Philippa Berry, Heshe Epstein, Yael Feldman, Greg Jay, Naphtali Loewenthal, and Sue Rosser for so generously giving me the benefit of their scholarship and advice, and to Richard Ziegfeld for an illuminating conversation in Ohio which set me off on a whole new train of thought. I am extraordinarily indebted to Amitai Aviram not only for his invaluable close readings of different versions of the ms. and for his acute and challenging questions, but also for explaining me to my word processor and it to me. Margaret Cannon, who knows just when to be all there and when to be absent, has been a pleasure to work with. And without Jens Holley, Rhonda Felder and Jo Cottingham at the University library, who indefatigably produced books from every corner of this country and valiantly suppressed their groans at the sight of me, it would have been impossible to write this book.

A version of Chapter 3 appeared in the 1992 issue of *Genders*; sections of Chapters 3 and 4 have been used in an essay in the 1993 issue of *Diacritics*.

As always, I am inexpressibly grateful to my husband, Jacob, for being a special place and making place, and to my vital young sons, Jonathan and Alan, for sharing me with 'that book again'.

1
Critical Theory and the Marxist Paradigm

'The acts of the fathers are a sign to the sons.'

Like the apparent departure from history in poststructuralism, the return to history in recent literary and cultural criticism has been effected within the parameters of the classical marxist problematique. As a result, the most various modes of modern historical and theoretical writing – marxist, *'marxisant'* and non-marxist – represent differences within the perimeters of a single complex field of discourse rather than disparate and unrelated camps. Current 'post-marxist' and post-poststructuralist work is making the perimeters of this field more visible while attempting, with varying degrees of success, to move beyond the frame of reference defined by the founding fathers.

The metaphor of a field with perimeters does not imply that marxist paradigms and assumptions necessarily remain identical throughout their various transformations or that there has been no innovation, no stretching of horizons or change of perspectives. The writings of classical marxism, Prague Structuralism, the *Annales* and post-*Annales* school, Bakhtin, the Frankfurt School, Reader Reception theory, French poststructuralism, American New Historicism and British Cultural Materialism are clearly not all 'the same'.[1] The metaphor of a field implies that there can be considerable change and innumerable local transformations within given parameters, and it implies considerable lability. Despite the Talmudic tendency of marxists to ratify their transformations by attaching them to Marx's biblical texts, even classical Marxism was generated by several generations of reinterpreting marxists. This is nowhere more evident than in matters pertaining to the relationship of literature to history and society where, as a glance back at Peter Demetz's once influential anthology will confirm, Marx' and Engels' observations were sparse, unsystematic, disconnected, sometimes contradictory and often aphoristic. If there is a 'marxist' view of the relationship of literature to history and society, it is due to a variety of others – from party leaders to European intellectuals – who reinterpreted, elaborated and systematized Marx and Engels' scattered observations for their particular times and places, supplementing lacks by drawing on other ideas from other texts and struggling with each other to fashion orthodoxies and counter-orthodoxies.

This process has continued, but in a different idiom and with greater *panache*. *Annales* school historians, Frankfurt School theorists, Poststructuralists, Reader Reception Theorists, New Historicists[2] and Cultural Materialists have reformulated marxist principles and extended them by drawing more and more widely on other ideas from other texts – texts of philosophy, ethnology, anthropology, linguistics, psychoanalysis and religion. They have produced a variety of transformations, inversions, displacements and reformulations, resolving some of the impasses they inherited, and reinscribing others. And they have made marxism perhaps the most imperialistic discursive formation today.[3]

The resemblances among all these schools of criticism and between these and traditional forms of marxist criticism are not always immediately obvious. One reason for this is that we tend to compare and contrast critical schools on the basis of a logic of identity and difference, rather than, as I will be doing here, on the basis of a Wittgensteinian logic of 'family resemblance.' In this logic, all characteristics do not necessarily recur everywhere, and they do not have to recur in completely identical form; instead, each family member shares resemblances, sometimes very general, sometimes very localized, with certain other family members, and resemblances are a matter of similarity rather than of sameness. Another reason for the obscuring of resemblances among critical schools is the modern tendency to market discursive products by advertising their novelty. We are always, it would seem, 'in the new': in the New Criticism, in the *Nouveau Roman*, in the new poststructuralist or deconstructive theory, in the 'new kind of history' of the *Annales* School, in the New Historicism of the California School, in the New Left or the New Right, in the new cultural politics of marxists in Thatcherite or post-Thatcherite Britain, in the new post-marxist cultural criticism, in the new era after an epistemic break. Our modern rhetoric of novelty is as ritualized and misleading as the rhetoric of *'auctoritas'* adopted by scholars until the 18th century, and it ill accords with the concurrent assertion that we are always ineluctably determined by the 'always already.'

The Old and the New, Repetition and Innovation, the Same and the Different are binary oppositions only to a desire moulded by a discursive and institutional economy which rewards originality, scorns repetition and sameness, and promotes its products by emphasizing their difference from yesterday's models. In practice, however, even our most 'seminal' thinkers do not construct their discourses *ex nihilo*; instead they transform materials they find already at hand. Our most novel discourses are always both old and new because they consist of more or less dramatic transformations – reworkings, reformulations, reinterpretations, recombinations or refashionings – of the given, the received, the already spoken and written and done. This is why it is always possible to trace filiations, to footnote sources and to discover predecessors, no matter whose work one is looking at.

In principle, the intertwining of repetition and innovation in texts means that one can enter history 'anywhere'; in practice, it means that one always enters history *in medias res*, without being able to justify the purely narrative assumption that there is a clear-cut before and after, or a straight forward chronological succession on the lines of 'And Hegel's writings begat Marx's writings, and Marx's writings begat Lenin's writings, and Lenin's writings begat . . . ' Texts, movements and practices escape such diachronies by remaining available for transformation well beyond their moment in a chronological sequence and by being reinterpreted and combined with other texts, movements and practices in different ways to suit a variety of local, temporal, political, and ideological circumstances. Texts, movements and practices also escape the logic of linear development insofar as the positions they represent persist or recur in some quarters even after they have been 'superseded' in others. In history, synchronic cuts always open onto non-synchronicities.

To speak of a marxist 'paradigm' of the relations between literature, culture, history and society even in the loose sense which I have been indicating is to start *in medias res* insofar as that paradigm only began to be formulated more or less systematically and in a manner which could be appropriated by Western intellectuals after a number of false starts (Plekhanov, Trotsky, Zhdanov, Lenin, Cauldwell etc.). It was constructed quite late in the marxist day, in the 1930s and 1940s, by transforming 'revisionist' marxists on the basis of what had gone before, both in marxist discourse and outside it. And in the course of the transformations and revisions to which it has since been subjected, many prior and once rejected positions have also been reactivated: for instance, Zhdanovism, once execrated by many for its insistence that socialist literature be used for the 'engineering of souls', reappears in poststructuralism as an insistence that 'writerly texts' can be used to change the discursive and social texts we are reproducing and to fashion a new 'politics of truth'.

Rather than give the marxist paradigm of the relation of literature, culture, society and history an artificial origin and an ineluctable diachronic development, therefore, I am going to show where different positions occurring at different points in the temporal sequence can be viewed as repetitions and variations of the same themes or as attempts to resolve the same difficulties. Although this approach involves 'bracketing' for the moment differences among critics or schools of critics which from other perspectives are unquestionably significant, it does have the advantage of counterbalancing the tendency of each 'school' of critics to underline their difference. And it makes it possible to foreground convergences, consensuses, limitations and questions before going on in other chapters to consider how what I am calling postcultural theories have succeeded both in moving beyond the perimeters of the marxist paradigm, and in imagining different possible questions and different possible answers.

In the marxist paradigm, discourse on literature is grafted *post festum* onto a dense and well developed body of theories about knowledge, culture, society, politics, history, language and 'man'. Discourse on literature has been expected to accord or fit in with these other theories, and it has therefore also changed with changes in them. This makes a certain amount of sense given the paradigm's most fundamental assumption about literature, which is that literature is always intimately interconnected with all that is not itself. But, as will become apparent below, it also means that assumptions about language, knowledge, culture, society, history and man always overdetermine both what literary texts are said to be and do and the sort of interconnections which are posited for them.

Society as a Whole

> In the social production of their life, men enter into definite relations that are indispensable and independent of their will, relations of production which correspond to a definite stage of development of their material productive forces. The sum total of these relations of production constitutes the economic structure of society, the real foundation, on which rises a legal and political superstructure and to which correspond definite forms of social consciousness. (Marx, 1970a: 20)

Passages such as these in Marx do not so much explain the relation of 'forms of consciousness' to 'material productive forces' in society as establish the *problematique*. For they assume an apparent paradox: on the one hand, that everything is interconnected in the social totality, and on the other, that the social totality is divided into a number of disparate strata or structures or spheres. And they leave it to others to determine precisely how these disparate parts may be said to interrelate in the whole.

One solution has been to argue that one part of the social whole is the key to all the others because it in some way makes all the other parts conform to itself. There have been two versions of this argument.

In the first version, (which relies heavily on Marx's metaphor of a multi-storeyed edifice which crumbles when its foundations are shaken), the economic base of a society determines everything else by making everything that is built on it 'correspond' to it in some way. Whether this occurs directly or only 'in the last instance' after complex mediations, and whether the development of different parts of the superstructure is viewed as equal or unequal, parts are interconnected in the whole by correspondences or 'homologies' which can be derived from or related to the material conditions of existence. The more sophisticated versions of this argument – I'm thinking most particularly of the Prague Structuralists, of Lukács, of Goldmann, of Lotman, and to some extent of the early Althusser – emphasize not only correspondences, but also the different internal structures of different superstructural spheres, the possibility of conflicts or contradictions among them, and their distance from the brute facts of material production. Some form of the theory of reflection[4] is generally used to solve the chalk and cheese problem of how the material and the mental can be homogenized, but society is essentially seen as what Althusser, in a last bow to this version of the argument, described as a 'complex structured totality' (Althusser, 1969: 120).[5]

The second version of the argument that one part of the whole is the key to all the others is an inversion of the first. In this version, the superstructure, or some aspect of it, determines everything else by making everything which is subject to it in the social totality 'correspond' to itself. Whether in the guise of some 'form of social consciousness' (a hegemonic ideology, instrumental reason, a particular episteme, logocentrism, social *energeia*) or of some legal or political or administrative structuration (fascism, centralized planning, disciplines), the superstructure imposes conformity on all aspects of social being. And then, once again, we have to do with homologies: between the principle of domination in subjective reason, in positivist science, in neo-Thomism, in social Darwinism and in the demand that individuals adapt to their social environment (Horkheimer, 1974); between the disciplines administered in the prisons, the barracks, the factories and the schools (Foucault, 1979); between Harriot's *Brief and True Report* and Shakespeare's Histories (Greenblatt, 1988); in the logocentrism and metaphysics of presence in the all the diverse texts of Western society (Derrida, 1976c or 1972). This version of the argument could be viewed as an extended commentary on Marx's observation in *The German Ideology* that 'the ideas of those who lack the means of mental production are in general subject to it'.[6]

In both versions of this argument, the whole is viewed as a reified set of relations which operate 'independently of (men's) will', and into which men are forced to enter, whether they will or no. But when hegemonic rule over the whole is displaced from the economic base to the superstructure, the chalk and cheese problem of homogenizing the mental and the material is resolved by denying that there is any real distinction to be made between basis and superstructure and by attributing materiality to mentality.[7] The principle favoured – a particular form of rationality, an ideological principle, a language, a discursive formation, a pattern of discipline – is seen as a 'material productive force'. It produces not only people's thoughts, expectations and identities, but also their everyday lives, social relations, and modes of production, and it makes any aspect of material existence which it cannot govern and appropriate, unthinkable, unspeakable, invisible and therefore non-existent. In this view, a material fact is only a 'fact' by permission of the superstructure.

The other solution to the difficulty of determining how parts interconnect in the social whole is to deny that any single part of society is the key to all the others, and to say that all parts determine each other. This immediately pluralizes and decenters the social totality. It pluralizes and decenters the totality because it means that each part can be determined in several different ways by any or all of the others. It also pluralizes and decenters the totality because it means that the whole need not be reduced to any 'simple formula' (Febvre, 1962: 365) and that parts need not be viewed homologously or 'expressively', as different manifestations of the same central and fundamental principle (Althusser, 1971: 63ff).[8] As in the more sophisticated versions of the base-determines-superstructure argument, differences between parts can be emphasized and so can the discontinuity, heterogeneity and mobility of parts. Indeed, these have to be emphasized to prevent the whole from falling back into the one-principle-is-the-key-to-everything argument, although in practice there is at least a partial return to this argument in the widespread tendency to take everything back to the political. The argument that all parts of society determine each other also makes it possible to deal with the chalk and cheese problem of mental and material production in a different way: by supposing that that these too are mutually determining. 'Material productive forces' now both produce 'social forms of consciousness' and are produced by them in a constant unpredictable motion.

This solution to the problem of how parts interrelate in the social whole shifts attention from the whole to the parts. Despite assertions to the contrary, it does not eliminate 'totality.' Totality no longer presents itself as unity or coherence, but it hides in the premise that it is possible or even meaningful to relate parts to each other. Totality hides as the assumption that everything in language, culture or society is articulated on everything else, however 'differentially' and therefore that one can move among parts and cross 'boundaries' at will. It shows its profile whenever poststructuralists open 'closure' onto an 'outside', whenever post-marxists work with the social as an 'impossible' or 'absent totalizing horizon' (Laclau and Mouffe, 1985) or as an imminent 'communitarian' finitude (Nancy, 1986 or 1982) and, more modestly, whenever critics claim that they are concerned with the entire field of semiotic phenomena.

Moreover, when attention is directed to the parts, the base-superstructure problematique is often reintroduced. The base no longer appears in its 'epochal' form, as a a stage of material production, but in the more local guise of particular social institutions (the family, the school, the culture industry, or whatever);[9] the superstructure no longer takes the form of strata or spheres, but that of specific ideological positions, forms of language, and modes of behaviour; and the task becomes that of showing how particular ideological positions, particular forms of behaviour, particular kinds of language, and particular institutional economies interconnect and interact.

Each of these views of the social totality could be said to predominate in one particular 'school' of critics. For instance, early marxist revisionists like Lukács, Goldmann and the early Althusser could be said to have worked within the base-determines-superstructure form of the argument that one part of the whole is the key to all the others. Poststructuralists could be said to have adopted the superstructure-determines-base form of this argument, while cultural materialists or historians like Darnton can be seen as following some members of the *Annales* School and of the Frankfurt School and the later Althusser in shifting attention from the whole to the parts. But theorists and schools of theorists also sometimes straddle different positions. For instance, while remaining fundamentally within the first model (where the base determines the complex structured totality), Lukács insisted as early as *History and Class Consciousness* that 'facts will only be facts within the framework of a system' and that ideology is a crucial determinant of the course of events (1971: 63). Foucault worked with the second model, where the superstructure determines the base, homologically, while also exploring the local interactions of practice and ideology in partial social institutions. Cultural materialists tend to focus on such local interactions (third model) but they give renewed emphasis to the notion of the economic base (first model) and also sometimes use, the superstructure determines base argument (second model).[10] And New Historicists posit 'the model of a dynamic, unstable and reciprocal relation between the discursive and material domains' (third model) (Montrose, 1989: 23), while concentrating largely on the 'linkages' between parts of the superstructure and on the way the superstructure produces practices (second model).

Such overlaps could be explained as an indication of the movement and development of theoretical thinking this century, as a

Critical Theory and the Marxist Paradigm

demonstration that theoretical texts are no longer bound by the logic of unity and non-contradiction, or, as Alvin Gouldner has suggested in *The Two Marxisms*, as elaborations of contradictory features in Marx's own texts. But however the matter is explained, it must be said that none of these three pre-comprehensions of the social totality has been entirely 'superseded' and that none of them has absolute ascendancy.

The Collective and the Individual

Despite much muddying of the waters by recent 'anti-humanists' anxious to distinguish themselves from social democrats and 'Marxist humanists', humanism is not to be equated with individualism. Humanism is an anti-theological, anti-metaphysical position which holds that 'the proper business of mankind is man' in this world, whereas individualism is a doctrine asserting the autonomy, independence, and often the uniqueness, of persons acting according to their own proper reason, volition or interests. Liberalism in the 19th and 20th centuries conflated humanism and individualism by arguing that the proper business of mankind is to foster the development and independence of self-regulating individuals. Marxist humanism countered this by conflating the human with the social. Like Renaissance humanism, it deindividualized 'man' by conceiving him as a genus possessing features which can also be predicated of other kinds or classes of things. As Marx observes in the 6th Thesis on Feuerbach: 'the essence of man is not an abstraction inherent in each particular individual. The real nature of man is the totality of social relations.'

In the 'humanist' marxist paradigm, then, 'man' is defined by features predicated of society: he 'is' what social existence, social relations, social consciousness, social knowledge, social language and socialized senses make him. As a 'social being', the individual is little more than a determinate particular embodiment of collective life and consciousness; his ideas, desires, interests and experiences are never properly or exclusively his own, but always held in common with others. And because 'men make their world' not immediately and as individuals, but collectively and in the last analysis, the social world always appears to have 'an independent existence *vis-à-vis* the individual' and to operate as 'an objective power above [him], growing out of [his] control, thwarting

[his] expectations and bringing [his] calculations to naught' (Marx, 1970b: 54).

Despite changes in terminology, there is no discontinuity between 'Marxist humanists' and anti-humanists with respect to the conflation of man and society or with respect to the position of individuals within the social system. For anti-humanists too, human subjects are what society has made them; they are subject to subjectivating forces which are outside their control and defined by the subject-positions available at a particular time. The difference between Marxist humanists and anti-humanists lies only in their *evaluation* of what Marx in *Kapital* calls 'socialized mankind'. For Marxist humanists, the realization that people always share their 'nature' their ideas, their reasons, their interests, and their forms of life with others and that they are, collectively and despite all appearances, participants in the production of social life, is liberating, empowering and disalienating. For anti-humanists, the same realization is appalling: to be socialized, to have the same mode of subjectivation, the same ideas, the same form of reason, the same mode of existence as others is to be programmed, spoken, subjected and forced to conform; it is the ultimate alienation. And to participate in the production of social life is merely to reproduce that which makes individuals the same. One might say, somewhat paradoxically perhaps, that in their evaluation of human sociality, anti-humanists implicitly and inadvertently fall back into the individualist conviction that each person is or should be self-determining and different from others – a conviction attacked and excluded by Marxist humanists, in the belief that people's true happiness lies in living, consciously and to the full, the sociality and communality which defines their essential nature.[11]

Setting aside this difference in evaluation, however, both 'Marxist humanists' and anti-humanists operate within the paradigmatic marxist premise that 'the individual is a social being' and that thinking and research must therefore be directed to demonstrating the ways in which, to borrow Lacan's words, 'the collective and the individual are the same thing'. Where the liberal individualist paradigm led researchers to display the self-determining uniqueness and originality of isolated and individualized figures ('great' writers, statesmen, philosophers, scientists, or whatever), the marxist paradigm led structuralists, poststructuralists, orthodox marxists, revisionist marxists, reader reception theorists, cultural materialists, anthropologists and New Historicists to seek the collective factor (the ideology, the cultural pattern, the unconscious structure, the narrative, the langue, the horizon of expectations, the interpretative community, the 'collective representations', the 'cognitive mapping' or whatever)[12] which defines, delimits and determines individual performance. Where the liberal individualist paradigm all but excluded the social and collective moment as extrinsic or peripheral to innovative individual achievement, the marxist paradigm all but excluded individual self-determination, innovation or difference from human achievement. If to be human is to be socialized, if people are essentially what social existence, social consciousness or unconsciousness, social knowledge, social language and social disciplines have made them, how can anyone be self-determining, innovative or different? How can anyone speak or think or want or imagine or work for anything new or other?

This difficulty has haunted the marxist problematique, both politically and philosophically, throughout this century, and it has produced a variety of suggested solutions – from Lenin's conception of the role of the Party and Rosa Luxemburg's 'voluntarism' to structuralist notions of individuality as systemic mutation, Bakhtinian notions of dialogy, Frankfurt School or poststructuralist definitions of individual difference as spaces of negation or non-being, and post-marxist theories of antagonism. But none of these suggested solutions has gone back to radically question the paradigmatic marxist conflation of the human with the social or the definition of man, generically and individually, as a completely socialized being.

The difficulty is displaced but not substantially altered by the coexistence in the marxist paradigm of two opposite scenarios of collective socialization. In one scenario, which can be described as monist or homogeneous, ideas and practices representing the ruling interests and justifying the ruling political forms dominate and socialize everyone in society. As Marx said in *The German Ideology*, 'the ideas of those who lack the means of mental production are, in general, subject to it' (1970b: 64). Here the dominant class (or classes) regulate the production and distribution of ideas, give them a form of universality, and subject everyone else to them. In the other scenario, which can be described as pluralist or heterogeneous, there are different class ideologies corresponding to the different positions of different classes in the division of labour and to their different shares in the collective cake: here socialization is a class matter, and if one happens to belong to a class 'excluded from society' and from its full share in the collective cake, one is, like other members of one's class, more or less 'forced into the most resolute opposition to all other classes' (Marx, 1970b: 39).

These two scenarios have remained constant in the marxist paradigm, despite changes in the language and in the actants. For instance, the position of domination in the monist scenario has been variously occupied by the aristocracy, the bourgeoisie, the proletariat, the bureaucracy, the technocracy, intellectuals, the West, the symbolic order, and the 'system'; similarly, the proletariat, the sub-proletariat, intellectuals, women, gays, racial minorities, the Third World, and the populace with its 'carnivalesque' culture have all figured as classes socialized into opposition.

The monist and pluralist scenarios function in the marxist paradigm like the wave and particle theories of light in modern science: although incompatible, each has its uses, and it is possible to move between them and to apply them 'strategically' as required. The monist scenario makes it possible, for instance, to describe hegemonies and forms of constraint, to seek homologies, to argue (like Zhdanovism) that the proletariat must use the production and distribution of ideas for the 'engineering' of souls, to explain that advanced capitalism does use the production and distribution of ideas for the 'engineering of souls', and to discover systems of constraint and modes of social engineering in past periods. The pluralist scenario, meanwhile, makes it possible to foreground social conflict, to ground the possibility or the necessity of revolution, to explain the possibility of counter-hegemonic groups or sub-cultures, to insist on the difference, heterogeneity, 'herterogeneity', incommensurability and heteroglossia of different parts of the collectivity, and to focus study on the different cultures and modes of subjectivation in different groups or on areas of resistance and disaffection in the past. But in both scenarios, the individual continues to be defined by the – larger or smaller – collectivity to which he or she is said to belong. And even when the divisions in society are multiplied and the principle of heterogeneity is extended – when classes are replaced by groupings and sub-groupings and individuals are said to belong simultaneously to a plurality of groupings or to occupy several subject-positions at the same time – the subsumption of the individual under the social lives on in the characterization of individuals as discontinuous or contradictory *combinatoires* of elements of what is 'always already' present in society.[13]

Well, what exactly has society made of man? The marxist paradigm again offers two possible models, one monist and the other more plural. Generalizing monistically from the perceived role of proletarians in capitalist society, the first model presents man as a producer. The primary function of socialized man is and has always been production – production first and foremost of the material means of subsistence, but production also of tools and instruments, of knowledge and ideas, of social and political forms, and of himself. In this model, 'religion, the family, the State, law, morality, science, art etc. are only *particular* forms of production', and while the division of labour may have separated 'mental production' from 'material production' it did not change the fundamentally productive character of all genuine human activity. In a just society, everyone would be what Marx calls 'a direct producer'; in unjust societies, there are unproductive groups, who live on the direct production of others. It is worth remembering that intellectuals were condemned as unproductive until Lukács, Althusser and Foucault rehabilitated them by stressing the parallels between material and intellectual production and the materially productive effects of knowledge. More recently, Gayatri Spivak has endeavoured to dignify childbearing in the same way, by describing it as production in the 'workshop of the womb'.[14] And the author, who died when he was completely displaced by the collectivity, lives on as a producer.

The second more pluralist model, which again generalizes from a perception of the proletariat in capitalist society, presents man as a being who is always alienated from his real self and forced to be other than he is. Alienated from the product of his labour, from other men, from his objectified and reified social world and from himself, and treated as little more than a commodity among competing commodities, man is fragmented and split off from his human truth and essence. Objectified in work which produces property for others in a world which confronts the individual as an autonomous power, man's human essence can only appear 'as a *loss* and as *servitude to the object*'. Poststructuralism and deconstruction reformulated alienation – speaking of it as as a profound split or division within the subject, as the death or loss of the self, as a decentering and pluralizing of man, or as the development in which man became an object to himself and to others. They also frequently revalorized alienation by making the subject's fragmentation and otherness from the other the conditions for difference, freedom and play (see Bannet, 1989). And in so doing, they renewed alienation's conceptual power, and gave it a further lease of life.

The Literary Text

> Economic and cultural relations – conception of the world – Form (in the artist as an *a priori* of creation) – Life as Formed – Public (here again the causal sequence: conception of the world – economic and cultural relations) . . . (Lukács, 1970: 74)

As this early formulation of the schema suggests, the marxist paradigm places literary texts in a network of relations: relations to conceptions of the world or ideologies or patterns of thought as they manifest themselves in other disciplines, in other texts and in other spheres of culture and society; relations to the economic and cultural circumstances in society; relations to the literary forms already in existence; relations to a Public, which is always conceived as reading the text from the standpoint of a particular conception of the world in particular economic and cultural circumstances. The text never exists 'in itself', in a vacuum.

Different critics and schools have emphasized different relations. For instance, structuralists have emphasized the relation to *a priori* forms, while Reader Reception Theorists have emphasized the relation to a Public or to a succession of Publics, each of which reads the text with its own conception of the world, 'horizon of expectations' or 'interpretative' mind-set. Poststructuralists, Deconstructionists and New Historicists have emphasized the relation to other texts in other disciplines or spheres of culture, and cultural materialists the relation to the economic and cultural circumstances of production and reception. Different critics and schools have also conceived of the conduit or vehicle of relation in different terms. They have sought what Derrida called 'corridors of meaning' (1981b: 95) either in ideology, or in *Gestalten,* or in language. But the principle of relation, the principle of articulating the 'inside' of literary texts onto one or more 'outsides', has remained a paradigmatic constant.

The principle of relating literary texts to what is 'outside' them is consistent with the paradigmatic assumptions that everything in the social totality is interrelated, and that the focus of research must be the collective determinants of individual performance. At the same time, it opens literary texts onto issues and concerns which are not merely 'literary' or 'aesthetic' in the conventional 19th and early 20th century sense. Even when autonomy and difference from other aspects of culture were still considered by marxists to be 'an irrevocable aspect of art', the assumption that 'art is defined by its relation to what is different from art' (Adorno, 1984a: 1, 4) led critics working within the marxist paradigm to cross disciplinary boundaries and to explore literary texts as instances of wider philosophical, ideological, social, historical, political and economic problems. From this point of view, the poststructuralist emphasis on 'intertextuality' has only foregrounded the paradigmatic marxist emphasis on interrelation and on literature's complicity with wider social, philosophical, ideological and political issues by erasing the moment of autonomy and difference retained by their marxist predecessors. Recently, Stephen Greenblatt has sought to restore the moment of autonomy and difference by suggesting that we might think in terms of an 'oscillation' between 'the establishment of distinct discursive domains' and 'the collapse of these domains into one another' (1989: 8).

In the marxist paradigm, there have been two basic models for describing the articulations of literary texts onto their 'outside'. In the first model, the literary text is treated as a more or less coherent and consistent demonstration or embodiment of a structure or Idea. The literary text's structure or Idea is then related directly, by a principle of 'reflection', or 'homology', or 'reproduction' or 'repetition', to structures or ideologies 'outside' the text. This 'outside' can be represented by a class, a group, an audience, by a particular mental, social or political configuration, by other texts, by some *a priori* narrative form, or whatever. More sophisticated versions of this model indicate differences as well as recurrences, and often try to explain them.

In the second model, the literary text is conceived as inconsistent and self-contradictory; it is always 'doing it without knowing it' or demonstrating something inadvertently and 'unconsciously'. For instance, despite itself and all unknowingly, 'critical realism' always brings out the contradictions of bourgeois life and ideology (Lukács, 1964); the ideological consciousness of literary texts secretes the presentiment of a utopian 'not-yet-conscious' (Bloch, 1988); great, critical modernist texts always demonstrate the impossibility of their own formal and ideological coherence (Adorno, 1984a); texts unconsciously 'stage' the limits of knowledge or ideology (Barthes (1982), Machery (1978), Balibar and Machery (1981), Eagleton (1986)); they deconstruct their own argument (Derrida (1976c), De Man (1983)).[15] Inconsistent and self-contradictory texts point in different directions; they oppose social norms or extant ideologies as well as reproduce them, differ from the 'always already' as well as repeat it. Inconsistency and self-contradiction fragment texts and allow them to relate in different ways to diverse aspects of what is 'outside' them.

These two models have never been completely distinct, and they have often been used together. For instance, what was once castigated as 'vulgar marxism' treated literary texts as direct expressions or reflections or re-presentations of a class ideology; but it also made it the critic's business to explain the contradictions and inconsistencies in this ideology, and its blindness to the real laws of history. More sophisticated revisionist marxists reversed this: they treated literary texts (or at least those they wished to preserve) as a contradictory mixture of blindness and insight, and made it the critic's business to explain the ways in which such texts 'really' reflected or reproduced class ideology and the economic and cultural circumstances of society or 'really' heralded utopia. In Horkheimer, Adorno and the Frankfurt School, more or less direct re-presentation of socially anchored ideological positions became the mark of texts produced by the culture industry, while contradiction, discontinuity, 'extreme inconsistency' and the simultaneous positing and negating of meanings became the mark of 'great' critical modern art.

Poststructuralism and deconstruction have, by and large worked with a similar division. They have tended to use the first model to establish conformities and to describe textual iterations of what Adorno called 'the modern world of total thraldom', and the second model to explore textual excursuses into opposition, critique, or utopia. But they have been more ambivalent than vulgar marxism or earlier revisionism about the locus of contradiction and inconsistency, suggesting both that literary texts simultaneously posit and negate established meanings and that this phenomenon is a function of their own 'writerly' operations on the text. Adorno, Febvre, poststructuralism and deconstruction, have also revaluated the second model's description of texts. Where traditional marxism saw the contradictions and inconsistency supposed by the second model as characteristic features of bourgeois ideology and as inevitable symptoms of the evils of capitalist society, Adorno, Febvre, poststructuralism and deconstruction have elaborated them as intimations of a pluralistic social ideal. The New Historicism has tended to regard inconsistency, self-contradiction and fragmentation as properties of all texts; but by using 'thick description' to reveal the codes or motive forces 'controlling the whole society', it has tended to fall back into homological applications of the first model. Although the ways in which literary texts are approached in the marxist paradigm have changed less than is generally supposed, there has been a marked extension of what is treated as a literary text. Since semiology and poststructuralism, all the texts of culture – whatever position they once occupied on the fact/fiction, high culture/low culture, academic/non-academic or disciplinary divides – and indeed all non-verbal semiological phenomena, are put in the paradigmatic place of the literary text and approached with the same methods and the same assumptions. Poststructuralist, postmarxist and New Historicist 'cultural critique' can be described as an application of marxist methods of literary criticism to a vastly expanded field of 'literature' where everything becomes 'text'.

Following Althusser, this change could be explained as marking a recognition that Marx himself used the same methods in approaching all texts, whether they were texts of political economy, texts of philosophy or texts of literature. Alternatively, the change could be explained as a break with conventional 'aesthetic' delimitations of 'literature', and as a return to what Raymond Williams has shown to be the word literature's pre-eighteenth century meaning, namely 'everything printed' (1977: ch. III).

But however it is explained, the positioning of all texts in the paradigmatic position of the literary text has been accompanied by the acquisition by all texts of negative features traditionally associated exclusively with the signifier 'literary'. Once in the paradigmatic position of the literary text, all social and cultural texts become constructions, fictions, artifices, narratives. All social and cultural texts are seen as deceptive, lying, and not real. All social and cultural texts are thought capable of making us suspend disbelief and of operating on us powerfully and to dangerous effect. And one of the tasks of the critic becomes the traditional, Platonic, Neo-Platonic and Christian task of warning us against literature's pernicious effects.

The text's relations to its 'outside' have also shifted with shifts in the marxist paradigm from a base-determines-superstructure model to the superstructure-creates-base or interactive models, and with corresponding shifts from 'scientific' to 'utopian' perceptions of history (see below). The former shift has led to increasing emphasis on the social functions and effects of literature – on literature's ability to create or fashion the social, political, ideological and material order

– while the latter shift has turned attention away from the text's relation to a past configuration in favour of its relation to a putative future configuration of social phenomena.

History: Utopian and Scientific

In the marxist paradigm, the whole of history is understood – and judged – in light of a projected future: proletarian revolution leading to a classless society. This future authorizes a particular reading of the past: the dominant class in each social order has, in time, been overthrown by the struggles of the class or classes it oppressed. But at the same time, read in this way, the past also demonstrates why the future must take its projected form: revolution against class domination has been the 'driving force of history', dominant classes have repeatedly been overthrown, and since this cannot end until class domination has been abolished, the goal of history must be revolution leading to a classless society. In this paradigm, therefore, the future explains the past, and the past, the future – or, to put it another way, that which is not shapes what has been, while what has been shows its lack, and indeed its need, of what is not. The present, meanwhile, figures as a threshold between the old and the new: it represents the *terminus ad quem* and the – promoted or retarded – possibility of overthrowing the past and ushering in the future.

For Marx, 'the truth, i.e. the reality and power, the "this-sidedness" of thinking' is 'proved' in practice (Second Thesis on Feuerbach). The question of whether thinking about history is true or not is settled in a perfectly practical way by events, so that events can also change the status of the thinking. As Marx points out in *The Poverty of Philosophy*, socialist 'theorists remain Utopians who improvize systems to remedy the distress of the oppressed classes' and who seek a 'regenerative science' in 'their own minds' until the moment that political, social and material conditions are ripe for the revolutionary constitution of a new society and things begin to happen before their eyes; but from that moment, their science 'has ceased to be doctrinaire and has become revolutionary' (Marx, 1971: 125). Whether socialist thinking about history is scientific or utopian, doctrinaire or revolutionary is determined in practice, and sometimes retroactively, by events.

In the course of this century, socialism's regenerative historical paradigm has changed its status several times. For many, events like the making of the Russian Revolution and the fantastic subsequent dogmatism of the Communist Party changed the status of the Marxist 'science' of history from 'doctrinaire' to 'revolutionary' and back to 'doctrinaire'; while unexpected developments like Western Capitalism's accomodation of Worker demands (in the Welfare State, for example) and the proletariat's choice of fascism or trade unionism over communism, changed the status of orthodox historical materialism from a this-sided practice to a utopian fiction. Alluding to Marx's famous statement that the point of philosophy is not to *interpret* the world but to *change* it, Adorno observed in his introduction to *Negative Dialectics* that, having missed its opportunity to change the world by realizing itself, philosophy survived what was supposed to be its 'end' by thinking its inability to comprehend reality in a positive conceptual totality and by valorizing (*beteuern*) negativity, otherness and non-identity with the real (Adorno, 1984b: 15). It was the failure of historical materialism, of the positive dialectic and of the supposedly 'scientific' laws of Marxist history to 'prove' their truth, reality and 'this-sidedness' in practice which forced those who nevertheless clung to marxist hopes to resort to a negative dialectic, to the valorization of that which is not, and to the assumption that all connective and causal accounts of history must (like orthodox historical materialism) prove to be fictions.

The marxist paradigm of history was not therefore abandoned. Instead, its status was changed from scientific to utopian, and some of its details were modified.

For instance, the adherence of large sections of the proletariat first to fascism and then to trade union 'reformism' and the oppositional politics of 'marginal' groups like students, women, gays and racial minorities suggested to poststructuralists and post-marxists that revolution is more likely to come from a variety of marginalized groups, cumulatively or in some sort of democratic hegemonic articulation, than from the proletariat as such. Instead of championing the proletariat, therefore, they have championed 'margins' and marginals. Or, to take another example, for many revisionists, Fascist and Communist totalitarianism and Gaullist *dirigisme* discredited Marx's sketchy vision of the classless society. As Lenin points out, Marx was a 'centralist', who relied on 'planning' to equalize economic and social relations in the classless society (Lenin, 1961: 142). But totalitarianism and *dirigisme* showed that, in practice, centralized planning is more likely to impose repressive conformities and to produce a dictator or a new dominant class of bureaucrats, or technocrats or Party officials, than to lead to the classless society. And communist and non-communist forms of 'state capitalism' discredited the notion that state ownership of the means of production is the key to liberty and social equality. *Annales* School historians, poststructuralists and post-marxists therefore came to envision the classless society in less economic and in more decentered, plural, differential, and political terms. Finally, the failure of revolutions this century either to materialize, or when they did, to lead to a really new and classless society, discredited the idea that a classless society is the end to which all history has, objectively and by virtue of its own inner dynamics, been moving.

But displaced from the level of events, deprived of its historical inevitability and reformulated as 'desirevolution' (Lyotard, 1973: 30), as utopia, as ideal, or as absence and lack, the classless society remains the goal of much theoretical and historical work. From this point of view, there is little difference between Lukács' observation (after Stalinism and the suppression of the Hungarian uprising) that socialism had become 'a mere abstraction, a mere ideal' for which he and a few other isolated individuals had to continue to work and hope (1971b: 652) and Ernesto Laclau and Chantal Mouffe's more recent assertion that the classless society (envisioned as a 'radical and plural democracy') remains the necessary horizon of left-wing thought and action because 'without "utopia", without the possibility of negating an order beyond the point that we are able to threaten it, there is no possibility at all of constituting a radical imaginary' (1985: 190).

As desire, as ideal, as utopia, as a radical imaginary, as lack, or as something 'other' than presence, and with its new indeterminate, plural, decentered, and differential structure, the classless society remains in place in the marxist paradigm of history. It continues to mark the position from which the past is read and judged, while the past continues to explain the need for such a goal. As a preached rather than as a promised future, and as a utopian social imaginary rather than as the end of history, the classless society continues to authorize particular readings of the past and to act, explicitly or implicitly, as the standard by which all past and present societies are judged and found wanting. It also continues to turn its exposition of the past into a justification of its now plural, decentered and differential ideals by critically unmasking and discrediting in the past and the present all modes of economic, political, social and ideological organization that fail to accord with it, and often by projecting its own structures into the past so that all texts and all societies become sites of plural, decentered and differential forces. In preserving the classless society as ideal, as lack, or as desire, the marxist paradigm overtly pays the price Marx warned socialist theorists about: its account of the past becomes an 'improvised system', a fiction divorced from confirmation by events. Historical analysis comes to depend for its 'truth' on what is not. It comes to derive its persuasive force from the moral conviction that it is necessary to 'remedy the distress of the oppressed classes' or from what Cary Nelson and Lawrence Grossberg have described as 'something like a commitment to revolutionary identification with the cause of the oppressed' (1988: 12). And historical narrative returns to its pre-nineteenth century moralizing or 'exemplar' mode, where the function of the past is primarily to teach the present practical lessons for the future. In this context, denials that words reflect reality and assertions that historical discourse is always fictional need to be read in the first instance as a recognition of the fictional and 'Utopian' status of theorists' own improvized regenerative systems in a world where events constantly disprove the truth, the reality and the 'this-sidedness' of regenerative thinking.

While the status of marxism's regenerative model of history has shifted from 'scientific' to 'utopian' the paradigmatic link between past and future, between was and is not, has remained intact. Other elements of the paradigm have remained constant too. For instance, certain issues continue to be foregrounded – like the thematics of economic, political or ideological domination and oppression. Post-marxism's innovation here has been to extend the thematics of domination to earlier marxisms, and to show that they too have not been exempt.[16] Similarly, certain structures continue to be priviledged – structures of conflict, contradiction, relation and homology, for instance. The value of the present continues to lie in its efforts to promote, rather than retard, a certain vision of the future. And there is a continuing tendency to attribute the 'power of knowledge' to what Milton would have called the historical 'argument' – whether the power of knowledge is conceived positivistically and 'scientifically' as the power to penetrate reality, or poststructurally as the power to create it.

Because in the marxist paradigm, a certain vision of society and culture is marked as 'right' – either in the sense that it is 'truly' going to happen, or in the sense that it morally ought to happen or both – all other visions of the world, of its mode of functioning and of its necessary or desirable course are marked as wrong. Everything is 'false consciousness' which does not promote or help to realize that vision of social justice which is either 'on the agenda of world history' or ought to be. And the task of historical discourse in the present becomes that of working for the future by exposing (that is to say, 'critiquing' 'unmasking' 'demythologizing' or 'deconstructing') and correcting the false consciousness of all past conceptions of world, ideologies, or discursive structures. In this context, the idea that everyone not party to the regenerative argument of the moment is trapped or blinded or spoken or bounded by a class consciousness, an ideology, a language, a world view, or a narrative which governs what can be known and understood and said in a particular class or culture at a particular time serves to legitimate the marxist paradigm. It explains why the logic of the marxist paradigm has not proved more universally self-evident, and justifies the subordination and colonization of all past discourse by the superior – critical (unmasking, demythologizing, deconstructive) and corrective – discourse derived from that paradigm.

At the same time, it is clear that once all past world views, ideologies, discursive structures, languages and modes of thought are marked as false, as blinkered, as inadequate or as lacking, and once the task of historical writing is conceived as that of demonstrating the inadequacies, lacunae, and falsity of all previous discursive and social formations, the past is precluded from figuring, positively, as an unsubordinated 'other'. It cannot, for instance, be explored 'in its own terms' or as a reservoir of alternative possibilities of being or of knowing. Nor can it be conceived as a marker in language and thought for what has come to be forgotten and what has fallen into disuetude, or allowed to challenge and show up the inadequacies and lacunae in the historical paradigm brought to it. This is not to say that no historian working within the marxist paradigm has had anything positive to say about the past – Lukács, Bakhtin, Bloch, Febvre, Horkheimer, Adorno, and the early Williams, for instance, often use the past as an alternative locus for important aspects of their utopian social ideals. But displacement of the ideal to the past is only another form of subordination and colonization of the past, another form of substitution of one's own problematique for that of an other, another way of using present discourse to operate on the past for the sake of the future.

Of course, not all historians working within the marxist paradigm are trying to promote marxist or post-marxists social ideals. Many New Historicists, for instance, have appropriated themes and structures from the marxist paradigm, as well as assumptions about the 'false consciousness' of historical texts, about the inevitably distorting character of ideological positions, and about the critical and corrective function of historical discourse in the present, while pursuing what can only be described as a conservative politics. But it is not fortuitous that 'true' reconstruction of the past has come to seem increasingly impossible as the utopian displacement of the marxist paradigm of history has come to be more and more widely accepted, by New Historicists and others, as a framework for discourse.[17]

Reconstruction of the past as such, without more or less direct subordination of the past to present concerns and future goals, was never the prime objective of Marxism's historical problematique, even in its 'scientific' mode. As Maurice Cornforth once put it, 'If historical materialism makes history into a science, this is because it is not only a theory about how to interpret history but also a theory about how to make history, and therefore the basis for the practical policy of the revolutionary class which is making history today' (1954: 9). True 'scientific' knowledge of the past was nevertheless thought to be possible because the truth of the marxist paradigm itself was thought to guarantee the truth of its interpretation of the past. In its utopian mode, the paradigm loses this claim to truth, while retaining the *a priori* marking of all past self-representations and all past discourses about the past as false consciousness. In these circumstances, 'true' reconstruction of any kind obviously becomes impossible. All discourses, whether in the past or about it, become equally inadequate as representations of what 'really' occurred; they become equally fictional. But they do so by virtue of the paradigm in use, and as a judgement by its operatives of what that paradigm can yield in the way of 'real' knowledge of the past.

At the same time, loss of truth about the past can be considered a minor inconvenience as long as it can be argued that the marxist paradigm of history retains its principal function, which is to be 'a theory about how to make history and therefore the basis for the practical policy of the revolutionary class which is making history today'. In its utopian version, therefore, the marxist paradigm of history legitimizes itself as a theory about how to make history, rather than as a theory about how to know it. Arguing that words create reality and that discourse is practice, it claims attention as an 'intervention' in history, rather than as a representation of it.

Many of those who have espoused the utopian version of the marxist paradigm of history and the negative dialectic have seen themselves as a new, left opposition to the doctrinaire dogmatism of the Communist Party. But, curiously, despite this stance of opposition and difference, their utopian version of the marxist paradigm has reproduced the same 'breach' between policy and reality, between words and facts, which Mikhail Gorbachev has described as one of the major political and theoretical failings of the Communist Party after Lenin (1987: 22, 76). For both poststructuralism and the Communist Party after Lenin, there is nothing in reality but saying makes it so.

Recently, there were signs of a revification of the 'scientific' version of the marxist paradigm of history. Mikhail Gorbachev insisted that 'what we need is not "pure", doctrinaire, invented socialism, but real Leninist socialism' and that 'historical science must undergo a major revision' (1987: 96, 49). The marxist paradigm of history as he described it was to be revised in the direction of greater 'openness'. For instance, it was to play down its own exclusive claim to truth: 'We do not claim to be the only ones to know the truth. Truth is sought in a joint quest and effort'; 'New tasks have to be tackled with no ready made answers'; 'we have no ready-made formulas' (Gorbachev, 1987: 167, 49, 65). The marxist paradigm as Gorbachev described it also posits the possibility that there may be something to be learned from others: 'Even the most extreme viewpoint contains something valuable and rational, for the person who upholds it honestly . . . in his own way reflects some real aspect of life'; 'there are no hints, recommendations and warnings that are more valuable than those you get straight from the people' (1987: 82, 73). And it insists on the value of constructive, as opposed to de(con)structive critique: 'relations between those who criticize and those who are criticized . . . should be relations of partnership based on mutual interests' (Gorbachev, 1987: 78).

Post-marxists too have begun to take the 'real' more seriously again, both as an Other which escapes domination and domestication and as something which can be known. They argue that the 'object' is 'to always reproduce the concrete in thought' and 'to give a better theorized account of historical reality' (Hall, 1988: 69, 65) and that 'we need systematically to understand' before we can hope to change (Mackinnon, 1988: 76). Postmarxist historians like Chartier argue that the emplotment of historical narratives is not a mark of fictionality and untruth, but 'a way of focussing on the possible intelligibility of historical phenomena . . . by means of intersecting traces that are still accessible to us' (1988: 45).[18] Postmarxists have also followed Gorbachev in insisting that 'there are no recipes' (Mouffe, 1988: 104) and in denying that everyone but themselves is or has always been in a state of 'false consciousness'. They now argue that it is necessary to try to work with the ideas, desires and needs really expressed by people, to 'look at what is happening "below"' and to 'learn to listen to this often silent speech enclosed within the urgency of survival' (Pecheux, 1988: 645). If this line is continued, we may well soon find ourselves insisting again that the ideologies, languages, narratives and mind-sets which we inhabit are not ineluctably condemned to behaving like Pater's 'thick walls through which no voice from the external world can ever penetrate', and that it is possible after all to hear voices from the past telling us valuable and rational things, and shedding light on some aspect of life.

But despite its greater openness, this most recent version of the marxist paradigm of history leaves revolution leading to the classless society in place as the goal of theory and practice, and the position from which history is understood and judged. *Perestroika* is another name for revolution leading to the classless society: it is a 'revolutionary restructuring' within and among nations to permit the equal, democratic and dynamic participation of 'diverse and variegated' groups, classes and nations in decision-making. Borrowing heavily from Euro-Communism and from the New Left's emphasis on plurality and *autogestion*, *perestroika* conceives of the classless society and the classless world as allowing for diversity and difference, and as involving collective 'self-government by the people' with 'control from below' while achieving a just 'balance of interests' among competing groups or nations who recognize their interdependence and cooperate for physical, ecological and economic survival.[19] Like earlier versions of the marxist paradigm, too, this newest version of the paradigm emphasizes the importance of taking practical measures in the present to 'make history' and to achieve these goals.

At the time of writing, the ontological status of this latest version of the marxist paradigm of history remains uncertain. Responding to the people's call for something other than marxism-leninism, Gorbachev told the Party's Central Committee that: 'We face the need for deep-rooted changes in our entire understanding of socialism. We are not going to find the answers to our questions within the framework of the old model.'[20] It remains undecidable at this time precisely which old model he meant.

The Critic and the Party

The Leninist Party was conceived as having a double task: on the one hand, it was to express the concerns, represent the interests and advance the cause of the proletariat; but on the other hand, it was to 'educate' the workers and lead them towards revolution by bringing them the revolutionary 'social democratic consciousness' they lacked 'from outside' (Lenin, 1971: 29).

This double task was early translated into a program for marxist 'critical philosophy'. In a book which exercised enormous influence, especially in France, Lukács, for instance, argued both that marxist theory was characterized by its ability to view everything in history and society from 'the vantage point' of the proletariat, and that the major task facing theory was 'the reform of consciousness' (1971a: 259). The state, the laws, the economy, the life-forms, the culture and the ideology of capitalist society were, he explained, 'second nature' to the proletariat; they appeared the 'only possible' environment of life and thought. Marxist Theory must therefore teach the proletariat that this is not the case: it must 'dissolve the rigid, unhistorical, natural appearance of social institutions' (Lukács, 1971a: 47) and denaturalize capitalist ideology, transforming facts and ideas into processes, demonstrating their facticity and making evident the possibility of change. Gramsci, who is now much read by post-marxists, took a similar line when he argued both that communism was an 'organic ideology' and that it faced a crucial 'educative task' in the cultural battle to transform the 'common sense' of the masses. Common sense had to be transformed because it consisted of the sedimentation of previous bourgeois philosophies, ideologies and systems of thought, and as such acted as the ground and preserver of the culture which needed to be overthrown (Gramsci, 1971: 160ff).

Detached from any necessary symbiotic link to the Party, and reformulated in diverse ways, this two-pronged program has remained the program of most modern theory and historiography.

Structurally, the vantage point of the proletariat represents a position 'outside' the *status quo* – or if one prefers both outside and inside the *status quo*. This is the case because in the marxist paradigm the proletariat is marked out while still inside capitalist society as the agent of the post-capitalist future outside capitalist society, and because it is conceived as the locus of oppression, disaffection, alienation, and resistance to bourgeois society. Structurally, the vantage point of the proletariat is the position of the dispossessed, the position of opposition, demolition and restitution. And as such, it can also be occupied by other groups – by ordinary people in the *Annales* school, by the non-Western world in Derrida, Said and Spivak, by the indeterminate Other of much French poststructuralism, by women in feminist theory, by gays in gay studies, by blacks in black studies. To speak from 'the vantage point of the proletariat' is in each case to express the concerns and advance the cause of the group in question. It is to show where that group has been dispossessed by society and by its official culture, to demolish conventional ways of viewing the past, and to restore to the group in question the visibility and the counter-history it heretofore lacked. Theory and historical narrative have become so closely identified with 'the vantage point of the proletariat' that any discourse which is not critical, not subversive or not restitutive in some way has come to seem intellectually and politically suspect.

Despite changes in the language, the method and the audience, 'the reform of consciousness' has also proceeded very much along the lines prescribed by Lenin. Theory no longer seeks to address itself directly to the proletariat or its substitutes. Instead, on the assumption that 'the educator himself must be educated' it addresses itself to those who teach the masses, teaching the teachers to question everything in their discipline, in the academy, in received ideologies and in society which has seemed 'second nature' or 'common sense' to them. Theory denaturalizes language, canonical texts, the symbolic order, *mentalités*, 'instrumental reason', Western metaphysics, the 'always already', bourgeois 'myths', master narratives, discursive formations, 'systems of interpretation and reinterpretation' or racist, patriarchal or homophobic ideologies and demonstrates their facticity. It dissolves the fixity of terms, of concepts, and of social institutions and shows them in process and in flux. It makes change seem possible and necessary. And it frequently also prepares for revolution by miming revolution – or as Lacan put it, by making the revolution 'in effigy' – through textual *renversements*, and through the verbal overturning and reversal of established hierarchies and dominant structures of language and thought.

The legacy of the Leninist Party lives on, too, in the idea that the education the masses require is really political education. The assumption that critics and teachers have a political function and a political responsibility has become a commonplace even among non-marxist theorists and historians, and so has the idea that all discourse and all teaching is political. The political dimension of education and discourse has come to override, even to eclipse, all other possible educative functions or responsibilities, and in many departments, Theory has come to demand the same sort of 'political correctness' of its students that the Leninist Party once demanded of its members. Partisanship has become the order of the day.

But there is little fixity here. Both on the Left and on the Right and both inside the academy and outside it, attempts are constantly being made to control critique, to direct critique, to authorize particular forms of critique while discrediting others, and to turn critique into a tool for the advancement of particular interests. This process establishes 'correctness' or more accurately, rival correctnesses. But correctnesses are also constantly being destabilized not only by recurrent struggles for academic hegemony and influence, but also by all the forces inside and outside the academy, which require critique to constantly transform and renew itself. To name just a few: the growing dependence of economies on 'critical thinking' as opposed to thinking which only reapplies a pre-determined model or 'truth;' the market demand for novel discursive academic products; the institutional demand for academic 'productivity;' changes in the political and social context; and the boredom-factor built into the paradigmatic repetition-compulsion. One would like to think too, with Lyotard, that transformation and renewal are also impelled by the 'summons' to trace a path to an 'I don't know what' which begins to take form only in the process of research and writing and thought (Lyotard, 1988: 12).

2
Limits of the Marxist Paradigm

> Certain questions are so aged that they can no longer age; they are only still – and very concretely – susceptible to an *other history*.
>
> Jean-Luc Nancy

The other has become a problem for postmodern cultural history. Speaking the singularity and difference of the other has become a problem for postmodern cultural history. Why? The answer which is most frequently given is that we live in hegemonic societies where disciplinary practices exclude otherness, preclude singularity and silence difference, and where we are inescapably caught in a net of language which speaks us. Another answer – an answer we rarely give and understandably seek to evade, the answer I will be exploring here – is that the newer kinds of cultural history (poststructuralist, cultural materialist, new historicist) are incapable of speaking singularity, because their premises and methods reduce everything and everyone to the Same.

We need to at least consider the possibility that if otherness has remained an abstract universal in the newer kinds of cultural history, if difference has remained indeterminate and if singularity has become the lack which justifies our narratives and critiques, it is *also* because the premises and methodology of these kinds of cultural history prevent them from adequately concretizing otherness, describing singularity, and giving voice to difference. In other words, while I am not denying the obvious fact that there are disciplinary practices and social pressures to conform, I am reopening the question of how postmodern cultural history is really placed in relation to conformity.

The question of singularity is a question about the limits of postmodern forms of cultural history, and of the marxist paradigm which they inhabit (see Chapter 1). But it is also more than this. For if the premises and methods of postmodern cultural history reduce everything and everyone to the Same, then this kind of cultural history has to be viewed as one of the languages which speak us and deprive us of singularity. And if that is the case, far from being a revolutionary, anti-hegemonic force, postmodern cultural history must be understood *in its own terms* either as a function and iteration of the hegemonic social systems it inhabits, or as a proponent of an ideology and methodology which constructs reality *as* a hegemonic society where singularity, difference and otherness cannot be spoken. The stakes in pursuing this line of inquiry are evidently high.

Poststructuralism and cultural history sought to move beyond the collective determinism in the marxist paradigm and to clear a space for difference by valorizing a plural, decentered and non-identical conception of the subject. This was seen as a solution for a while – in part, as Roland Barthes pointed out, because if individuals cannot speak or be without citing the always already of language and culture, they can at least be thought to 'originalize themselves' by the unique way they fragment and combine cultural citations. The plural and decentered subject made it possible to think difference as a particular combination of languages, group-affiliations and subject-positions, and to conceive of singular beings as having multiple, potentially divergent or contradictory, relations to different aspects of the social text. But this, as everyone soon came to understand, also prevented difference from being radically different, since no *combinatoire*, however polyvalent, could be wholly other than what was always already present in language and culture. Considered merely as a site upon which elements of the always already intersect, the plural and decentered subject could not help falling back into some version of the Same. This meant, in turn, that the otherness of the other, the other's singularity and difference, could only be marked as non-being and non-presence. The subject could only be 'himself', his 'real' self, where he was not – not a social being. If people are fundamentally or essentially socialized beings (even in their unconscious), then their real singular non-socialized self is nowhere in being, and it can only be described as absent, indeterminate, indefinite, and incapable of being spoken.[1]

The plural, decentered and non-identical subject does not, however, contain these ideological and political significations as an invariable essence. Like an empty signifier, this form or structure of subjecthood can be given a variety of different significations in different intellectual and cultural con-texts.[2] This becomes apparent as soon as we look behind and beyond the debates of the present, to the very different ideological significations which have been associated with the plural and decentered subject in the past. For postmodernism has not, as we tend to assume, been displacing the centered, rational humanist subject of the Enlightenment with a 'new' plural and decentered subject; it has only been displacing the Enlightenment humanist subject with the very subject that the Enlightenment subject had displaced before. And despite the surprise, disorientation and excitement initially produced by his postmodern deployment, the plural and decentered subject, who lacks any intrinsic essence or proper form, is no more 'new' than the idea, which we now associate with Marx, that 'man is not any inborn image of himself, but many images coming from the outside' (Pico, 1977: 6).

The plural, multiform and always destructible subject who can 'fashion, fabricate and transform himself into the shape of all flesh and into the character of any creature' because he is nothing but the potentiality to become like anything that already is, is – at least according to Pico della Mirandola whom I have been quoting – as old as the Chaldeans and the Pythagoreans, as the secret rites of the Athenians and the secret wisdom of the Hebrews. In some recently discovered Gnostic Gospels, this non-identical subject speaks with the voice of a female divinity:

> For I am the first and the last.
> I am the honoured one and the scorned one.
> I am the whore and the holy one.
> I am the wife and the virgin . . .
> I am the barren one,
> and many are her sons,
> I am the silence that is incomprehensible . . .
> I am the utterance of my name.
>   (in Pagels, 1979: xvii)

In the course of its long pre-modern history, this subject has not only been both male and female, and both human and divine. It has also been Pagan, Christian and Jewish; of the party of the Church and of that of the Devil; religious and secular; an emblem of wisdom and a sign of madness.

This plural and infinitely diverse subject – not the single, self-identical rational subject now attributed to humanism – was the subject that Renaissance humanists declared the wonder of the world: 'Who does not wonder at this chameleon that we are?' (Pico, 1977: 5). If Renaissance humanists described man as a microcosm, it was not because he possessed any determinate and self-enclosed nature proper to himself, but because he incarnated and could actualize in himself and in his life any or all of the plural modes of being always already outside him in nature and in culture. Man was a wonder not because reason made him nature's master, but because he had 'no fixed seat nor form of [his] own' and could therefore 'live every kind of life' (Pico, 1977: 5, 4). And the same qualities which made man the site at which all modes of being intersect made him free. It was precisely because he had 'no fixed seat, nor form of [his] own' that man was free to 'possess any seat, or any form' that he could desire. It was precisely because he was not confined by the bounds' of any single determinate mode of being but 'infinite in faculty, in form and moving' (Hamlet, II, ii, 320) that he was at liberty to 'fix the limits of nature for [him]self' and to change at will.

The ideological significations attached to the plural and decentered subject here are almost diametrically opposed to those attached to him in postmodern cultural history today. And if we bracket, for a while, the assumption that we have got it right and they got it wrong, or that theirs was false consciousness and ours is not, this difference raises some intriguing questions: how, in our hands, did a wonder of the world, an emblem of human freedom, become a mere *combinatoire* of cultural citations? By what contractions, reductions, exclusions and displacements did a plural, decentered and infinitely mobile structure of subjectivity – which was initially introduced into the marxist paradigm to make singularity and difference visible and intelligible again – lose most, if not all of its freedom and difference? And what can we learn about the premises and methods we are employing from the process by which we accomplished this ideological transformation?

By going back to this completely *pre*-modern conception of the subject in a multitude of different texts, in a variety of fields, through a rapid succession of critical modes both prior and subsequent to poststructuralism, and in the course of a by now quite considerable number of years, the 20th century has given the once *passé* plural, decentered and non-identical subject what Nancy calls 'another history' a postmodern history – or perhaps, more accurately, a tissue of different but not unconnected postmodern histories. None of these postmodern histories attempts to reconstruct the 'original' history of the plural and decentered subject in any simple, naive or conventional way – this is perhaps the mark of their common postmodernism. And I am not going to try to do so here either. Instead, I am going to select from the wealth of modern material three instantiations of the plural, decentered and non-identical subject, which seem to me to demonstrate particularly clearly how the ideological signification of this subject is transformed from freedom to social determinism as it becomes more and more fully appropriated by the premises and methods of the marxist paradigm.

The line connecting Lucien Febvre's 'new kind of history' to Michel Foucault's poststructuralist history, and Michel Foucault to Stephen Greenblatt's New Historicism can be described, at least from one point of view, as a line of influence. This is useful for, as we all know, lines give (hi)stories a plot, or if one prefers, what Milton called an 'argument'. But lines are not only a matter of filiation; they are also traditionally composed of points or moments. And it is also as moments representing alternative constructions of the protean subject in relation to the social text within the marxist paradigm, and thus as constructions which can be repeated by others at other moments, that we will be considering the work of Febvre, Foucault and Greenblatt. In the final part of this chapter, we will close the historical distance between the two diverse histories of the protean subject by considering how methods of analysis within the marxist paradigm repeat those of an earlier era.

Febvre, Foucault, Greenblatt

My story begins with Lucien Febvre, founder of the *Annales* school of history. Febvre's Renaissance histories can conveniently be treated as a matrix in which the modern figure of the protean and decentered subject emerges not only in conjunction with a set of now commonplace marxist or *marxisant* positions on society, history and historical narrative, but as an attempt to challenge some of them. Febvre's work therefore makes it possible both to foreground some of the *a priori* limitations and exclusions to which this figure was subjected when he was recast for the 'new kind of history', and to consider some of the ways in which this 'new kind of history' used the Renaissance figure to challenge and change the marxist paradigm.

The protean Renaissance subject reemerges in Febvre's histories in conjunction with that repositioning of history and the historian which reduces the past to a strategic instrument and makes the historian a creative writer intervening politically in his present. Febvre argued that the historian must consider the past in light of his 'precise knowledge of contemporary facts and of the contemporary world' (1962: 198) and that he must use history both to 'call into question the answers that have been given' (1982: 1) and to pave the way for a more congenial future. Like the critic in the marxist paradigm, then, Febvre's historian was writing to uproot false consciousness and to change the world.

Febvre sought to help the world move towards becoming one, complex, diverse and interconnected global society without national boundaries. His dream was not only of a classless society, but of a classless, nationless and completely interconnected world, where what happens in one place is seen to be dependent on what happens everywhere else. To make this, to him utopian, possibility visible and intelligible, he had to challenge the one-dimensional determinism and the 'simple' notion of unity inherent both in marxism and in psychoanalysis during the '30s and '40s.

The plural and decentered Renaissance subject provided a way of challenging social determinism and the unified view of the subject, because while the plural Renaissance subject was determined or 'socialized' by all that was outside him in nature and culture, he was also relatively free, un-unified and self-determining. But to refashion this subject to his new ideological ends, Febvre had to exclude the Renaissance subject's prior ideological functions and reduce him to a relatively limited number of structural characteristics: synchronic multiplicity, continual diachronic difference, and dynamic interchange with his environment.

To subvert the 'simple' deterministic notion of unity in marxism and psychoanalysis, Febvre attached the synchronic multiplicity and continual diachronic difference of the Renaissance humanist subject to the marxist premise that 'being determines consciousness', and that consciousness therefore changes with changes in being. This move severed the Renaissance subject from all his previous links to the animal and spiritual kingdoms, and severely curtailed his freedom by confining him within the temporal bounds of a purely social and material order. But it enabled Febvre to pluralize both 'being' and 'consciousness' by expanding the latter to encompass every aspect of man's mental, psychological and emotional life, and the former to include all aspects of life in society without privileging the economic. It also enabled Febvre to use the marxist premise that 'being determines consciousness' both against ego-centered psychology and against marxism itself. For if man's mental, psychological and emotional lives really change with changes in the social and material order, then a modern ego-centered psychology based on observation of the sedentary, urban, refined and solitary people of the present can hardly be said to apply to the nomadic, rural, overcrowded and unrefined people of the Renaissance. If all aspects of human consciousness change with changes in the social and material order, then categories of analysis like class, party or ideology which are derived from the observation of modern capitalist societies can hardly be said to apply unequivocally to the social and material orders of the past.[3] If both material being and consciousness are constantly changing, it becomes absurd and unnecessary to try to 'open all locks with any single key' (1962: 365).

Febvre often preferred to minimize the radical implications of his call for a 'historical psychology' and of his break with universalizing concepts of man and society: 'Nothing is lost if everything simply changes shape' (1973: 15). But Febvre knew that 'man' was lost: 'For history' he wrote, 'man does not exist, only men' (1977: 2). And Febvre knew that all passably stable, transhistorical categories and truths were lost. Historians, he wrote, must 'realize . . . that the "universe" is no more absolute than the "spirit" or the "individual" but that it is constantly being transformed through the inventions and civilizations produced by human groups' (1973: 10). Both man and his world lost anything that might be considered proper to them. But what was gained was the image of a more plural, diverse and fluid world.

Febvre rewrote 16th-century France as a period when everything and everyone was constantly changing shape: 'Their world was one where nothing was strictly defined, where entities lost their boundaries, and in the twinkling of an eye, without much protest, change shape, appearance, size, even "domain" as we would say' (1982: 438). Febvre portrays Luther as the quintessential 16th-century man in this respect: 'He proceeds – indeed leaps – from one paradox to another. He bounds with ease, with agility, with fearful abandon from the most desperate doubt to the most confiding belief, from excited acceptance of hell and damnation to the most tranquil swooning in the arms of divinity, from fear to love, from death to life' (undated: 58–9). Febvre's dynamic 'polyphonic and contrapunctal' portraits of Luther, of Rabelais, of classes in the Renaissance and of Renaissance society as a whole, made his portraits of history portraits of the sort of fluid, plural, complex, diverse and interconnected global society which he hoped and believed was on the agenda of world history. These portraits emphasized that every entity and every subject is 'at once one and multiple, prodigiously diversified in its activities and possessing, like Panurge, a million strings to its bow' (1962: 354). And they served to demonstrate that there is no simple economic or psychological determinism, but an 'interdependence of phenomena' (1962: 365) which connects everything to everything else in multiple different ways.

For Febvre, therefore, history was full of plural unities without any dominating or regulating centre. Instead of deconstructing unities as poststructuralists later sought to do, Febvre reconstructed them in their positivity, as non-simple, non-centered entities whose elements converged, diverged, agreed, disagreed, collided and transformed each other in innumerable ways. Instead of deferring meaning, he allowed historical subjects to assume multiple, even incompatible, sometimes divergent and sometimes convergent meanings. And instead of assuming that the subject had ever been present as a bounded, self-enclosed identity, he described historical subjects in multiple, diverse, transforming dynamic interactions with others and with the variety of men, ideas, conventions and ideologies always already outside them in the society of the time.

If the subject is protean in Febvre's work, it is also because he is always being formed and transformed by the people, circumstances, events, ideas, conventions and languages which he is constantly encountering and which he, in turn, is constantly acting and changing himself to transform. Against those who would argue that men are simply the product of an economic system, of a class ideology, a human nature or a language which precedes them, Febvre insisted that: 'Nothing is dictated, inexorably dictated.' He granted that no man, however exceptional, can think just anything or be just anything in every period and in every society; but he insisted with equal vigour that this does not mean that everything is always already determined. Against the simple determinism which held that people are little more than the product of an economic system, of an ideology or of a psyche which precedes them and acts on them, Febvre argued for a 'complicated play of actions and reactions', with the given shaping and constantly reshaping the subject, and the subject constantly shaping and reshaping elements of the given.

Foucault used the 'same' plural and decentered subject for more immediately and more classically revolutionary ends. Where Febvre portrayed the world as one diverse, interconnected global society, Foucault strove to make possible a revolution in his own country, the outcome of which would be decided by marginalized and subjected groups. To show how subjects were oppressed by the status quo and how they could act to change it, Foucault married Febvrian plurality and fluidity of actions and reactions within the confines of the social and material order to a Gramscian notion of social hegemony, which further reduced the plurality of the subject and made singularity and difference all but unintelligible.

Foucault used the protean subject's diachronic difference in a 'historical psychology' not only to make possible a more or less direct critical analysis of the present, but also to demonstrate that, as paradigms of subjectivation have been changed in the past, so they can be changed in the present. Conceiving of the past as a 'historical succession of models of subjectivation' (1980: 74) enabled Foucault to show that the modern anthropological figure of man as a living, working, speaking, sexual being who is always an object to himself, is a mere episode in the history of human subjectivation. And this, in turn, enabled Foucault to argue for the death of man in his modern anthropological form, and to insist that we can 'promote new forms of subjectivity through the refusal of the kind of individuality which has been imposed on us for centuries' (1982: 208). The protean subject, with his synchronic multiplicity and his dynamic interchange with his environment, was also the form of subjectivation that Foucault promoted towards the end of his life as a means of 'refusing the kind of individuality which has been imposed on us for centuries'.

In some respects, different though the language is, it is as though Foucault had transposed Febvre's fluid image of plural and decentered Renaissance subjects in the fluid society of Renaissance France or Germany to the France of the '70s, substituting the complex play of power for Febvre's complex play of actions and reactions. Foucault's 'new' kind of subject inhabits a mobile and dynamic 'field' of interrelations in which power is everywhere and comes from everywhere. In each of his plural and diverse power-relations (in the family, at work, with doctors or teachers, in the realm of discourse, practice etc), the subject acts and is acted upon, is determined and determines, conforms or resists. Consequently, each subject's 'shape' can be a function of the diverse ways in which he is acted upon or has been acted upon by his different relations to others and by the diverse ways in which he acts or has acted upon others. Each plural subject's shape depends on the extent of his conformities and resistances, and changes with these local conformities and resistances.

The liberating, revolutionary and empowering potential of this plural and shape-changing subject are clear. For such subjects can work and 'struggle on their own terrain and on the basis of their own proper activity (or passivity)'. They can potentially 'engage in a struggle that concerns their own interests, whose objectives they clearly understand and whose methods only they can determine'. Each subject can potentially 'engage in a struggle against a particularized power, the constraints and controls that are exerted against him' (1977a: 12; 1977b: 216). Each can do a plurality of specific and local things, if he will, even he cannot achieve a classical marxist or maoist revolution; and in the end, as the result of the specific and local actions of innumerable shape-changing subjects, the shape of society might itself be changed.

Yet empowering and liberating as this seems, and in some ways really is, in the context Foucault gave it, it also involves severe restrictions on the subject. For to funnel the protean subject to revolutionary grass-roots struggle and to *renversement* of the given, Foucault further confined the subject to two possible modes of action – conformity or resistance – and to two possible modes of relation – exercising power and being subject to power. And he excluded all other possible modes of action and relation. Foucault's plural, decentered and shape-changing subjects are, for instance, incapable of negotiation, cooperation or duplicity.

At the same time, to show why revolution was desirable and necessary in the present, Foucault had to present historical formations as total systems of subjection which continue to dominate the present. Where Febvre presented society and history as an unbounded ocean of flux within which certain configurations and *mentalités*,

Limits of the Marxist Paradigm

which were neither binding nor permanent, could at times be distinguished, Foucault therefore began from the opposite premise, the premise that history is a series of more or less stable hegemonic configurations – a Nietzschean series of systems of interpretation and reinterpretation. He then gave these hegemonic systems of interpretation and reinterpretation even great rigidity and solidity by conceiving of them as structured, unconscious, uncontrollable and all-encompassing determinants of subjectivation. The result was threefold.

The first result of this hegemonic construction of subjectivation was, in practice, to exclude heterogeneity. Class, or ethnic or criminal sub-cultures are silenced by this construction of history. Such sub-cultures emerge in Foucault's histories only in isolated acts of resistance – when 'the people' pull 'patients' off the scaffold, indulge in scattered acts of petty theft, or wander the countryside threatening the public order. 'The people' have no life of their own outside the hegemonic order, no culture or practices other than those imposed on them by the various technologies of power, no traditions of otherness, no dialects or habits of speech or forms of humour, no means of giving Caesar his due while using Caesar to their own advantage, no capacity for living simultaneously in different cultural orders. Even criminals and delinquents are denuded of their distinctive social and discursive practices and presented only as they appear under the panoptic eye of hegemonic institutions. It is no doubt true that information about such groups is far from prominent in official histories and official archives; but, as Annales school history, Foucault's own book on Raymond Roussel, and the work of feminists and of people in Black Studies shows, much information about the lives and cultures of such groups and of singular people among them can in fact be retrieved, if the historian only will. While presenting hegemonic discursive formations as silencing sub-groups and individuals, Foucault was in fact also silencing them himself.

The second result of Foucault's hegemonic construction of society and history is to disempower the plural and decentered subject again. All Foucault's historical models of interpretation and subjectivation are full of examples of subjects acting and being acted upon in diverse ways. The difference between past models and the revolutionary model Foucault was trying to develop is that in the past the multiplicity of diverse actions and reactions by subjects are always portrayed as subordinate to a single principle (measure, inquiry, or examination; correspondence, difference, or sameness; a particular view of reason or unreason etc). This principle – which is 'unconscious' in the sense that people are unaware of it as such, and 'anonymous' in the sense that it is planned by no-one – is shown to operate as a law which 'governs' the different statements that can be made, the different truths that can be found, the behaviour which is permitted or proscribed, the form of subjectivation which is imposed, and the forms of treatment and control which are in force during the period of its ascendancy. Domination, control and the power of selection and exclusion are thus built into each historical formation as Foucault describes it. And when they are not excluded altogether, difference, innovation and individual initiative (the invention of a new treatment for the insane, for instance) are always subordinate to and incorporated by the workings of the episteme or historical formation in force. This is what makes each historical formation a 'system of subjection', and it is what Foucault's new shape-changing subjects are supposed to resist and overthrow. The problem is that there is nothing in Foucault's new form of subjectivation to prevent the various local actions and reactions of innumerable shape-changing subjects from reconstituting or unconsciously obeying some anonymous and unconscious principle which, in retrospect, will be seen to have governed the different statements they made, the different truths they found, the behaviour that was permitted and proscribed and so on.[4] And there is nothing to prevent difference and singularity from continuing to be reabsorbed into the Same.

Finally, the hegemonic construction of society, history and subjectivation makes it impossible to explain either how docile, disciplined, confessing and totally subjected bodies in a completely carceral society can also be or become plural, shape-changing and resisting subjects, or how any subject can in such circumstances 'think the unthought'. Febvre had made individual freedom and original in-put into history and society – the creativity of a Rabelais or the inspiration of a Luther – possible in two ways. First, he had left them essentially unexplained in terms of *mentalités* and 'historical psychology'. In Febvre's work, silence on this point marked not an exclusion, but an opening, the place where the fortuitous, the exceptional and the inexplicable could enter history. Secondly, he allowed historical subjects both to be fashioned by what was already in the social world and to contribute to fashioning what did not yet exist. Foucault, on the other hand, divided these two aspects of the

Limits of the Marxist Paradigm

subject from each other. He further limited the plurality of historical subjects by excluding from their subjectivation imagination, creativity, play and the power of conceiving of anything that is not. But on the Nietzschean principle that 'we can destroy only as creators', he appropriated creativity, innovation and play exclusively to himself. While everyone else was spoken by the language, the conventions, the disciplines always already produced by hegemonic discursive systems, the poststructuralist theorist-historian remained free to 'think the unthought', to 'fiction a politics that does not yet exist', to fashion a 'new politics of truth', and to effectively intervene in his present to change history and society. This made the poststructuralist theorist-historian's freedom to 'think the unthought' and to fiction anything that does not yet exist as mysterious and as socio-historically unintelligible as the resistance of completely docile and subjugated bodies or the historical possibility of protean subjects.

Stephen Greenblatt, founder of American New Historicism in the '80s, succeeded both in putting the plural and decentered subject back into the past – most particularly, back into the Renaissance where he had been found – and in explaining socio-historically much that Foucault left unintelligible. But he achieved these successes at a further, and this time lethal, cost to the protean subject. His very success in explaining both the existence of plural and decentered subjects and their resistance as effects of social fashioning led him to a reaffirmation of the marxist paradigm in its most extreme and deterministic form. This is all the more noteworthy because Greenblatt is anything but a marxist.

To put the plural and decentered subject back into the Renaissance, Greenblatt modified Foucault's view of history as a series of cultural hegemonies by borrowing Althusser's notion of overdetermination. He posited that the men of the English Renaissance were subject not to one subjectifying authority, but to multiple authorities with different disciplines and different technologies for the production of identities. Greenblatt's Renaissance in *Renaissance Self-Fashioning* is like Foucault's revolutionary present insofar as it is a plural 'field' dominated by institutions which produce subjects by mechanisms of discipline and control, in which power is constantly being confronted with resistance. Greenblatt's Renaissance is also like Febvre's insofar as it is a period of diversity and conflict, when boundaries are still largely unfixed and subjects can change their shape, their appearance, their 'domain' in the twinkling of an eye.

But these traits of the Renaissance are now presented as being intrinsically related to the various institutionalized disciplines for self-fashioning provided by the Catholic Church and the Protestant Bible, by the Court and the Queen, by penitential exercises and imitations of the life of Christ, by conduct manuals and courtship rituals. If subjects in this Renaissance were shape-changers, it was because they occupied several institutional 'domains', because they were constantly moving between them and refashioning themselves accordingly, and because they could put on, put off and 'play' their various identities. The plural and shape-changing subject, whose behaviour is now mildly reminiscent of the 'role psychology' of the '60s, was historically possible only because he was always already 'overdetermined'.

Greenblatt also modified Foucault to explain the possibility of resistance. In *Renaissance Self-Fashioning*, resistance is no longer what it was in Foucault, namely the mysterious struggle of individuals on their 'own' terrain. It is itself a form of conformity. Greenblatt's book is full of men who actively, dramatically and tragically resisted the power of the monarch or of the Church, but Greenblatt shows that in every case, they resisted in the name of obedience to another authority and to another discipline for self-fashioning. Tyndale resisted the power of the Catholic Church in obedience to the law of Christ and to the discipline of self-fashioning inherent in the Protestant Bible. More resisted the King in obedience to the law of the Catholic Church and the discipline of the *consensus fidelium*. And imitation of Christ provided all sides with a way of shaping the self for resistance. Not only were those who resisted power in *Renaissance Self-Fashioning* always resisting power in obedience to another 'higher' power, but Greenblatt argues that their resistance was always an inverted mirror image of the authoritarian 'disciplinary paradigm' they were resisting. At the same time, if resistance permitted Greenblatt's Renaissance subjects to assert selfhood in the sense of a single self-fashioned identity, it permitted them to do so only by stopping the play of shape-changing self-fashionings. And they could stop the play of shape-changing self-fashionings only by choosing one of the possible authoritative models of the self at their disposal, and by resisting – to the death, and in death – any power that demanded further changes of shape.

There is no mystery about what the protean subject has lost here. To put him back into the Renaissance and to explain his resistance, Greenblatt had to deprive that subject of autonomy, of freedom, of all possibility of difference, and of any self of his 'own'. As far as Greenblatt was concerned, if a man moved among institutional domains refashioning himself accordingly, he was left 'nothing' behind the plural play of fictional poses. For a man to express and fix his identity by following an authority to the death or by identifying himself with a single model of self-fashioning external to the self was an abnegation or loss of self. And for the assertion of identity to depend on a choice among extant models of selfhood was an intolerable limitation of human freedom. As Greenblatt observes in his epilogue: 'Whenever I focussed sharply upon a moment of apparently autonomous self-fashioning, I found not an epiphany of identity freely chosen, but a cultural artefact. If there were traces of free choice, the choice was among possiblities whose range was strictly delineated by the social and ideological system in force' (1980: 256).

In his earliest book, *Sir Walter Raleigh: the Renaissance Man and His Roles*, Greenblatt had approached the same protean and shape-changing Renaissance subject with different premises and a different method, and he had reached completely different conclusions. In that book, the protean subject who fictions identities and acts out different roles was presented as the sole author and director of the multiple parts he played in a 'stage-play world'. Apparently free of all limitations on his ability to fiction his own history and to invent ways to dramatize his resistance to the world, the protean Renaissance subject had been a 'token of (man's) power to transform nature and to fashion his own identity' and of the 'belief in man's power to control his own destiny' (1973: 31, 30).

It was only once he began working with Geertz's restatement of the marxist premise that people are only what society makes them – 'there is no such thing as a human nature independent of culture' – that Greenblatt's Renaissance protean subject became a 'cultural artefact' who could only choose among extant possibilities. And from here it was but a short step to the complete collapse of the individual into the social and to the position, in Lacan's words, that 'the collective and the individual are the same thing' (Lacan, 1978: 43).

Greenblatt took this short step in his latest book, *Shakespearean Negotiations: The Circulation of Social Energy in Renaissance England* (1988) by transferring all the traits of the protean and shape-changing subject to the collective domain. Even the life-force is now transferred to the collectivity: this is said to possess an *energeia* (the social energy of the subtitle) which 'circulates' to permit movement, change and the illusion of life. The human subject's freedom to create and innovate is likewise transferred to the collectivity: there is 'a sustained collective improvization' (1988: 14), 'a collective making of distinct cultural practices' (1988: 5), and 'a collective production of literary pleasure and interests' (1988: 4). Broadly to be identified with the plurality of parallel and divergent forces in Renaissance society, social energy is constantly changing shapes and redefining boundaries as it 'circulates', enabling 'exchanges' to take place and permitting collective beliefs, experiences and practices to move from one medium to another. Social energy is concerned with nothing so much as negotiating the survival of its own authoritarian fictions, making itself responsible in its cunning not only for the production of subjected bodies, but for the 'constant production of its own radical subversion and the powerful containment of that subversion' (1988: 41). The collective subject thus becomes the subject of history (the Hegelian subtext here is evident). It becomes a subject which, in its plurality and dynamic changefulness produces and contains not only all historical subjects, practices and beliefs, but also all possibility of difference, resistance and change. And then, as Greenblatt says, adopting the collective voice: 'There is subversion, no end of subversion, but not for us' (1988: 39). We're back at complete social determination, but at a social determination more total than even Marx or Foucault envisaged. And the plural, decentered and non-identical subject, whose function was once to challenge collective determinism by reasserting the possibility of freedom, singularity and difference, becomes entirely buried in the collective determination of the whole.

The Quest for Likeness

These three instantiations of the plural and decentered subject suggest that the subject loses plurality, freedom, particularity and difference as he is defined more completely in terms of the social and cultural order. Let us recap.

To consider the protean Renaissance humanist subject in relation to the marxist premise that 'social being determines consciousness' and thus to contain him within the bounds of a purely social and temporal order, the plurality of the protean subject had to be pared down. The Renaissance humanist subject's prior ideological functions had to be minimized or excluded, and his links to the animal and spiritual orders severed. Embraced by the *mentalités* and configurations of the social order, the subject can no longer think or be 'just anything'. His possibilities are limited by social givens, but these are not inexorable and all-determining. The subject retains freedom, singularity and difference (a) insofar as interrelations in the social order are explored on the level of the local and the particular, where 'the interdependence of phenomena' appears as a fluid and 'complicated play of actions and reactions' and (b) insofar as some elements in the subject's behaviour and thinking are allowed to remain outside the order of social givens.

To consider the protean subject in relation to hegemonic social systems of subjectivation, the plurality of the protean subject had to be further reduced. Many of the subject's possible psychological dimensions and social modes of relation had to be ignored or truncated – for instance, duplicity, negotiation, and the power of conceiving of anything that is not. Attention is focused on larger patterns of conformity, and on the ways in which, despite and through a complicated play of actions and reactions, people are fashioned alike. In this context, difference appears either as something silenced by the hegemonic homogenizing mechanisms of society (passive non-conformity) or as resistance (active non-conformity). Thus here too, difference appears as what is outside the social order as such.

It is only when the protean subject is left nothing besides the plurality of his conformities that he is entirely encapsulated by the social and cultural text, without hope of issue. When subjects are described as being like extant models of subjectivation even in their resistance, and when all singular reactions are attributed to one of the multiple possibilities within the social order, there is complete incorporation of difference. As Louis Montrose has put it: 'social systems are produced and reproduced in the interactive social practices of individuals and groups; . . . collective structures may enable as well as constrain individual agency' (in Veeser, 1989: 21). Thus if subjects are able to act or react or be different, this is only because they have been *enabled* to do so by the social and ideological system in force. Here difference itself becomes nothing but a moment in the reproduction of the Same.

The progressive collapse of the individual into the collective and of difference into the Same could be explained (away) as an expression of ideology and politics – as a question of the sort of intervention critics are making in their present (Greenblatt's politics, for instance, are clearly a great deal more conservative than Foucault's), or as an instance of finding what the regime of truth of a particular intellectual group leads one to expect to find. But to explain it this way would be to evade the question raised by these particular instantiations of the plural and decentered subject: the question of why the subject's scope contracts and his capacity for difference diminishes as the emphasis on what subjects have in common with others in the social order increases.

To put it more provocatively, my (hi)story suggests that the protean subject is absorbed into the collectivity and deprived of singularity and difference *to the extent* that man is assumed to be what society makes him and described with the aid of a methodology primarily designed to discover resemblances. The methodology in question did not originate with Marx, and I think that we will see how it works more clearly if we 'defamiliarize' it by discussing it in the scholastic terminology of an earlier era.

The strength both of what Aquinas called 'natural philosophy' and of what Marx called 'materialist philosophy' has lain in identifying what 'living things have in common' (Aquinas, 1959: 44) with each other and with their natural or social and cultural environment. To do this more effectively, both rejected the Platonic thesis that ideas can also in some way exist separately from 'real things' and both compared extant subjects to each other and to 'already existing' forms of being. It matters little here that in one case the human subject is compared to what already exists in nature and discovered to have his powers of nourishment, growth and reproduction in common with plants, and that in the other case he is compared to what already exists in language, society or culture and discovered to be like an extant model of subjectivation or like other members of his or her socio-economic group. What matters is that the presumption of likeness is a precondition for discovering 'what living things have in common' with each other and with their natural or social environment, while the effect of seeking 'what living things have in common' with each other and with their natural or cultural environment is inevitably to reinforce the presumption that living things are like each other and like their environment.

Within the marxist paradigm, we are still caught in this circularity. Likeness is our premise, we look for likeness and we find likeness; we find likeness and we confirm our premise. Otherness, or what is not like, remains outside our parameters; within our parameters differences can only appear as distinctions or contrasts among phenomena or groups of phenomena which predominantly share their likeness. Or, to put it differently, to accomodate our comparative methodology, we delineate the subject in such a way as to foreground areas of likeness among subjects and between subjects and cultural con-texts. Then we forget that we have done this, and generalize our methodologically useful one-dimensional working fiction into an all-encompassing and non-exclusionary truth about man and society. When we begin to recognize that we are caught in the circularity of our own premises and language we despair: reality can never be known; our narratives are fictions; it is impossible to speak difference and singularity; language (whose language?) cannot speak otherness; there is nothing but likeness – likeness between what we see of men and the social environment (narratives, ideologies, fictions, languages) which fill our sights.

But this is not all. For to make it possible claim that human subjects are like 'already existing' forms of being, whether natural or cultural, both natural philosophy and materialist philosophy also had to develop another hypothesis: the hypothesis that what is 'inside' the subject is like what is 'outside' the subject. For instance, in *De Anima*, Aristotle said that 'the soul is somehow like all that exists' (233) because 'like' can only be 'known by like' (69) and 'acted upon by like' (233). And in his Commentary, Aquinas explains: 'knowledge is caused by the knower containing a likeness of the thing known; for the latter must be in the knower somehow . . . all knowledge implies that the thing known is somehow present in the knower (present by similitude), the knower's actuality as such being the actuality of the thing known' (Aquinas, 1959: 71, 250). Similitude thus makes it possible to cross the boundary between subject and non subject; similitude inhabits the subject and, by inhabiting the subject, makes comparison possible between what is 'in' the subject and what is 'outside' him.

The assumption about similarity here is not merely that similitude between inside and outside makes our knowledge of the subject possible, but also that the subject himself cannot know anything that is unlike, or cannot know anything while it is still unlike. Unlikeness, or in modern parlance, Otherness, cannot be present in thought, in subjects or in language, for the subject in some sense becomes his knowledge, and in becoming his knowledge, eliminates all unlikeness. One cannot know anything (an object, an ideology, a model of subjectivation) or be acted upon by anything (an environment, a discursive practice) without either becoming like it, or making it like oneself. Any initial difference or dissimilarity between subject and not-subject must therefore be removed in the process of coming to know something or in the process of 'being acted upon' by it. Aristotle argues that the soul 'is acted upon insofar as (something) is not like; it becomes like in being acted upon and is then such as the other' (1959: 247). And Aquinas insists that 'although at the start of any action the agent and patient are contrary, when the action is finished, they are similar. For the agent, in acting, assimilates the patient' (1959: 456).

It matters little as far as this is concerned whether we argue that the subject is the mastering agent – 'his soul being able to assimilate all forms of being' – or whether we argue inversely that the subject is the subjected patient, who is assimilated to and actualized by what Aquinas calls 'some active agent already existing'. The result is the same whether the subject assimilates forms of being or forms of being assimilate the subject, whether man makes his world and recognizes himself in it or whether the world makes man in its image by acting upon him, or whether we use Aquinas' language or that of the Marxist paradigm. In both cases, subjects and forms of being are assimilated to each other, and each only is in and as its identity with the other. Unlikeness, the possibility of singularity and difference, already difficult enough to ground within a methodology designed to identify likeness, becomes all the more difficult to justify or discover as the doctrine of assimilation – the doctrine that 'the soul becomes like in being acted upon and is then such as the other' – is more closely adhered to.

The postmodern equivalent to the scholastic assumption that 'the soul becomes like in being acted upon and is then such as the other' is the assumption that social institutions are overwhelming successful in acting upon subjects, and that disciplines, discursive formations and socialization inevitably make subjects like themselves. Our assumption is, in other words, that there are no failures and no only moderate successes.[5] This assumption can only be described as anachronistic, not to say regressive in relation to such things as statistics and probability theory. Statistics, for instance, register, even if they do not satisfactorily explain, the incidence of untypical behaviour in members of the 'same' group. Statistics show that everyone does not become like in being acted upon, even if our marketing people and social services wish that they would. And by showing that uniformity and predictability are far from being inevitable, probability theory indicates that the 'laws' and theories we once predicated on likeness and on recurrence of the Same are uncertain at best. Can we fail to conclude at the very least that theories predicated on likeness and on the conviction that 'the soul becomes like in being acted upon' belong to an earlier model of science, a model which has preserved its authority in the marxist paradigm and in the postmodern cultural histories which still inhabit it long after it has lost its authority elsewhere?

If singularity cannot be spoken, if otherness has remained an abstract universal and difference has remained indeterminate in postmodern thinking, it is not only a function of the particular kind of 'scientific' or historical questions we have been asking, and a result of the particular kind of comparative method we have been using. It is also the result of the very success, effectivity and *usefulness* of a particular kind of cultural and historical research. We do need to know what living things have and have had in common in different cultures and at different times. We do need to identify ideologies, disciplinary practices, regimes of truth and group factors which socialize us in particular ways. We do need to be made aware of the conformities and uniformities in our lives and of the operation of the forces which act upon us to make us 'like'.

But we also need to understand that in identifying conformities and uniformities, we are seeking and foregrounding likenesses and then projecting those likenesses onto 'reality' or history or culture as all there can be and all there is. We need to understand that in so doing, we too are playing a part in suppressing difference and in making singularity invisible and unspeakable. We need to remember the limits inherent in our premises, in our method and in our paradigm, and look for ways of speaking singularity, difference and otherness elsewhere.

3

The Other Body of Man in Derrida, Levinas, Lacoue-Labarthe, Nancy and Borch-Jakobsen

> Upon comprehending their words, I hastened and delayed not, and I fulfilled their beckonings . . . And I rendered it from the dismal language of Kedar to the language of glorious gold.
>
> Alharizi

(De)construction is deconstruction with a significant difference. Depending on one's orientation, this difference could be described socio-historically in terms of a difference of generation, location and political climate, or theoretically as a redeployment of deconstruction for (re)generative work. Deconstruction was a transatlantic phenomenon issuing from Derrida's kabbalistic revisions of Heidegger in the late '60s and early '70s in direct or indirect response to an international mood of rebellion against the 'system'. (De)construction is a still largely untranslated French phenomenon of the later '70s and '80s, which issues from a more or less cohesive intellectual group that includes Philippe Lacoue-Labarthe, Jean-Luc Nancy, Derrida and Levinas; and it speaks to those who understand why a return to the hierarchical, humanist, man-centered *status quo ante* is unacceptable, but not why it must remain impossible to affirm an other self, an other truth, an other ethics or a God other than the conventional patriarchal figure of institutionalized religions. Lacoue-Labarthe marked this change when he observed in 1975 that: 'What should be practised is something like a (de)construction, (something) less critical than positive, or to put it this way, *not very negative* . . . What should be *upheld* all the way is the philosophical *thesis* itself according to which *there must* – always – be truth and knowledge' (1975; 254). (De)construction could be described as deconstruction affirming that truth and knowledge can again be born(e) to language and to Man, as long as it is clear that these terms – truth, knowledge, language, Man, affirmation – are to be understood other-wise.[1]

For after deconstruction, truth cannot return in her traditional logocentric forms. Truth cannot unveil herself and display her naked charms to the rapacious gaze of man or present herself as a clear and distinct idea to the mind's eye. She cannot be layed out in philosophical propositions or adequately represented in language or in sensuous form. *Savoir* (knowledge) can no longer be identified with *sa-voir* – literally, his seeing; homonimically (*ça-voir*), seeing it. And speculation therefore has to lose its specularity. If knowledge is 'I see', if it represents a subject's identification, determination or com-prehension of what an object presented to it 'is', then, like deconstruction, (de)construction must be called a non- knowledge. For (de)construction affirms a truth and knowledge which is always other than historical concepts, identities, ideologies and languages – a truth and knowledge which infinitely exceed presence, the word and the finite mind of man, and which, as a consequence, are no longer properly speaking truth and knowledge at all. And, as Levinas points out, to try to contain what infinitely exceeds finitude in 'a *savoir* which assimilates' or an 'apprehension and a grasp' is to restore it to immanence and to the 'I think' and to blot out 'the-idea-of-the-infinite-in-us' (1982: 8).

On the other hand, unlike deconstruction, (de)construction neither inhabits nor privileges the negative – even in the sense implied by the now popular but inaccurate term 'negative theology'. Its *pas-de-plus*, its further step and further negation, is a negation of negativity, a denial that negations of the metaphysics of presence can take philosophy a step beyond metaphysics or beyond the evidence of presence. As Levinas pointed out, with a gentle reproachful glance at deconstruction, negation may open what is onto a void; but since it remains within the dialectic of being and non-being as a determination of being, it can always be recuperated by being *as* being: there *is* a void. (1974: 3) 'Nothing' can become present.[2] Nancy argued more aggressively that 'indexes of decomposition, deconstruction, displacement or outflanking of the system . . . indexes such as those which go by the names "text", "signifier", "lack", "trace" etc., are converted into values, erected into truths and hypostatized into substances'. And he insisted that 'this conversion is prescribed by the economy of the very first discourses which proposed these indexes, not just in the repetitions and borrowings of epigones' (1976: 7). Concepts like 'arche-writing' only aggravate the situation as far as he is concerned, by suggesting that there is an 'outside' to logocentric discourse from which undecidability can come into discourse and present itself as truth. To preserve such an 'outside' is to remain within the shadow of metaphysics.

For (de)construction, truth is neither to be found in the positivity of *ça-voir* nor in its negation. Truth is 'beyond' the dialectic of being and not being in the sense that it traces a relation to what both is and is not in being. *In*-finite means both *not*-finite and *in*-(the)-finite. The Infinite is both transcendent and immanent: neither entirely present as being nor entirely absent from being in some sort of 'outside' and neither fully evident to beings nor completely hidden from them. A certain doubleness and an uncertain oscillation always mark and re-mark its approach.

Wholly Other than historical truths or knowledge or language, that which infinitely exceeds them repeatedly enters history, language and the finite mind of man, but not in the ways we have come to expect. It does not come as a truth which in-forms history, or manifests itself *as* history, or even 'has' a history, as Foucault and Marx assumed; and it does not remain pure and uncontaminated by history, as it generally did in metaphysics. Instead, it 'traverses' history, in the sense that it keeps sounding through the historically bounded languages and the historically fashioned minds of men, accompanying and interrupting the social production of subjects and works, and allowing history to be transited towards an other meaning which itself non- historical (Derrida, 1978: 25). That which is wholly other than history and man repeatedly traverses history by repeatedly traversing language and man. It is a recurrent visitant: a *Geist* or ghost or guest or spirit which has always already come through man and through language and which, when called ('*Viens*'), can always, eternally, return to man and to language again. In this sense too, it both is and is not in being.

In sounding the possibility of such return, French (de)constructive texts of the late '70s and '80s deconstruct the modern – marxist and capitalist – figure of man as a Worker or producer of Works, as well

The Other Body of Man

as the postmodern figure of man as a subjected subject. They take us to a beyond of the marxist paradigm against which the politics, the limits and the premature totalizations of a paradigm which assumes that what manifests itself in ideology, in culture and in society is all there is, emerge into view. And they suggest that man can also be other than what society, history, ideology and language make him. Against the quest for likeness in the marxist paradigm, (de)constructive texts mark the possibility of a person's unlikeness to her/his rational, rationalizable and socialized self, as well as the possibility of each person's unlikeness to every other.

French (de)constructive texts of the '80s also lead us to a beyond of Freudian and Lacanian psychoanalysis, against which this 'scientifically' promoted attempt to get back in touch with one's 'true' self emerges as an institutionalized cult of masturbation and obsessive egoism. Drawing on an ancient kabbalistic figure, they construct an alternative anatomy of man, which is both 'material' and linked to an 'unconscious' in a completely different way. (De)constructive texts also dramatize the *tukhe* – the encounter between analyst and analysand which for Lacan was at the heart of the psychoanalytical experience – in a way which both confirms the possibility of hearing the incohate otherness of the subject who is 'no-one' sending his insistent message through an alien symbolic order, and completely revises what it means to be a subject, to be no-one, to send a message, to speak through language, to hear and to encounter. And these revisions, in turn, change what it means to write and to read that which comes to us through language from an other.

This does not exhaust all that (de)constructive texts 'do' or imply, nor, in principle, can one do so. For one thing, Derrida observed quite early on that what one might call 'plural deployment' is 'a strategic necessity' when diverse 'hegemonic pretensions' were competing for dominance (1976b: 105, 103); and (de)constructive work has, in fact, extended into a variety of areas which were previously dominated in Paris by other signatures. For another thing, Derrida in particular has demonstrated a marked preference for 'matrixes' which are 'powerful' in the sense that they 'account for more meaning' (in Easthope, 1988: 238) and have 'the greatest potential, variability, undecidability, plurivocality, etc., so that each time it returns it will be as different as possible' (1985d: 158). Such matrixes are infinitely suggestive and variously applicable, not narrowly targeted and interpretable in only one way. (De)construction is also still very much in process, with the result that, despite the recurrence of certain cruxes and of its characteristic double-speak, its responses to many issues are still being worked through. What follows, therefore, can only, in principle, claim to take suggestive bit(e)s of (de)construction, and to piece them together into a possible way of hearing what has been proffered. Having said that, we will allow Lacoue-Labarthe's (de)constructive critiques to lead us out of the marxist paradigm, and then turn to (de)constructions's alternative anatomy of man and to its impact on Freudian-Lacanian psychoanalysis. Finally, we will consider some problems raised by the way (de)construction (en)genders the Law, and by the not unconnected issue of its style. Some of (de)construction's other implications for writing and reading in the academy will be discussed in Chapter 6.

Man the Producer and the Poet

In 'Typographies' and in the collection of his essays called *L'imitation des Modernes*, Lacoue-Labarthe mocks our Western, marxist and capitalist, obsession with Works by showing how many work- and production-related German and French words derive from the roots *stellen* (to place upright, to take a stand) and *Stand* (standing, upright position). For example, in German *herstellen*, to produce, literally means 'to set up here' with the added connotation of mastery and virility (*Herr*) which also inhabits *techne*, understood as the art of mastering or dominating givens to produce new givens. *Darstellung* and *Vorstellung* – presentation, literary representation and imagination – literally 'set something up here, before us' while the object, (*Gegenstand*) and the present (*Gegenstand*) are literally what stands over and against us. To take a stand (*Stand*) or a position (*Stellung*) or to install something also assume an *Aufstellung*, the erection of something which will stand – a stance, a *Gestalt*, a framework, a schema, a figure, a statue, a statute, a stand (*Gestell*) or a stele, a monument in the form of a colossal column. Labarthe's elaborate and erudite *Witz* at the expense of man's phallocentric obsession with putting things up that will stand erect (like man as opposed to animals or man as opposed to woman) also gleefully reminds us that what has been so lovingly and precariously erected can decline and fall (*tombe*) and that every stele is not only a monument but also a tomb.[3]

One of the serious functions of this *Witz* is to underline the extent

The Other Body of Man

to which attention has been redirected in the marxist paradigm from the question 'Who is the producer?' to the question 'What is the product?', and to unmask the dubious theoretical and political interests which are served by this redirection of the question. Lacoue-Labarthe argues that emphasis on man's monumental works 'displaces the emphasis from the producer to the product, and speaks of the producing subject in terms of the product, in order to be done with the producer, the dangerous poet' (1975: 218). And using the poet as the emblem of man as a producer of works (because *poiesis* means making or production), he suggests that in displacing our emphasis in this way we are repeating Platonic gestures of exclusion, for similar reasons and with similar theoretical and political results.

When we displace attention from the producer to the product or speak of the producer *as* a product, he argues, we focus on more or less stable objectifications and monumentalizations in order to evade the really radical and destabilizing implications of *poiesis*. For if indeed all human making or production (*poiesis*) is imitative – if man makes by imitating what is already in being, if all identities are constructed in imitation of others or in imitation of extant models of subjectivation, and if man therefore merely mirrors reality or ideology – then man as a maker or producer is nothing in his own right. He is nothing that can stand erect, independent and alone. He is 'not really a subject (but) a non-subject or subject-less subject, which is also to say a multiplied subject, infinitely plural, since the gift of nothing is identical to the gift of everything, the gift of impropriety is the gift of general appropriation and presentation . . . the more he [the poet, the maker, the actor] is nothing, the more he can be everything' (Lacoue-Labarthe, 1986: 29). Followed to its logical conclusion, the subject who produces or reproduces himself, society or texts by imitation of what is already in being escapes definition, delimitation and schematization. Whereas the product can be fixed and grasped, identified and schematized, the producer 'himself' cannot.

In banishing poets from his Republic, Lacoue-Labarthe argues, Plato was banishing an incarnation of this fundamental impropriety and instability of the subject who, because he is nothing in and of himself, can be like anything or everything. Plato was making the poet a sacrificial victim for the subject's 'absolute, endless and bottomless vicariousness' which is 'something like infinite substitution and circulation: the defaulting of essence' (1975: 246). For

Plato wanted his Republic to be a stable and orderly society where the guardians are guardians, the soldiers soldiers and the workers workers. He wanted subjects to be identifiable in terms of their socialization, and he wanted to be able to place and define subjects in terms of determinate, psychological, sociological, biological and anthropological attributes. This is why, having failed to banish mimesis with the poet, Plato tried to prevent mimetic mirrors (which, for Lacoue-Labarthe represent the mimetician) from being turned on everything and anything improperly and unstably, by fixing his own mirror to the wall of a cave, where it can no longer turn, but only reflect, however obscurely, stable, static and unchanging truths.

The implication is that we repeat these Platonic gestures when we assimilate the subject to his products, whether we do so by identifying the producer with his products or by banishing him altogether. To banish the producing subject by claiming that he is always already spoken by language or always in any case already dead, is to banish the dangerous possibility that *poiesis* issues from nothing that is like a subject or a self, and that the primary poetic gift, the necessary poetic gift, is the gift of self-abnegation and self-obliteration (*desistance*). And to identify the producing subject with his products, is to conveniently 'forget' that *poiesis* involves substitution – that Plato 'is' no more Socrates or the Sophist than man 'is' a given model of subjectivation – in order to make the producing subject as visible, as identifiable and as capable of reappropriation as his product. For once the subject is as visible as his product, his impropriety can be mastered by categorizing and identifying him in determinate anthropological terms (psychological, sociological, political and historical). To identify the producer with his product – a language, a set of practices, modes of subjectivation – is always to control the infinite vicariousness of *poiesis* by installing theory or history or philosophy safely in the realm of what is manifest and evident, where they can define identities, establish classes, discover likenesses and construct schemata. To assimilate the producing subject to the product is to fix our theoretical or historical mirrors to a wall where they reflect plurality as stasis, and the entombment of all producing subjects.

Lacoue-Labarthe also indicates that in treating the subject as a subjected or as a socialized product, we are carefully suppressing the radical implications of human malleability. Postmodern psychology and cultural history have taught us that that if man always 'accedes to himself by submitting to the model of the other' then he is what he is only by virtue of the other. They have brought us to think of man as unresisting clay, as a *subjectum*, a substratum or support on which anything can be imprinted. Man is thought to be 'constituted in the same way as a figure is imprinted on malleable matter when it is stamped with a type, or 'typed" so that his psyche is only 'the instrument of another, the support, the matrix, or the malleable matter where the imprint is made' (1986: 99–100). We consider this subjection of the subject to typing and imprinting an evil. In the anthropological order, malleability, passivity and receptivity are associated with feminization and with depropriation of the sovereign rights of the rational and conscious self. When we speak of subjects as products of social typing and imprinting, we confront this 'evil', but we also leave ourselves an opening for regaining mastery and control. If we have been feminized, if we have been typed, if we have lost self-determination, we reassure ourselves, we can become conscious of our condition, take deliberate, active, political measures, promote a new form of subjectivity and regain our virility.

What we exclude with horror is the more radical possibility of some sort of immemorial psychic or genetic preinscription of the *subjectum*, which opens the subject to a *Geist* – a spirit, vision or visitation – which cannot be reduced to history or language or society, and makes the subject a receiver for a telecommunication which comes from elsewhere. Like Plato, we want to be done with poetic inspiration and fear the implications of being possessed by an Other. Women, madmen and poets are possessed. They yield to another, and allow their bodies and voices to serve as instruments of another. If we redirect our attention away from the poet, it is because we want to be done with inspiration, feminization, and poetic madness – 'the dangerous poet' in all her forms.

Banishing the poet from his Republic, Plato is, like us, banishing inspiration and feminization, and with them the socially disruptive and destabilizing possibility that persons can be possessed by a *Geist*, a spirit, visitant or vision, which is beyond rational, social and political control. Plato wants to control the malleability of the subject both in theory and in practice. He wants to control education and, with it, the models and myths to which subjects are exposed. He wants to reform society by im-printing subjects according to rational, theoretically determined models. Like Heidegger after him, and with similar fascist and totalitarian implications, Plato thinks of philosophy as a *Führung* of the people; and like Marx, he believes that man and society can and must, actively, deliberately and rationally, be remade under the guidance of the political philosopher. Poetic inspiration and feminization constitute a threat to such *Führung*. For the possibility of possession represents the possibility of evading rational, historical, political and social control. The person who serves as an instrument for a spirit other than the current spirit of politics and society, is also something other than a tame instrument of the polis.

To assimilate the producer to the product is not only to suppress and control the possibility of subversive otherness; it is also to suppress the possibility of singularity. Nancy, Derrida and Levinas are all very insistent on this point. 'When we understand man on the basis of his works,' says Levinas, 'his life and works mask him' because a man's works disguise the way he 'presents himself, without reference to anything, distinct from any other being' (1965: 153, 152). 'The anthropological profusion of the subject' Nancy complains, merely serves to 'mask and suppress the question – or rather the voice – of someone who is neither a subject nor the Subject' (1979:13). And Derrida insists more cryptically and more programmatically that 'the relation to the product cannot structurally be cut off from the relation to the producing subjectivity, however indeterminate and anonymous this may be: implication of a signature which is not identical with the extrinsic requirements of (psychological, sociological, historical etc) empiricism' (1975: 64).

Levinas and Derrida both accuse historicising marxist and postmarxist approaches of defacement, depropriation and burial of the producing subject: 'Historiography,' says Levinas, 'only recounts the way survivors appropriate the work of dead wills and testaments; it rests on the accomplished usurpation of the victors, i.e. the survivors, and tells a story of enslavement by forgetting the life fighting against slavery' (1965: 204). And Derrida says that 'history puts to death and treats the dead . . . (it) is the science of the father. It occupies the place of the dead, the place of the father' (1982a: 22). To illustrate the death of the subject in pluralizing histories, Derrida parodies the way such histories fragment authors and their works when they relate them to a variety of other common extant psychological, sociological, ideological and cultural phenomena, by fragmenting proper names, including his own, into syllables which repeat or recall other common words in language. To liken a writer or a work to a variety of other social, cultural and ideological phenomena is to efface the singularity of the signatory, even while one is erecting him into a monument. Derrida also mocks the logic of historical 'reconstructions' or 'restitutions' of the past (see Derrida, 1978). First, he suggests, we detach products from their producer and leave them, abandoned like the shoes in a Van Gogh painting, silent and staring, on a museum wall; but then, because we cannot tolerate the awful anonymity and indetermination of the abandoned product, we try to link it to a real subject and to give it a material base. Shoes, after all, are supposed to walk upon the ground. We treat the work as a fetich, as a detachable and reattachable appendage when we say: 'these abandoned shoes are the shoes of a peasant – like Van Gogh, they are grounded in the soil of the fields' or 'no, these shoes are the shoes of a townsman – like Van Gogh, they have their material base in the city.' And we ignore 'what the thing *says*' (Derrida, 1978: 330).

But how is it possible for a person to live anything, think anything or say anything which is irreducible to anthropomorphic concepts, knowledge and history? How is it possible for something wholly other to come into being and into beings? It is to this question that we now turn.

Man's Spectral Double

Derrida speaks the coming of what is Wholly Other than history, society and subjectivation as an event, an affirmation and a telecommunication which comes into being and into beings from elsewhere. The terms being and beings here are to be understood in their most concrete and material sense – in the sense of: 'yet in my flesh shall I see God' (Job, 19: 26). In Derrida's texts, the Wholly Other comes to the material human body: to the ears and the mouth, to the hands and the feet, to the psyche and to the blood, to the sexual organs and to the body's heat. Difference comes to the body as a spectral body which is carried by the body normally exposed to and by *sa-voir*. It 'haunts' the body as an other of the body or as a double of the body, which deconstructs all conventional knowledge and language of the body, while regenerating it and revealing it as the bearer of an other thought, an other speech and an other mode of action.

The Other comes to the *subjectum* – to the subject as that extant material substance or 'docile body' which is bound to history and culture and language and subjectivation, and which is manifestly present in the world. But its effect is to reveal that the *subjectum* is *also* constituted as a *hyperkeimenon* (support, substratum) or, in kabbalistic terms as a *merkhava* (chariot) for that which hides beneath or beyond substance and its accidents, beneath or beyond society and its changing models of subjectivation, beneath and beyond what we know as the 'self' or the 'subject'. As Lacoue-Labarthe explains:

> What interests us . . . is that which is *also* called into play in the subject, while being absolutely irreducible to any subjectivity (that is also to say to any objectivity) whatsoever; that which, in the subject, deserts (has always deserted) the subject *himself* and which, prior to all 'self-possession' (and in a manner other than that of dispossession) is the dissolution, the undoing of the subject in the subject or *as* the subject.' (1979: 151)

In many of Derrida's texts of the late '70s and '80s, 'what is *also* called into play in the subject' is symbolized by the feminine.[4] And this *also* must be emphasized. Man's spectral or feminine body is not something external to his body: it is a difference within the same, or the same body which is also different. The feminine body and the masculine body, the spiritual body and the egotological body, the psychic body and the psychological body share and infinitely differentiate the same corpus of writing, the same language and the same flesh: 'I am (the) both, (the) double, I sign double, my writings and I make two. I am the (masculine) dead and the living (feminine) . . . ' (1982a: 21). The subject and his words belong to the dead order of the Father – to the order of finite, determinate and manifest being, the order of erections, representations and identifications, the order of history, socialization and subjectivation, the order of the Same. And *at the same time* they *also* belong to the living order of the Mother – the order of concealment, withdrawal and unrepresentability, the order of psychic and spiritual life, the order of ethics and the Wholly Other. The subject inhabits both orders, speaks both languages simultaneously. There are (at least) two in one: *la vie la mort*.

Derrida's texts are therefore characterized by what I am calling double-speak and by *double ententes*, as well as by fragmentation inasmuch as different texts focus on the regeneration of different body-parts. To do what I am about to do – piece together at least part of the fragmented body of Derrida's bisexual *Doppelgänger* from the diverse essays in which it is disseminated, and recover a philosophico-poetic fable of bodily-spiritual transformation from the play of language in which it is couched – is to translate Derrida's double-speak into a much less ambiguous narrative which is not present *as such* in any single Derridean text. This is both a distortion and not a distortion, since, as Derrida has pointed out, 'a certain narrativity is to be found at the heart of even the simplest affirmation' (1987a: 110).

Derrida uses the syntax of the blood, borrowed, in part, from Blanchot to speak the first step away from the order of the father, which Lacoue-Labarthe calls *desistance*, Heidegger *Gelassenheit* and mystics 'the loss of self'. By assonance, the blood (*sang*) indicates the need for a withdrawal or subtraction (*sans*) within the subject from what we know of the subject. 'The effect of the *sans*', says Derrida, is to make 'the same word and the same thing appear removed from themselves, withdrawn (*soustrait*, also subtracted) from their reference and their identity, while continuing to let themselves be traversed in their old body towards a wholly other concealed in them' (1986b: 90). Withdrawal from the manifest being of the subject, from his identity, socio-historical selfhood, and what we regard as his 'reality', reveals the spectral body which haunts the subject as a me-less-me or me-without-ego (*moi-sans-moi*) and as a reality-less-reality (*réalité-sans-réalité*). As withdrawal and subtraction from self-possession and self-presence, the *sans* does not occur without the spilling of some blood (*sang*): 'the *sans* cuts out the thing and deprives it of itself' (1986b: 195). There is a death-sentence and a sacrificial killing (*tu-toi*, kill your self) or effacement of the self. The subject removed and distanced from the ego, from consciousness, and from all sense of self is dead in these terms: 'When death has come from the other, *I my* (*je m'*) is no longer possible . . . I is always called *I dead* (*je mort*)' (1986b: 80).

However, the *sans* is not only a mark of withdrawal and subtraction from the manifest identity of the subject; it is also a mark of the separation and participation of two distinct and opposed dimensions in the same bodily shell. The *sans* 're-marks the same X (X-less-X), without annulling it, with the wholly other which parts it from itself' (1986b: 91). And in this respect, the *sans* is also a *sans-sans-sans* (a without-without-without) or a *sans-sans-manque* (a without-without-lack) (1986b: 151). It marks not a negation but an affirmation, the possibility of an event or advent. In Judaism, the blood is traditionally the seat of the life or the soul of a body. In Derrida, this second *sans* leads 'towards a *living* (*un vivre*, also: food, provision, supplies, an allowance) which is finally intransitive and which is equivalent to (*vaut*, also: is worth) "perhaps even dying"' (1986b: 44). In Nancy's *Ego Sum*, the soul's relation to the body is understood in terms of the circulation of the blood.

Spectral feet take the step (*pas*) designated by the blood. They make the crossing (*passage*, also *pas-sage*, wise step) from the self-possessed island of the ego (*il, île*) towards that other shore where the event or the advent occurs. Like the *sans*, therefore, the step (*pas*) in question is both a removal from something or of something (a *pas-à-pas*, step-by-not), and an affirmation (*pas-ne-pas*, not-not) of the possibility of stepping beyond the bounds of subjectivity and subjectivation (*pas-au-delà*).

The beyond here is not transcendental – 'the no-beyond (*pas-d'au-delà*) is the beyond itself' (1986b: 44). The beyond is neither outside man nor outside living. If anything, it is a surplus of living, a sur-living (*survivre*)[5] and sur-truth (*sur-vérité*) (1986b: 167), charged with the sense of extension or expansion which comes of moving into a different, unbounded medium where 'the Thing takes place without having a place' (1986b: 181). The step into the beyond (*au-delà*) is a step into a different medium or dimension. The medium of the *au-delà* is water (*eau*), which is 'an infinite metaphor' or 'metaphor of the infinite', not only because by a happy chance *eau-de-là* (water from there) is almost literally a translation of the biblical word for heaven (*sham-mayim*) but also because, as one might expect from an infinite metaphor, it leads the step in an extraordinary number of directions. Water leads, for instance, to the sea (*mer*) and to the mother (*mère*), and to all manner of generative and merging and submerging liquids and fluids (galactic, seminal, parturient waters). By assonance, *au/eau* becomes the O – the nothing from which everything comes and to which everything returns, the O of the Wholly Other, that is nothing like what we know and the zero of self-effacement. As a pictogram, the letter O is also the round hole in the ego (m*o*i), in the word (m*o*t) and in the thing (ch*o*se), the hole of death (m*o*rt), and the opening of the gift (d*o*n). And as a pas-sage to all these Os, the step (*pas*) also requires a certain *pas*-sivity.

For the gift (*don*) comes to the ears (*ouï*, heard) in their passivity. It comes to the 'docility of a listening . . . a receptive modality, an attention to what it is given to hear rather than to (and prior to) the entrepreneurial and inquisitorial activity of a request or inquest'

(1987c: 645–6). The gift comes as a call ('*Viens*') or recall which is no sooner heard than assented to (*oui, oui*, aye, aye; hear, hear). The call is echoed by assent (*amen*, literally, I believe) because its very advent is an affirmation of the Eternal I am: '*Gott spricht immer nur Ja*. God only ever says Aye (or: I am).' As Derrida emphasizes, the German word *Ja* (*oui*, aye) is also a Hebrew word for God, *Jah*. The event is the advent of the *oui*, of *Jah*, of the affirmation Aye Jah Am (1987c: 640). This affirmation (in Hebrew, *ken*) is the indwelling of God (in Hebrew, *Shekhena*), the proximity of God within man, or as Levinas might say, the idea-of-the-infinite-in-us.[6] The *Shekhena* is feminine, like the sea and the mother (*la mer, la mère*) and like the French words for truth (*la vérité*), thought (*la pensée*), speech (*la parole*) and voice (*la voix*).

This she who is many shes comes to man as a feminine figure or as a feminine voice, questioning, calling ('*Viens*'), and signalling the reality-less-reality of the affirmation which dwells in man.[7] This feminine is not God 'in person'. The *Shekhena* is at best a threshhold or outer court of Godliness, and a messenger or an envoy of Godliness in man. The infinite and supernal *Ein Sof* (literally, no end, infinite) is not *Shekhena* but *Ayin* – Nothing. Lacking all material substance and all finite determinations, the *Ayin* is unnamable, unknowable, unrepresentable, inexpressible and infinitely distant from man. But, as Levinas says, 'the infinite is not (out there) first to reveal itself afterwards. Its infini-tion is produced as revelation, as the placing in *me* of its idea' (1965: xv). The *Shekhena* reveals the infinite in the finite and opens finitude onto infinity. As Derrida says: 'the near from-come distances . . . Distance is here at the heart of the Thing' (1986b: 28).

Man's assent (*oui*) is therefore always already a response to a prior hearing (*ouï, Jah*); it is always 'in the first place secondary, coming after a demand, a question, or another *oui*' (1987c: 649). But hearing (*ouï*) and affirming (*oui*), affirmation (*Jah*) and affirmation (*ja*) are also practically simultaneous. Similarly, the event or advent is always a re-cital or re-citation; it has always occurred before in another's experience or in another's text. But it also happens each time for the first time. It is absolutely singular each time. This singularity, each time, for each person, makes the event an *Ereignis* or *Er-eignis*, literally his own. It makes each person absolutely 'unique and irreplacable' (Levinas, 1982: 55) in his response-ibility. Each person's acquiescence to the call and the demand – *oui, oui*, I return, *hineini*, here I am, (Aye/I) come; send me – is a singular undertaking and a personal pledge, 'a sort of archi-engagement, alliance, consent, promise' (1987c: 647).

This engagement and this response-ibility come to the male organ as the ring of circum-cision, the incision in the flesh of the covenanted bond. They also come as a ring to the hand. The ring (*anneau*) on the finger (*doigt*) founds the alliance (*alliance*, also: marriage, wedding ring) not only in an annihilation, an annulation and return of the subject, but also as infinite obligation (*doit*, debt). The debt is infinite because man is always finite, imperfect, never finished emptying himself of his self, and therefore always unequal to the demands made upon him by his alliance with the-idea-of-the-infinite-in-us. 'Demanding all and nothing, the thing (*chose*) places the debtor (the one who would like to say *my* cause (*chose*)) in a situation of absolute heteronomy and in an infinitely unequal alliance' (1984a: 49). But notwithstanding its inequality to the task, the ring-bearing hand must bear witness; it must be an emissary of the thought and the thing. The hand must give a sign, send a sign (*envoi*) or better yet, be a sign (*Zeichen, zeigen*) in the biblical sense of 'bind it as a sign upon your hand' (Deut. 6:9) and in Levinas' sense of 'I am testimony, or trace, or glory of the Infinite . . . it is I who express the Infinite, precisely by giving a sign of the gift of the sign' (1982: 122).

Above all, the hand must give. For both Derrida and Levinas, the hand is the seat of *chesed*, of infinite and disinterested generosity and goodness: 'the hand belongs to the essence of the gift, by a giving which gives, if that's possible, without taking anything at all' (Derrida 1987c: 428). But here they part company. For Levinas, the essence of giving is to give other people something: usually the bread from one's mouth. For Derrida, the essence of giving is not transitive: the hand gives itself up (*se donne*). The hand gives a hand to others, usually by handing on the gift of the sign; but then it hands over. It leaves matters in the hands of others, giving up all possibility of manipulation or constraint, giving up even its need to give. As Infinite *chesed* gives Being (*es gibt Sein*) while leaving (*laisser, lassen*) beings to have an apparently separate and independent existence, so Derrida's hand gives dependably (*Verlassenheit*) but with abandonment (*Verlassenheit*).

Moreover, where Levinas speaks of giving with both hands, Derrida makes a traditional kabbalistic distinction between the left hand and the right. While the right hand (*chesed*) gives, the left hand (*gevurah*) is obliged to hold back. Its task is to contract and limit the outflowing of *chesed*, concealing the full force of the 'inexpressible' behind a partition or curtain. While the right hand gives the sign, the revelation, therefore, the left hand withdraws or conceals the supernal mystery behind a curtain or veil of undecidability. For traditionally, the 'secret must and must not be allowed to divulge itself . . . It must not be divulged, but it must also be made known, or rather this 'must' 'must not', 'must not not' must be allowed to be known' (1987c: 557). Derrida is less than enthusiastic about the political and pedagogical implications of this tradition, which he thinks makes the veil of rhetoric a shield for an elite against the masses. But he finds that in sharing (*partage*) the secret, the secret 'partitions (*partage*) itself' insofar as 'it can only appear, even to one person, by beginning to vanish, to divulge itself, therefore, by dissimulating itself, as a secret, in showing itself' (1987c: 558).

When this difficulty comes to the lips, that is to say to language (in Hebrew *safa* means both lip and language), it turns the event, the advent of the-idea-of-the-infinite-in-us, into poesie. Philosophy becomes again what it was in the bible, in *hagadah* and in *kabbalah*: metaphor, fable, narrative, parable, allegory, allusion. For, seductive and rather flirtatious behind her dissimulating veil, 'the feminine (the truth) does not allow herself to be taken' (1979: 56) either on the stylus of the dogmatic philosopher who seeks to penetrate her with his 'discourses in pro and contra' or in the specular mirror of the language of presence. She evades the grasp. Philosophy becomes literature because *inventio* is required to persuade her to give herself *as another* and *for another*.[8]

Metaphor, fable and allegory give the Other *as another* because they neither mirror nor create the Other in any onto-theological sense. They do not invent that which 'alone invents the world . . . and which invents us' (1987c: 60). Instead, allegory and fable constantly indicate their own fictionality, their own dependence on language, and the fact that they are themselves inventions – inventions 'which make themselves inventions of truth, truth of/from fable, fable of/from truth, truth of/from the truth *as fable*' (1987c: 30). Thus Derrida's fable about the doubling of ego and guest, of same and other, in the same flesh, in the same text, in the same word, is also always and only an invention. It is an invention about invention of/from the Other, an invention about the truth of invention, and the invention of truth as an invention from 'the other without me, beyond me, in me' (1987c: 11).

Metaphor, fable and allegory are also required to persuade the truth to give herself *for another*. Fable and allegory are performative, and as Derrida conjugates the word, philosophical invention is related to *venir* and *avénement*, to the advent of the event. Philosophy (if this can still be called philosophy) is an *ars inveniendi*, an art of letting come in.[9] To give a sign of the giving of the sign, each text has to be an event: it has to allow an affirmation to come which can awaken the *oui* in others. It has to be an *invention de l'autre*: an invention *of* the other in the sense that it 'lets an as yet unanticipatable alterity come (in)' (1987c: 53) and an invention *from* the other in the sense that it proceeds from an 'other without me, beyond me, in me' (1987c: 11). Or, to put it differently, the philosopher's pen-is has to be inverted into a vagina, into a channel or passage for the other, who enters being and time through him. His is not the masculine role of mastering truth or penetrating her, but the feminine role of bearing the truth to others and of serving as the channel for its coming. (De)construction is dedicated to:

> an invention of/from the other who traverses the economy of the same; that is, by miming or repeating the same, (it) gives a venue to the other, leaves the other to come. Please note that I say *leaves the other to come* for, if the other is precisely that which does not get invented, deconstructive initiative or inventiveness can only consist in opening, in de-enclosing, in destabilizing structures of foreclosure to leave a passage for the other. One does not make the other come; one leaves the other to come by preparing for its coming. (1987c: 60)

But of course, what comes through (de)construction's inventions has always already come to the lips and to language before. Derrida's figure of 'man as the psyche of God' (1987c: 58) or of the psyche as the man of God re-invents Kabbalism's psychic body of the upright man (*yosher*). His doubling of the psychic body and the psycho-sociological-historical body repeats Chasidism's metaphor of man as having two psyches or two souls – an animal soul which gives life to the prophane body and the prophane world and participates in its values, and a divine soul which, unsatisfied by this world and these values, always calls man back to a wholly different truth and wholly different values.[10] Derrida's 'event' reverberates with echoes of innumerable texts in different religious traditions which recount the mystic's encounter with God, as well as with echoes of the writings of a long line of philosophers.

And in association with man as poet or writer passing on what has come to him from elsewhere, it also re-calls the now abandoned and denigrated figures of the inspired poet and poet-prophet.

There is nothing new about this if we insist on looking for the new where we conventionally expect to find it – namely, in the invention of some new thing or in the creation as if *ex nihilo* of something heretofore unknown, unthought, unspoken or un-done. The invention in question is a re-invention, a repetition, a re-citing and a re-turn of what has always already come to man, to language and to texts many times before. But there are also differences. I will indicate two of them here, and leave some of the others for the last section of this chapter.

One difference is that what is returning in these texts is an other past, an other tradition with an other imaginary of man and an other imaginary of the author. Or, if one prefers, what is being returned is tradition's other, the author's other, history's other, and the present's other, in the sense that it is other than what is considered reasonable and possible within our current and historically projected economy of the Same. The figure of the inspired poet haunts the modern figure of the author, and the image of man doing God's work in response to God's call, haunts the the modern figure of man as Worker and Producer as their long-buried spectres. In-spiration, in-vention 'from the other without me, beyond me, in me' haunts our modern 'techno-onto-anthropo-theological concept of invention' as its now impossible other.

Thus, and this is the second difference, though the event and its imaginary return, they return differently. And they must – always – return differently. For one thing, while the event may return and return again, circling back like a ring (*anneau*), like an anniversary, or like the year (*année*), it always returns on a certain date, a date which is unique. Each time, the sign has to be transmitted, handed on at a different historical moment, in a different tongue, and in different social, political, economic and ideological circumstances. These distinguish each coming from other comings, and help to make each 'what it must be, 'primary', unique, uniquely unique, opening *in its turn, in vicem, vice versa*, on its date, each time the first time/turn (*fois, vices, ves, volta, Mal* etc.)' (1987c: 650).

Moreover, the event always comes to a singular person, as a response and response-ibility which comes to him for the first time, and to him alone: 'The only: singularity, solitude, secret of the encounter' (1986a: 18). It is as a unique and irreplaceable singularity that one turns back (in Hebrew, *tshuvah*, usually translated repentance, means return) to the Other within/without one and it is as a unique and irreplaceable singularity that one gives the sign of the gift of the sign which allows the Other to return to language, to discourse and to others at this date. In this sense too, each time (*volta*), each turn (*volta*) to the Other, each return of the Other is the first time, unique. The singular person is never merely an example of a general law. His 'example remains irreplaceable' because 'the example only gives an example if it is not to be taken for any other. It gives the example, the only possible example, in that he is the only one to give it: the only' (1986a: 18-19).

Psychology and Psyche-ology

The (de)constructive turn or return to the other within/without one could be described as a return to a certain 'unconscious', and we might imagine it, in Lacanian psychoanalytic terms, as a return of the subject to the last signifier, the Other, who is also the subject's 'true self'.[11] Many (de)constructive texts are designed to disabuse us of this assumption, to distinguish its teachings from psychoanalysis, and to show why the psychoanalytic displacement of the subject 'himself' from consciousness to the unconscious is theoretically, morally and politically suspect.

In an early essay, 'La Trace de l'Autre' Levinas contrasted 'the story of Abraham leaving his homeland for ever for an unknown land and forbidding his servant to bring even his son back to this point of departure' with 'the myth of Ulysses returning to Ithaca' (610). Ulysses' circular movement of return to his homebase, he suggested, is analogical to the circular movement of egoism, which starts from the self and brings everything back to the self. As Lacoue-Labarthe, Nancy and Derrida were quick to realize, there is also an analogy here to the circular movement of the speculative dialectic, where the Subject externalizes himself only to return to himself by incorporating what is other than himself, as well as to the circular marxist movement of appropriation by which man makes his world, objectifying himself by his labour and recognizing himself in the products of his labour. By contrast, Abraham journeys outwards from his point of departure and, having left his home behind him, he never tries to send or bring anything back. This unrecuperated movement towards the other, with its abnegation, is, Levinas suggests, the ethical movement itself.

(De)construction argues that psychoanalysis only repeats and institutionalizes the circular, narcissistic movement of the speculative dialectic. Most obviously, the classical Freudian doctrine of *Wo es war soll ich werden* describes a trajectory in which the conscious subject, separated and distanced from his true unconscious self, gets back in touch with himself by gradually returning to his 'truth'. Despite the fact that the Lacanian subject is constituted on the basis of a fundamental absence or lack, the goal of Lacan's dialectic is the same as Freud's and Hegel's: 'reintegration and accord or reconciliation' (Lacoue-Labarthe and Nancy, 1973: 13, 128) or 'a certain reappropriation and a certain readequation (which) will reconstitute the proper, the place, meaning and truth that have become distant from themselves for the time of a detour or a non-delivery'[12] (Derrida, 1980: 182). For the purpose of a Lacanian analysis is to get the subject to ultimately hear and recognize the insistent message that his unconscious has been sending him through all the detours and games of language: I, the real subject, am not, because my true self has been lost (castrated) by false identifications with others. In *Grammatologie*, Derrida cautiously and ironically suggested a parallel between Rousseau's masturbation with images of absent beauties who were substitutes, supplements, for his lost mother and the Lacanian analysand's pursuit, through a succession of false images of the self, of 'full speech' (*parole pleine*) where the subject touches on his original castration, his original loss of self. In 'Speculer-sur Freud' he mockingly compares the circular path of the speculative and psychoanalytic trajectory to the famous game in which, for hours, Freud's grandson would throw a cotton spool away from him to make it disappear and then pull it back to make it reappear (*Fort/Da*). Little Ernst too played at expelling or losing something (his instrument, his phallus, himself) for the pleasure of returning (it) to himself. Little Ernst's pleasure too lay in the 'reapparition of his own proper instrument, with all the threads in his hand' (1980: 339). There is no real loss of self here, no self-abnegation, no 'exappropriation' only deferred reappropriation and mastery. Displaced to the unconscious, the ego in its egoism continues to bring everything back to itself.

By contrast, (de)construction describes the life of the psyche as an Abrahamic journey, emphasizing not only that the journey undertaken at God's command is a journey outwards without return – thus a sending or mission (*envoi*) – but also that it does not issue from anything like a self. As an envoy, each person in his singularity is not an 'envoy of himself' (1987c: 137), but an envoy of the other which, like Abraham's homebase, is always in retreat in relation to where he is. The departure which initiates the journey of being, the mission of life itself, is therefore a genuine departure, a genuine break. In sending being and beings into being, God also withdraws or retreats from them in order to leave them (*lassen, verlassen*) to be apparently independent and self-contained entities – without this separation between God and the world, there would, according to *kabbalah*, be no world and no separate beings or things because everything would be reabsorbed into God. There is in (de)construction, therefore, no possibility of return to that which has retreated or withdrawn, to the homeland from which the journey issues, no possibility of reappropriation or mastery. And in being itself, there are only 'envoys of the other, others. Inventions of/from the other' (1987c: 137). Men are inventions of the Other, sent into being by the Other, as 'emissions from the other, from the other in them without them' (1987c: 141).

At the 'kernel' of man, there is therefore not another subject who can become conscious of himself as the subject of the unconscious or the unconscious subject; there is a fundamental retreat, a fundamental non-being, or *Ayin* or unrepresentability, from which men, like the world, emerge into being. For Kabbalism, the soul 'itself' as it issues from infinity is, like God, basically unrepresentable and unknowable – it can only present itself through its finite effects on thought, speech and action. And, as Nicolas Abraham points out very traditionally, this means that anything that presents itself as the subject or as the I or as thought, speech or action, only constitutes 'the husk of an inaccessible kernel'. It is this living kernel of unrepresentability that (de)construction salutes in the crypt of the text, and it is in 'the disappearing appearance' of the author's retreat that (de)construction marks his singularity. There is here a very different kind of *Fort/Da* from that of psychoanalysis: an oscillating now-you-see-me-now-you-don't which only dimly outlines a dark generative space where all presence, all images and all re-presentations of self vanish.

(De)constructive texts also deconstruct psychoanalysis by bringing out the social and political implications of psychoanalysis's failure to take the unconscious beyond representations and identifications. The problem with this fundamental theatricality both of the conscious mind and of the 'other scene' of the unconscious in traditional psychoanalysis is not only that man is for ever encouraged to seek himself in his self-representations rather than understanding himself as a 'representative' an 'envoy', of any Thing beyond them. The problem is also – as Lacoue-Labarthe, Nancy and Mikkel Borch-Jakobsen (who has built on their work and brought out its implications) have argued – that self-representations are also mimetic identifications. And structures of identification are, according to psychoanalysis itself, always murderous structures of rivalry and hatred.

In dreams, when the unconscious subject desires what another person desires, it represents itself in that person's place, and in that sense kills or eliminates the other person. Similarly, identifying with another person or 'acceding to oneself through the model of the other' provokes rivalry and hatred because when a subject sees himself in another or as another, his ego and his separateness disappear, and to see himself in his ego and separateness again, he requires the disappearance of the other. As Lacan said: 'the aggressive tension of this "me or other" is absolutely integrated into every aspect of the function of man's imagination' (1978: 110).

Lacan saw the Oedipal phase as a resolution of this dilemma, but Lacoue-Labarthe, Nancy and Borsch-Jakobsen argue that the Oedipal phase only perpetuates the dilemma by placing the son in a situation of identification and rivalry with the model, the father. And this rivalry can still only be resolved either by the son eliminating the father in order to take his place (as in the murder of the Urvater by the original tribal band) or by the son incorporating or assimilating or swallowing the father as an 'ego ideal' in yet another version of the narcissistic, reappropriating speculative dialectic. If the Oedipal phase is supposed to constitute the child's entry into society, language and law, and if we are socialized by mimetic identifications, then we are socialized unsociably and anti-socially, the law can only be a law of violence, and society can only be a place of murderous rivalry, competition, and hatred where everyone seeks to swallow everyone else up to get the upper hand.

The situation changes, however, if we consider that 'the subject of desire has no proper identity before the identification which makes him come, blindly, to the place of the other (who is therefore not other)' (Borch-Jakobsen, 1982: 65). For if instead of positing, as Lacan did, that there is something like a subject behind dream representations pulling the strings like a puppeteer, we assume that the subject is completely caught up in the scene of the fantasme and totally identified with the puppets, then the subject is not putting himself in the place of an other, but immediately taking himself to be the other. If this is the case, there is no mimetic distance between the self and the other, and no question of rivalry and hatred. And if, instead of supposing, as Freud and Lacan did, that a child is something or someone before his identifications with others, we assume that the child only comes into being with his identifications and as his identifications, then the child's identifications become possible, like the poet's mimesis, only by virtue of a fundamental *Ayin* or irrepresentability or absence of determination, an initial 'retreat of identity'.

For Lacoue-Labarthe and Nancy, only 'identification with the retreat of identity' beyond and behind all figures and models makes the social bond possible (Lacoue-Labarthe and Nancy, 1981b: 69). Once people define themselves in relation to what is always already in retreat – the retreat of identity, the retreat of truth and the retreat of God – people share (*partage*) what divides (*partage*) and dis-sociates them. They share their finitude, their abandonment, their exposure, their impotence and their mortality. And this is what ultimately makes community not only necessary, but possible. As Nancy explains:

> it is with the retreat of the gods that community comes: a group of people standing before its gods does not think of itself as a community in the sense that it does not seek the presence of its bond in itself; instead, it experiences itself as a group (a family, a tribe, a people) in the face of the god who holds and reserves apart from it the truth and force of its bond . . . as soon as I name my god or appear before him, I am by virtue of this, placed with other mortals like myself.' (1987: 41)

Where Marx and Feuerbach argued that men must reappropriate the essence which they alienate in God, Nancy argues that alienation of the essence is the *sine qua non* of community. For when men try to reappropriate the essence – when they try to appropriate for themselves supreme power and knowledge, or worship Man or Society or a particular human philosophy or human ideology as their God – social life becomes what Marx somewhere called 'the war of the greedy' and politics becomes the rivalry of political groups all claiming the right to enforce their will because they alone possess 'the truth'. If, on the other hand, supreme power and knowledge remain the exclusive preserve of an unrepresentable God, they can be claimed by no man and by no political group. All men then stand before God in the same pas-sivity, in the same nullity, in the same indebtedness and the same destitution, as emissaries of the other. All men are exposed to God and to each other in their singularity and in their dispersal, in their response-ibility, and in unforced, and therefore non- violent, obedience to that which gives them the Law.

(En)gendering the Law

The problem with this is that in (de)construction, the Law too is in retreat from identity, and men therefore have to return to give the law. In (de)constructive texts to date, God gives being (*es gibt Sein*); God does not give the Law or indeed, any determinate gift. It is only by answering the call within/without him that each singular man comes to moral duty (*devoir*) and to responsibility to and for others, and this call is, in principle, without any determinate content as such. This rids (de)construction of transcendentals, universals, authorities and dogmas. But, as becomes apparent when Derrida figures the Law as a Law of Gender,[13] it also subverts both the possibility of otherness and the possibility of making any moral, social, psychological, political or gender difference.

In (de)constructive texts, the retreat of identity is symbolized by the mother. Ontologically, this symbolism can be explained by the fact that coming into being as a finite and separate person involves becoming physically separate from the mother – birth and weaning are separations from the mother, and when the mother leaves the child, this is experienced as withdrawal and abandonment. But the point of the symbolism is that, like God in his retreat from being and beings, the mother gives her child the gift of life, the gift of finitude, the gift of separate existence, by her withdrawal; her gift is the gift of division or dis-sociation, the gift of allowing people to be separate and other. Moreover, like death, the mother symbolizes the basic invisibility, unfigurability and unrepresentability of the origin, of the truth, of God in retreat from the world: 'death can no more present itself as such 'in person' than the sex of the woman, of the mother' (Lacoue-Labarthe, 1979: 206). The mother serves as a re-citation of the Supernal Mother in kabbalism who is, among other things, a homonym for some of the concealed, transcendent aspects of the God who did not even show Moses his face. As a homonym or homology for God, the mother is 'the faceless figure who gives rise to all the figures by losing herself in the background of the scene like an anonymous personnage' (Derrida, 1982a: 38). She is 'the figure without figure, the disappearing origin of all figures, the fundament without fundament against which, at every moment, the life of the I flaps and emerges' (Derrida, 1986b: 176). And as Levinas, Derrida and Lacoue-Labarthe repeatedly point out, this means that real women are not what they are talking about.

If the basic 'retreat of identity' on the basis of which the subject comes into being is symbolized by the mother, and the finite representations and ego-identifications of the subject are symbolized by the father, then the psyche can be described as bisexual from its inception: 'I am my father and my mother.' The subject belongs both to the order of the father – to the order of finite, determinate and manifest being – insofar as he is 'husk', and to the order of the mother – to the order of concealment, withdrawal and representability – insofar as he is 'kernel'. For Derrida, this bisexuality is more fundamental than manifest biological, sociological or historical sexual differentiation, and it means that basically 'there is no truth as such in the sexual difference as such of man or of woman as such' (Derrida, 1979: 104). Biological, sociological or historical sexual differences belong to the ontological order of the father, and so do feminisms which remain anchored in problems of sexual difference: 'Feminism is the operation by which woman wants to resemble man, the dogmatic philosopher who asserts truth, science, objectivity, that is the whole virile illusion . . . ' (1979: 64). For the 'virile' order of the father is always already secondary and subordinate to that of the mother, since it is the mother who, by her withdrawal, gives being (*gibt Sein*) to the order of the father. The father is therefore always already the mother's son, and it is the son, in his separation and forgetfulness of the mother, who engenders himself as the Father.

(De)constructive psyche-ology tries to puncture this forgetfulness and to return us to the mother, to the fundamental retreat which gives beings their being and their mission. The encounter with the mother therefore dominates the life of the psyche, making 'genders pass one into the other' (1986b: 280) in a way which is supposed to deconstruct the Oedipus. For in the coming of the event, in the call of the *shekhena* (also known as the mother in kabbalism) to the psyche, the feminine emerges from her absolute retreat to become what Lacoue-Labarthe calls 'the active mother'. She takes the active role of the masculine to emanate, influence and fertilize her sons with her gift of the sign. Her sons (the subjects to which she has given life as separate beings) thus become her daughters (the 'lower mother' in kabbalism, sometimes described as 'the sea (*mer, mère*) into which all the rivers stream'). They become passive recipients of what has entered them through her – 'insofar as I say *oui, oui*, I am a woman and beautiful'. These sons turned daughters also become engendering mothers in their turn, vaginal passages through which the gift of the sign issues into the manifest world: '"I" have the chance of being woman, of changing sex' says Derrida, 'Trans-sexuality permits me to engender, in a manner which is more than metaphorical and transferential. "I" can give birth' (1986b: 281). In the life of the psyche, therefore, there is not only a sex-change operation, but also permanent incest: there is a hymen between the Supernal Mother (the *deus absconditus*) and her son (man in his finitude), and between her son and her daughter insofar as the son (the ego) desires to be one with his sister (the psyche in its passivity as recipient of the call). There is also a love-affair between two women who are mother (*shekhena*) and daughter (the psyche who yearns for her and is a mother in her turn). This 'mixture of genders' is, Derrida suggests, the 'law' of the psyche and the law of life, and it is supposed to deconstruct the Oedipus.

The problem with this 'mixture of genders' is that it is not really a mixture of genders at all. (De)construction's 'mother' remains a virgin protecting her purity, her intactness, her wholeness and her impenetrability by fleeing the father – the order of finitude, of determinacy and of representations – as her own downfall. (De)construction's 'mother' is an expression of a purely masculine 'desire for the intact kernel which does not exist, the desire for the untouchable, for virginity' (Derrida, 1982a: 116). This is why in inverting their pen-ises into vaginas, (de)constructive writers remain passages for nothing but blood (*sang*), the mark of the great without (*sans*) – without the father, without figure, without presence, without representability, without finitude of any sort. With each return of the blood, the sign is given that no finite and determinate living child can be born.

For (de)construction's 'mother' does not give birth to any finite body of Law. The tabernacle is empty, says Derrida, and man, owing the law (*devant la loi*), only stands before, outside (*devant*) the gates of the law. 'The God who touches man touches him to leave him to himself' says Nancy (1987: 22). 'The revelation of the infinite leads to the acceptance of no dogmatic content' says Levinas (1965: xiii). The moral law, says Nancy, has no form except that of its own retreat: 'there is nothing here which can serve as a criterion for truth' and 'what the law orders cannot be described' (1983: 105, 151). The feminine gives herself, says Derrida, only in and as 're-citals of the affirmation (*oui, oui*) of life, where the *oui* says nothing, describes nothing of itself, other than the performance of its own event of affirmation' (1986b: 180, 149).

This leaves the sons in a stronger and more commanding position than before. First, it leaves them in command of the mother and her law: 'The law in its feminine aspect . . . is born of him for whom she becomes the law.' 'The law . . . is not other than me (the me representative of the law); it is the child of his affirmation' (Derrida, 1986b: 283, 284). 'He says she is unsaturable, he who is the author of the law to which he submits, he who engenders her, he his mother who can no longer say "I" . . . ' (Derrida, 1986b: 285) 'The world is what one says of it. After one's own manner' (Lacoue-Labarthe, 1979: 20).

Secondly, by supposedly allying themselves with the mother in her retreat from the father, the sons take command of the father too. For if the mother is nothing but a fundamental 'retreat of identity', if she has never allied herself with the limiting and figural force of the father, if she has never 'descended in wondrous fashion' (Lament. I: 9) differentiating and limiting the outflowings of pure voice into distinct and intelligible articulations, then there is no 'truth' to any determinate moral command or to the words of any prophet. The words of Moses, of the prophets – or indeed of anyone who has served as a 'chariot of God' before Levinas, Derrida and company – and all determinate spiritual and moral injunctions, including the Ten Commandments, can be dismissed as being 'outside' the law of the mother, and as belonging to the stranger, the father. And the fate of the father at the hands of his sons is well known: 'No Scripture can be of any use to us, either by virtue of some decoded message, or of some mystery held in reserve. There is no longer a Book . . . The writing which we practise, which obliges us and is in-finite in us, in no way picks up on the Scriptures . . . it longer speaks of anything but its own insistence which is neither human nor divine' (Nancy, 1987: 51). Levinas, Derrida and Lacoue-Labarthe are not so extreme:

The Other Body of Man

Levinas describes 'the relationship between God and man' as 'a relationship between minds who meet through instruction, through the Torah' (in Friedlander, 1990: 85). Derrida remains haunted by Scriptural and Kabbalistic sources, and Lacoue-Labarthe by the Dionysian Mysteries of Ancient Greece. But they too retreat from 'Narcissus to Echo' only to make Echo a stick with which to beat the father in order to erect their own writing and their own indeterminate affirmation in his place. Far from deconstructing the Oedipus, therefore, (de)construction falls back into it, and far from abnegating self, it ultimately only reinstitutes a 'feminine' self in another, masculin and even more commanding place.

If there were in (de)construction a genuine 'mixture of genders' if the mother also joined herself to the father to delimit the gift of the gift of the sign and to say something more differentiated than *oui*, the empire of her sons would be ended. The sons would no longer be able to glory in their own submission to a higher duty (*devoir*) which, conveniently empty of all content and all specificity, leaves them to invent and do whatever they wish, subject to nothing but themselves – even if it's a higher or better or other part of themselves. When 'there is nothing which can serve as a criterion for truth', when 'what the law orders cannot be described' when 'the world is what one says of it after one's own manner' then every man is left to think, say and do 'what seems good in his own eyes' or rather, for (de)construction, what sounds good in his own ears. This does not take us a step beyond where we are – thinking, saying and doing whatever seems good to us is precisely what we have come to think morality is. And this notion of morality has not achieved encouraging results.

Delimitation of the gift of the sign would delimit obedience to the call: not 'Come' but 'Go to Nineveh' or 'Go to Pharaoh' and 'tell them . . . ' But to rethink this would not only mean rethinking the possibility of being given directions, the possibility of freely accepting limits, boundaries and restraints, and the possibility of being called to do specific, risky or unpleasant things which even one's higher self has absolutely no desire to do. It would also mean recognizing that nothing can be given without some inevitably inadequate, fragmentary, determinate form – even the (de)constructive 'sign of gift of the sign'. To give being (*es gibt Sein*), God had not only to withdraw from the world, but also to delimit his gifts. To give being is always to give something which has measure and limit, something which falls short, a living child. This is one of the things which makes morality such an 'impossible possibility'. As every mother knows, the difficulty, the impossibility of giving, begins precisely where her pure, absolute, indeterminate desire to give everything and nothing has to be delimited and dispersed into a host of inevitably deficient and unrepresentative specific acts. As Irigaray understood (see Chapter 4), ethics cannot re-enter history, society and human life without also confronting questions of finitude, differentiation and limit.

Another problem also arises from the absolute retreat of the Law. On the one hand, (de)construction's turn away from the Law and its emphasis on obeying an imperative which comes from within/without each of us in our singularity and gives each of us our law, returns us to something like individual responsibility and to something resembling conscience. It not only grounds singularity in response-ibility, but as we will see in a moment, also has social and political bearing. But on the other hand, the retreat of the Law is also a *partage* (separation, division) of the Law from *partage* – from anything can be, or has ever been, publicly and openly shared and accepted. And it could be argued that in banishing the Law and in emphasizing the inner call to singular men of a more or less unspecified moral/spiritual duty, (de)construction is merely repeating the founding gesture first of Christianity and then of Protestantism in a way which ultimately subverts its hopes of social revolution. When each man hears the Law wholly after his own fashion, and then only if he is prepared to listen, social change can only come additively as the singular *tchuvah* or return of each of the multiplicity of human atoms to an other within/without them.[14]

(De)construction does have revolutionary bearing, and in this respect, the imperative within/without us turns out, after all, not to be wholly without content. The call of/from the other within/without us (who is, in this context, God and/or other people) is a call turn away from the pursuit of egotistical self-interest and the 'war of the greedy' to 'place oneself . . . on absolute and utopian ground, where disinterestedness is possible' (Levinas, 1982: 22). It is a call to return to *chesed* – kindness, compassion, giving and generosity – in our treatment of others, to gratitude for what we have been given by the Other and by others, and to response-ibility to and for others. And this is a revolutionary call. For the possibility that man can turn or return (*retour, volte*) at any time (*volta*), at every moment, from same to other and from self to others is also the permanent possibility of a *revolt* and *revolution* which would materially transform human relations.

Clearly, this is not a marxist or postmarxist concept of social revolution. But it does suggest, against Marx, that the impulse or 'imperative' to help others, to act responsibly towards others, to sacrifice oneself for others, and to seek social justice for others – for the proletarian, the orphan, the widow, the suffering and the oppressed – cannot be explained, much less achieved, by recourse to the psychological or historical subject's rational calculations, instrumental thinking, self-interest, economic interests or class consciousness. The call to seek social justice for others comes to us from elsewhere. From this point of view, the marxian protest against social oppression and demand for a just society itself figures not as a product of logocentric thinking and of historical consciousness, but as testimony of an 'ontological interruption' and 'dislocation' (Levinas, 1982: 26) which acts through men but comes to them – repeatedly – from elsewhere.

By making the quest for a good society a response to the call of the other within/without one, (de)construction suggests that morality is not reasonable or self-serving behaviour; that ethics neither reflect social reality nor are grounded in it; and that a just society cannot be imposed on merely psychological and historical subjects by violence, by legislation and by socialization. To achieve a revolution in social and human relations, to achieve community, politics have to call on something, call for something wholly other in every singular being. And since a revolution is never achieved once and for all, the revolutionary turn to an other 'I' and 'an other us' also has to return again and again, at each moment, in each singular situation where singular people interact, each time for the first time.

This may correct the error of revolutionaries who have assumed that if one can *only once* change society for the better, people will automatically become better and happier too – only to find their revolutionized societies falling back into violence, barbarism, cruelty and injustice because the people in them have not changed at all. But (de)construction also seems to be repeating an error of the Church which is the inverted mirror image of the other: the error of assuming that if one only concentrates on saving individual souls and on encouraging people to act charitably towards one another, society will automatically be saved too. Each approach is one-sided; and both approaches leave society unredeemed. Perhaps it is time we realized that one is not going to work without the other. We have to be able to hear a Law which can be shared and divided, a Law which can join and distinguish us, as well as a law within/without each of us – however difficult it is to rethink at this date the possibility of a Law which does not obviate plurality and difference. (De)construction is still working on questions of society, law, and revolution; one can only hope that this is not its last word.

Double-Speak and Undecidability

To write of Derrida, or indeed of (de)construction, in such terms is a transgression. One may write like Derrida; one may develop or apply some element of his writings; one may weave generalities around and about Derrida; but to write as if Derrida, or the spectral body of Derrida, had any *vouloir-dire* is as wrong, as shocking, as daring to lift the cloak which conceals a parent's nakedness. As Alice Jardine has put it:

> Derrida is a philosopher of the unrepresentable and, pausing at the threshold of any new question, he makes sure that he himself remains so. Few critics find the where-with-all to write *on* Derrida – one is forced to write for him or with him. This is in large part because of the way the Derridean text infects its reader, binding him or her in a contagious mimetic relationship. (Traces here). One can never be sure when or where it is Derrida speaking or writing.' (1985: 181)

So let us examine the coat of many colours with which Jacques conceals his corpus. Let us ask how/why his corpus effects this cloak of undecidability and whether – within, behind or beyond it – there is any *ouï-dire*, any hearsay or I-say, any possibility of hearing something being said or affirmed by 'Derrida'.

In the Derridean texts with which I have been working, undecidability is largely, but not solely, produced by double-speak.[15] Double-speak mimes in language the oscillation of a truth which *at the same time* is and is not in being, the doubleness of a subject who is at once self-same and other, and the esoteric style of writing in which the mystery, the secret, must and must not be revealed.[16] It is also indebted to a theory about the way the singular I gives signs of itself in language which comes from Levinas.

For Levinas, every act of expression or externalization in language is also a failed act and the speaker or writer's singularity is always therefore in some sense 'in retreat' in relation to what is manifest, thematized, and 'objective' in his words and his works. When we look into someone's eyes as they speak, we sense that beyond the common words they are using and beyond their physical likeness to other human beings, only this particular person is speaking to me now. We recognize that what manifests itself in a person's language is not identical to this 'face' or aspect of the person which reaches out to us from behind or beyond what they actually say. There is always, Levinas argues, a singular person offering a singular sign and making a singular appeal through his words and his works; his singularity always 'accompanies' his words and his works in some way. But at the same time, to carry the sign and the appeal to others, the word has to be held in common. And inasmuch as it is held in common, the word effaces the uniqueness of persons and detaches singular messages from the *hic et nunc* of their profferance and from the possession and control of their speakers. Once detached in this way, the word and the work come to depend for their meaning on others who can do violence to them, usurp them, treat them as objects of exchange or place them in completely different contexts of their own. But, Levinas argues, the word and the work do not, for all that, cease to carry a singular sign and a singular appeal. Thus, as Derrida puts it after his fashion, language is like a sponge: 'On the one hand, the sponge sponges out the proper name [of the singular speaker], places it outside itself, effaces it and loses it, sullies it too to make it into a common name ... But simultaneously, the sponge can retain the name, absorb it, shelter it in itself and guard it' (1984a: 66).

Inasmuch as the word or the work not only effaces the singular message and appeal of their signatory, but also retains them to speak 'its/his most proper cause or thing, in its/his own name' (1986a: 22), the word or the work speaks double. Beyond the historical-anthropological models and masks, beyond the common use of words and beyond the signature which authentifies the property of the work, there is always another signature, a singular signature issuing from the singular *Er-eignis* to which the work gives passage. Encrypted in the word and the work, this other signature, this singular signature of the other, 'ventriloquates' through the manifest language of concepts or arguments or through the common or expected meanings of words. This other signature signs by sending signs through other signs; it signs by doubling one sign with an other.[17]

This other signature offers itself to the ear more than to the eye. One way it is heard is by hearing double, by hearing 'two words in one' (Derrida, 1987a: 9). One hears *double ententes*: the singular *ouï* implied in the common *oui*, or the *ça-voir* which inhabits *savoir*, the double-meanings in puns. Similarly, one hears one argument – about invention of/from the other for instance (in the title essay of *Psyche. Invention de l'autre*) – here and there doubling or re-marking another, more conventional, argument in the same essay about institutional and technological concepts of invention.[18] Two signs, two meanings, two arguments, two signatures sound at the same time, in the same word or in the same text; they are bound together in the same word or in the same text (this is one meaning of 'double-bind') so that it is not a matter of hearing one *or* the other, as it was for Lacan. Rather it is a matter of hearing both one and the other, plus the distance or difference, the heterogeneity or opposition, between them. One hears two bands of signs, two bands of meaning, as one hears music stereophonically: two distinct voices from two different speakers, and the way each sounds against the other.[19] When one hears this curious doubling which Lacoue-Labarthe dubs paradox and Nancy syncopation, one is therefore also 'listening with a third ear'.

But hearing the other signature, the other sign, is also a matter of another sort of tonality – it is a matter of hearing a certain tone of affirmation. As Derrida observes: 'there is no signature without *oui*' (1987a: 121). This *oui* is a *oui* of confirmation – 'yes, that's it, that is what I am saying, I am indeed speaking, yes, here . . . ' (1987a: 124) – which need not appear in so many words and generally only sounds through other words or arguments. Empty of all meaning and all substance, it signals itself by almost imperceptibly punctuating a word, an argument, an idea, or an image as if to say: 'Yes, I'm signing this one, I'm behind this one, I'm allied with this one, this is what I believe too' so that 'the question of the *oui* always comes back to that of the *doxa*, to that in opinion which opines' (1987a: 98). One can obviously also write without signing in this way, without implicating any aye/I in what one is saying, thus intimating 'No, no, I'm not here, I'm telling you this for whatever reason, but I'm not answerable for it and you don't hear me here.' In this stereophonic music, therefore, the balance between speakers alters from moment to moment; there is a 'double dissymmetry'

(Derrida, 1982b: 76) or a disymmetry in the doubling, such that one signature, one meaning, one argument never permanently prevails over the other, and one has to continue to listen to both and to the constantly changing dissymetry of emphasis between them. It is, therefore, possible, in principle, to hear the signature of an other Derrida in these texts – to hear where something is being said or affirmed which is other than what we have come to expect of Derrida. But at the same time, it is never possible to be certain that one has heard him aright.

One level of undecidability comes from the fact that Derrida in general writes on another text – a text of Heidegger, or Nietzsche, or Blanchot, or Joyce, or Ponge – in such a way that his text and their text, his argument and their argument, 'his' affirmation and 'their' affirmation, blend, bleed into each other, contaminate each other. This means that one can never be absolutely sure whose affirmation one is hearing: is it Derrida's or Heidegger's, Derrida's or Nietzsche's, or are they both affirming in the same word, the same thing, at once? To complicate matters further, if the text is on Heidegger, for instance, there are at least four in the text – Heidegger's self and other, and Derrida's self and other – more *Doppelgänger* still, if the text also introduces a bit of Nietzsche or of Plato. And it is from this weave of selves and others, that that which is Wholly Other comes. The Other comes as a sign given by an other, or by the other in the other, to an other who is also Derrida. And this makes it undecidable whether the affirmation of the Other is merely something that 'Derrida' received from an other, from another text or from the *Ereignis* of an other – thus if he is merely repeating an affirmation he has received, at second-hand, from someone else – or whether 'Derrida' is giving the other (Heidegger, Nietszche) this dimension of otherness and allowing the Other to be heard through the particular way he is repeating their arguments – thus in-venting, introducing into the other an encounter with the Other which is more properly his own encounter with the Other and the other. It might also be the case that both are occurring at the same time, and that these two possibilities, while distinct, are also bound together as each other's condition of possibility: in other words, it may be that one can only receive something oneself because one has already received it from an other, and that one hears it in an other because one has already received it oneself.

Another level of undecidability relates to the undecidability of tonalities. Tonalities may haunt language, may inhabit it, but, especially in written texts, they are insubstantial supplements of sound or emphasis which are not susceptible to proof; as Derrida repeatedly insists, they depend on another *ouï* – on the hearing and affirmation (yes, it's there) of someone else, who responds to them and hears them *as* affirmations of whatever it may be. Moreover, as Derrida observes with pointed reference to his name (or one of them, at least), there are different tonalities of *oui-dire*, one of which is *oui-rire*. Inasmuch as any *oui-dire* could also be a *oui-rire*, this other Derrida, who sounds so different from himself, might be yey-saying, affirming what he affirms laughingly, unseriously, to set people up and have them on. Or he might be both affirming something seriously and laughing at it, at us, at himself at the same time. His laughter and/or his affirmation might be joyous or mocking, or both at the same time. Just what Derrida is 'really' doing, just what he really 'wants to say' thus becomes undecidable: 'one cannot decide between two *oui* (two affirmations, or two modalities of affirmation) which *must* resemble one another like twins, or simulacra, one as the gramophonics of the other' (1987a: 141). In other words, even if we can decide where 'Derrida' is, after all, affirming something wholly other than the Derrida we think we know, we cannot decide quite what position he is taking with regard to what he affirms.

For instance, is the *oui* – Aye, Jah, come – of the old-new fable of/from truth discussed above being 'used or cited' in 'Derrida?' And if it is being cited, are Derrida's re-citations mocking, parodic – not therefore something that Derrida is proffering 'seriously?' Or are they an attempt to allow something to return in such a way that it can be heard again, afresh, as if for the first time, as something to which we can turn again in the present? Or perhaps Derrida's re-citations of this old-new *Jah* only constitute a work of mourning? And if they do, is Derrida only incorporating in his corpus what he has received from his Jewish heritage as something which is forever lost to him and to us, or is he perhaps encrypting a 'desire for memory, desire as the memory of desire and desire of/from a memory?' (1987a: 90). As Derrida points out, if his *oui* might be used or cited undecidably, 'you still do not know what I wanted to *say* or wanted to *do* by beginning with this phrase [*oui, oui*]' (1987a: 58).

This particular undecidability, unlike the other, pertains to positionality, not to affirmations. It is an undecidability about Derrida's 'real position' on what he affirms. And this undecidability not only prevents Derrida's 'message' from being unequivocal; it also effectively allows 'Derrida' to 'be' however we hear him. It enables 'Derrida' to be whatever Derrida we want to hear and affirm, whatever Derrida we choose to legitimate by our counter-signatures. If we argue that Derrida is not only giving, but also taking back all these signs of an encounter, an event and an Other, and that there is in his writings a 'tonal dissymmetry' which gives the edge to the moment of taking back, then we still have the old, familiar deconstructive Derrida. This is more or less what Samuel Weber argues when he says that in *Envois*, there is a *'vouloir-rien-dire'* (a wanting to say nothing) because Derrida 'tells us *nothing*, doesn't take a step without then, with the next step, retracting it' (1984: 42).

There is a great deal to be said for binding together opposite possibilities or dimensions, and for the texture of undecidability. For instance, the binding together in the same word or the same text of two signatures, one singular, the other social and subjectivated, suggests that there need be no question here of giving up the immense gains of the marxist paradigm, with respect to understanding subjects and texts in relation to their social and historical contexts, to fall back into some sort of cult of singularity. It suggests that we can and must continue to hear the socio-historical and collective dimension of a text or a writer, as well as the imprint of singularity which marks each writer's difference from every other and the distance or difference between the two.[20] At the same time, to hear the singularity of others as the discontinuous punctuation of spectral affirmations – yes, I'm behind this particular bit of this text – means that one can no longer totalize or represent or capture the singularity of the other in a mastering discourse, or assert that one has any competence in determining the other's truth or untruth. To hear the singularity of writers in spectral and discontinuous aye/I's, is to be able to affirm the singularity of writers without immediately dissolving singularity into a purely collective and socio-historically determined phenomenon. I also think that we do, in practice, get at least some of our sense of other people and at least some of our sense of a writer's meaning(s) from listening out for them in this way.

On the other hand, that blurring or bleeding of different writers' signatures or affirmations into each other which makes it undecidable who is affirming what, suggests that we might also return to what Nancy calls a 'communism' of ideas. This is a provocative old-new term for the pre-copyright conviction that truths (or ideas, or phrases) are not the property of any one writer, but belong to all, so that there is no difficulty about citing or repeating ideas or affirmations without attribution, and no point in worrying about who said what first. In conjunction with this, the undecidability about Derrida's own position with regard to his affirmations not only opens what are essentially binary structures onto a plurality of different ways of hearing what they mean, but also defers response-ibility for the lesson(s) to be learned from Derrida's texts to us. It engages us to think with him, and to be co-responsible for what we affirm with or through him; and it reminds us that we are not absolved from responsibility for affirmations because we only repeat them and are not their proprietors or inventors.

Moreover, inasmuch as the structure of the double also presents itself as a structure of double-binds, it could be considered a re-mark on the present. For the present, which is itself double (a gift and *Gift*, poison), is full of double-binds: Conform and be a unique individual; invent something wholly other and be sure that your invention can be repeated, marketed, institutionalized; teach the truth and don't teach truth; repeat old writings and make them new; be a guardian of the past and a purveyor of the future. From this point of view, (de)construction does not go beyond the present, except – and this is not negligible – to explore such mixed messages and to suggest that double-binds can be, at the same time, our catastrophe and our chance.

But for there to be a chance, we also have to go beyond undecidability and beyond double-binds. For all its virtues, the cloak of undecidability is also a protective cloak, a cloak behind which it is easy to hide. As Schneider suggests, it can mark 'the desire to be heard and the terror of being heard too well' (1985: 17). In relation to Levinas' teaching that 'the relationship between God and man is . . . a relationship between minds who meet through instruction, through the Torah' and in relation to his injunction to 'love the Torah more than God' (in.Friedlander, 1990, 85, 90), undecidability can also be an expression of the double-bind of loving certain texts of Jewish tradition and Western philosophy and desiring to teach and repeat them, without living, or desiring to live, the relationship they signal. This is like endlessly loving, rewriting and meeting minds through the *Kama Sutra*, without ever going to bed with anyone. Undecidability can also be a mask for undecidedness, indecisiveness, and evasiveness.

Derrida has acknowledged that there is a down-side to undecidability:

> To make the undecidable an assured value, an instrument of greater worth than the particular situation in which it is necessary (for example, against binary logic, the dialectic or philosophy), as some people may now be tempted to do, is to put oneself in a double-bind to the point of paralysis . . . The double-bind: when it is pulled to extremes, there is a danger of cramp; it becomes cadaverous and empty (*cadaverise à vide*) between two incompatible desires, the condition of possibility and impossibility of erections. The play [of possibility and impossibility of erections or of incompatible desires] is then paralysed by the undecidable which, however, also opens a space for it. (1976b: 110)

(De)construction's way out of the 'bad' paralyzing undecidability Derrida describes has been to use undecidability to open a space in which erections are and are not discernible, by allowing opposite poles – presence and absence, being and not-being – to oscillate undecidably against each other. But this does not really save it from the 'bad' undecidability Derrida describes. (De)construction's play of linked opposites, its undecidable paradoxes, may disrupt assertive binary and dialectical logics. But the (de)constructive game also leaves conventional logic in place inasmuch as its oscillating *fort/da* depends on the law of the excluded middle. It is the presence of an excluded middle which constructs the simultaneity of opposite terms as paradoxes, and thus locks us into double-binds. And it is the law of the excluded middle, the law of cavernous emptiness between, which persuades us that anything appearing between opposites must be ghostly.

To try to resolve double-binds by oscillating between opposite sides is to fall back into the worst kind of undecidability: undecidedness and paralysis. And to try to resolve double-binds by tonal dissymmetries which give one side of the opposition a slight edge over the other, is only to spectrally echo the traditional way out of double-binds – either/or – which the structure of the double-bind itself deconstructs and which, for good reason, the whole of postmodernism decried. To have any chance of dealing with double-binds other-wise, we need a wholly other logic, a logic capable of saying both/and.

4
The Logic of Both/And

> Truth must encompass all opposites. It is
> the quality that enables any component
> to join with its antithesis.
>
> R. Shalom DovBer Schneersohn

The distance which separates contemporary feminist thinking about the Other from the thinking current at the outset of the feminist movement can be indicated by juxtaposing two statements. The first is Simone de Beauvoir's famous statement in *The Second Sex*: 'He is the Subject, he is the Absolute – she is the Other.' The second is the no less memorable recent statement by Barbara Christian: 'many of us have never conceived of ourselves only as somebody's *other*'[1] (1988: 70).

On the basis of the first statement, where woman's Otherness is defined in binary opposition to man, woman could only be understood as that which is absent from language and excluded from culture. Exploring women's Otherness in these terms, feminisms showed us how her-story has been excluded from his-story, and her stories from his canon. Feminisms showed us that in his theology, God has been a Father and a man; that in his philosophies of reason and culture, she has been identified with nature, instinct and Un-reason; that in his imaginary, he is the active, she the passive element; that in his psychology, her 'normal' development involves a break with her motherbody and motherworld in favour of an identification with his body, his desire and his ideals; that in his language, Man is the all-inclusive and supposedly universal term. Defined as the male subject's Other, woman remained 'the preserve of a purely negative otherness' (le Doeuf, 1987: 198) Like the feminine in (de)construction's symbology, woman remained invisible, unspeakable, indeterminate, and unidentifiable in terms of any extant identity or subjectivity. Conceived as the Other of

The Logic of Both/And

the extant male subject, woman could be nothing but a void of subjectivity, or as Kristeva has put it: 'a woman cannot be.' With the refusal to 'conceive of ourselves only as somebody's *other*' however, another possibility opened up. It became possible to start mapping the void in order to make visible and identifiable what had remained invisible and unidentified before. It became possible to think of women's otherness in completely different terms: as an other experience, an other mode of identity, an other body-image, an other theology, an other psychology, an other theology, an other manner of thinking and writing. It became possible, in other words, to think of women's Otherness as specific and determinate otherness proper to specific and determinate women as such.

During the past ten or fifteen years, American and French feminisms have, by and large, gone about recovering women's specific otherness from the void in different ways. American feminisms have generally preferred to retrieve women's lost historical experiences by empirical sociological and historical research, while French feminisms have tended, more poetically and philosophically, to try to reconstruct the specificity of feminine experience by speaking the mystery of the (m)other body in her absolute biological difference. Much has been made of the differences between American and French feminists, and indeed of the differences among different groups of feminists in each country (marxist, socialist, liberal, cultural, essentialist, etc.).[2] But there have been convergences too, convergences not only with regard to the quest for women's specificity/ies, or with regard to the delineation of those specificities, but also with regard to the need for an other theoretical imaginary. As Sandra Harding explains: 'it has never been women's experiences that have provided the grounding for any of the theories from which we borrow. It is not women's experiences that have generated the problems these theories attempt to solve . . . When we begin inquiries with women's experience instead of men's, we quickly encounter phenomena . . . that were made invisible by the concepts and categories of those theories' (1986: 646).[3]

There seems to be widespread agreement too that, to move beyond the dominant patrilinear theoretical imaginary, women need to do two things: we need to find a way of describing our difference and differences without falling back into binary oppositions which exclude or subsume an other, and we need to rethink the possibility of human agency. The theoretical debate among feminists about how this may be done is only just beginning. But it seems to me that, in practice, women have already succeeded in finding (at least) one solution to these problems which deserves closer attention. In the process of trying to speak or describe the specificity of women's experience, it seems to me that American and French feminists have already begun to develop an other theoretical imaginary – a theoretical imaginary grounded in women's own experience as that Other which was excluded from language – and that they have succeeded in eliminating some of the major shortcomings of the theories considered in previous chapters. I am calling the theoretical imaginary in question the Logic of Both/And.

Since this logic emerged in different feminisms, more or less simultaneously, in the process of trying to describe or imagine a woman's identity, a woman's psychology, a woman's experience of the body, a woman's God/ess, a woman's morality or woman's labour, we will begin by considering it briefly and necessarily selectively as it appears in work of this type. We will then consider Irigaray's '80s' critique of Derrida's fable of the body and the way the Logic of Both/And is elaborated in her alternative feminist fable. Finally we will discuss how the Logic of Both/And resolves theoretical difficulties and how it applies to the study of singular subjects in history and society.

Both/And in some Anglo-American Feminisms

When Eric Neumann explored the Archetypal Feminine in his study of *The Great Mother* in 1955, he pointed out in passing that, in principle, this archetype allows binary oppositions to coexist: 'Just as the Great Mother can be terrible as well as good, so the Archetypal Feminine is not only a giver and protector of life but, as container, holds fast and takes back. As the symbol of the black and white egg indicates, the Feminine contains opposites, and the world actually lives because it combines earth and heaven, night and day, death and life' (45). But intellectually and experientally, Neumann could make no sense of the logic of both/and which is operative here. He therefore hastened back to the safety of binary oppositions. He restored the Feminine to her accustomed place in binary opposition to male culture and consciousness, by making her an embodiment of the repressed male unconscious. He consigned both the Feminine as container of opposites and the 'matriarchal' understanding that the material world combines opposites to a category which he called the 'undifferentiated uroboric mother' so that, as a 'primitive' and 'undifferentiated' aspect of the Great Goddess, the uroboric could be opposed to later and more 'differentiated' forms. Finally, he constructed an elaborate chart dichotomizing the Great Mother into separate and contrasting figures: the life-giving earth mother versus the terrible devouring mother, and the all-encompassing uroboric mother versus the mother of transformations and spiritual mysteries.

Feminists, on the other hand, have insisted that such dichotomies are only artificially differentiated aspects of the Mother and that they belong together. In feminist writings, the Great Mother once again combines opposites: she is both womb and tomb, both beneficent and devouring, the one whose breasts never run dry, who gives and nurtures all life, and she who sends her children to their death, who watches them spill the blood that dissolves life and takes them back into herself. Both material and spiritual, both mother and virgin, she is both the weaver of children and of clothes, and the weaver of songs and fates, both the transformer of food and the transformer of consciousness, both potter and pot, both wise woman and witch.

This makes sense to feminists intellectually and experientially, because they have found that such opposites are conjoined not only in the Great Mother Goddess, but in mothers themselves. Feminists have found that female subjects can and do live both poles of binary opposites. They have found that, considered concretely and experientally, women's lives, women's labour and women's experiences cannot be placed neatly on one-side of any binary opposition – private/public, natural/cultural, personal/political, individual/collective, home/workplace or whatever – because women's lives and experience straddle such oppositions, without becoming 'undifferentiated' or sinking into indeterminacy as a result. As Joan W. Scott has put it: 'opposites conceal the extent to which things represented as oppositional are interdependent' (1988: 35).

Thus where phallocentric thinking has polarized the good mother and the bad mother, and prettified motherhood by identifying 'true' 'normative' motherhood with goodness, sweetness and light, feminist writings have found that the mother's experience is double at almost every level. Adrienne Rich was among the first to describe her experience as a mother in terms of both 'anxiety, physical weariness, self-blame, boredom' and 'passionate love, delight in my children's spirited bodies and minds' and to analyze motherhood as both naturally and institutionally defined. Since then, feminists as diverse in other ways as Mary O'Brien, Ann Donchin, Nor Hall, Hilary Rose, Kathryn Allen Rabbuzi, Jean Bethke Elshtain and Rayes Lazaro have gone further. They have drawn attention not only to the 'hatred as well as love' that inheres in the mother-child relationship, but also to the way women's labour – both in giving birth and in sustaining life – has been both physical and mental, both material and emotional, both biologically and socially determined, both natural and cultural, both vexing and joyous, both the source of women's oppression and a source of possible liberation.[4] Meanwhile, historical and cross-cultural feminist research has also begun to suggest that the one-sided and monologically categorizable mother – the purely domestic mother outside the labour force – has been something of an historical and cultural exception, confined to certain classes in certain periods of Greek and Western culture. Such research is beginning to show that the vast majority of women, today as in the past, must be viewed both as mothers and as other than mothers as well: spinners and potters, basket weavers and agricultural workers, and breadwinners in innumerable other ways.[5]

The radical implications of understanding women's lives and experiences as both one thing and another are indicated by Mary O'Brien: 'I had been taught in the male tradition to think dualistically. We understand things by their opposites or we must separate one thing from the other before we can understand why it is that particular thing, or we must simply face the fact that we as individuals are doomed to be dualistically constituted because we stand opposed to the "Other." . . . (But) the midwife in me said again and again: birth is cultural, it is a unity of natural and cultural processes . . . It is also integration between knowing and doing. Women may not be able to stop what they are doing, but they know what they are doing' (1989: 21–2). The logic of Both/And therefore deconstructs dualistic thinking by speaking the complexity of experience where things which have been represented as opposed are present together, interdependent and intertwined. The Logic of Both/And rests on the experience that 'the world actually lives' because it combines earth and heaven, night and day, death and life, nature and culture, knowing and doing, private and public, individual and collective, and all the other abstract oppositions enshrined in what Mary O'Brien calls 'male-stream thought'.

This sense of the coexistence and interdependence of opposites reappears in many feminist writings as a defining characteristic of female identity. Where men define self in opposition to other, women are understood as constructing their identities as a relation to others, in which self is defined with or through others. Whitbeck has explained: 'Since an other is not taken to be opposite to the self, the character of the self does not uniquely define the character of the other by opposition to it: others may be similar or dissimilar in an unlimited variety of ways . . . the relationship is not fundamentally dyadic at all, and is better expressed as a self-others relation, because relations, past and present, realized and sought, are constitutive of the self' (in Freeland: 1986: 79). Diverse feminists now agree that the subject conceived as a single, autonomous individual – the 'disengaged self' or 'unencumbered subject' confronting what is 'other' than himself – is a male not a female subject.[6] The reasons given for the more relational and 'encumbered' construction of female selfhood differ: feminists say that it is because of the physical-biological bonding of mother and child, or because the psychological development of little girls differs from that of little boys, or because women have been historically and culturally responsible for the nurturing of others, or because her genital organs are 'two lips – two but not divisible into one(s)'. But whatever the cause, the effect of relational subjecthood is to give women 'more flexible or permeable ego boundaries' than men, and to orient them to relationships where 'each party in the relationship is responsible for ensuring some aspect of the other's welfare'. As Smith and Valenze have put it in their study of 19th-century working women, this means that for women '"mutuality' (is) a form of individuality based on interdependence and recognition of other agents as part of one's own agency' (1988: 278).[7] This construction of 'individuality' does not swallow up the other, any more than it exists in rivalry with the other. It accomodates both self and other, and allows both self and other to coexist. As Cixoux has said: 'preserving in life the other who trusts her/himself to her, visits her, a woman can love an other as an other. She can love an other for being other, for being an other, without any necessary abasement to the same, to herself . . . ' (1975: 159).

The Logic of Both/And also seems to be a recurrent feminist response to problems of truth and effectiveness raised both by deconstruction and by political action. What many feminists seemed to have learned from deconstruction and from attempts to act as feminists on the basis of particular political positions is 'the incomplete character of all theorization' (Le Doeuf, 1987: 208). As Leslie Wahl Rabine explains: 'Although it is necessary for feminists to take positions, every position can be analyzed as lacking a full truth or fully correct politics . . . Over the past several years, feminists have found, when we have attempted to put these positions into practice, that each one is somehow unsatisfactory and incomplete' (1988: 26–7). When pro-choice legislation can be used to provide a rationale for forced sterilizations among the poor, when feminist-backed no fault divorce legislation contributes to the feminization of poverty, when differences among women can be 'a source of fragmentation and disunity as well as a creative source of resistance and change' (Sawicki, 1986: 36), then tidy, stable, one-sided theories and practices clearly won't do.

Many feminists on both sides of the Atlantic have come to the conclusion that one-sided choices, universalizing truths, stable master theories and univocal, consistent systems or positions are unsatisfactory and incomplete because they exclude or ignore the both/and complexity of life. These are some American feminist voices: 'the social-political order as an interwoven tissue of conjoining and conflicting contradictions . . . cannot be represented by stable positions' (Rabine, 1988: 27); 'Feminist analytical categories should be unstable – consistent and coherent theories in an unstable and incoherent world are obstacles both to our understanding and to our social practices' (Harding, 1986: 649). And these are some French feminist voices: 'there is a proliferation of systems – economic, political, juridical, intellectual – and each considers itself determinant; only life is excluded from them in order to maintain a model that eliminates everything that does not conform to it' (Claudine Hermann, 1976: 88). 'Why must we choose between two extremes that are mutually dependent? Why let ourselves be locked into a choice of opposites that are two sides of the same coin, which is the exclusion of woman?' (Xaviere Gauthier, 1976: 202). Increasingly, feminists are looking for both/and solutions. They are beginning to argue, for instance, that women are both different and equal, or that we need both French and American feminist approaches, or that white middle class women have been both privileged and excluded, or that possessive power can be both life-preserving and destructive of the other.[8]

Both/And in Irigaray

Exclusion of the both/and complexity of life is also one of Irigaray's major criticisms of (de)construction's fable of the feminine as the spectral body and bride of man[9] (see previous chapter): 'Your only woman/wife: eternity . . . But if all your love is for eternity, why remain on this earth? Is this not always always desire of a spectre rather than desire of the living? And to transmute beyond the body? Without stopping off at this life? . . . Aren't you always skipping over the question 'In what am I alive?' to ask yourself 'how sur-live?' (1980: 29, 30, 33, 35) The reason that (de)construction leaves the living behind, she continues, is that the Other, the feminine, is never allowed to say anything but 'oui' to whatever men say of her. For were those feminine 'immemorial waters' to be allowed to speak, they would say something wholly different. They would say that, like life itself, they are both/and: 'Same am since forever, and at the same time, always different. And thus come and go, change and remain, continue and return, without any circle . . . And without one ever prevailing over the other, and without wanting one rather than the other. For they do not separate. Which is not to say that they are confused with each other' (1980: 20).

If (de)construction only understands the 'immemorial mèr(e)' (sea, mother) as a mysterious abyss, an absence and a withdrawal, says Irigaray, it is because this abyss and this withdrawal marks the space of a forgetting: 'A forgetting of your birth. No longer knowing if you descend from a monkey or a worm, unless you be a hybrid of vegetable and spectre' (1980: 18). What Derrida's fable is really seeking in God and in the maternal-feminine is a return of the son's first intra-uterine home. For the womb is the place where the mother 'in person' is not, except as that incessant transfusion of life which comes to him insensibly, as he lies suspended, sightless and hearing, in the dark, abyssal waters. The womb is the place where 'the Thing happens' where the child is given the gift – life, body, housing, nourishment, warmth – before it has even called, while the mother remains hidden, anonymous, unknowable, behind that first veil, the placenta. 'In this sojourn, no face-to-face with her [with the Other, with the (M)Other] is possible' (1983: 31–2). Once born of her, the son refuses to think through the cutting of her and his umbilical cord, the rupture of his and their placenta and the absolute impossibility of return. And so he keeps trying to recreate a link, a life-line, to that mèr(e), to that experience within the mother's body, by means of the ear, by means of the body, by means of allegory, by means of God. Irigaray's emphasis on what takes place in the mother's belly also reminds us that Derrida has significantly omitted to give his spectral feminine body a womb.

And what of the feminine envoys in Derrida's fable, those angels or messengers who come to man from the beyond, whose gift of the gift of the sign he is supposed to pass on? There are good angels and there are bad angels, says Irigaray. The bad angels are 'those who want to become similar to God, interrupting the mediation between, placing themselves between' (1983: 40). And what else is Derrida doing but placing himself between? In the fable, the feminine brings him unspoken messages, incriptions written on fragments of the body. He wraps them in his own veil of language, re-presents them after his own fashion, insisting that she can only speak through him. He therefore swallows her, appropriates her, subjects her to his own pleasure, 'the pleasure of the child-God'. The son has again taken command of the woman and the mother, as the Father did before him, and once again, 'the maternal feminine only serves as a mediation for the generation of the son' (1984: 70). Derrida has fallen back into the position of mastery, which dominates discourse and assimilates the (m)other. 'Miming the maternal-feminine comes down to dissembling it/oneself as other in a strategy which reestablishes royal sovereignty' (1980: 172). By once again bringing what is outside the masculine self inside, Derrida returns the Other to the Same.[10]

Or, to put it differently, in Derrida's fable, the real woman has been obliterated in favour of a spectral fantasm, with the result that the real woman has, as usual, not been allowed to speak her difference: 'You took me into yourself . . . Your body is my prison . . . I had not begun to exist. I was only your sheath (*gaine*), your reverse side, your inversion. Your mime. The double, redoubling of your organ . . . And you filled me with your voids. You heaped me with your lacks' (1982: 17, 18, 74). 'You' – the man, the philosopher, he who appropriates her as a spectral double of himself – also prevents her from beginning to exist by using all the old masculine stereotypes of woman: woman as the receptive vessel, woman as the passive channel through which something comes. But her organ, says Irigaray, is not a passage or a hole. It is a muquous and elastic vase whose form changes, as she requires, as indeed does her womb with the growth of her child. Her containing flesh moulds

The Logic of Both/And

the other – the man, the child – from within. Her flesh is mobile, active, interactive. Clearly, when a man uses female symbology, he cannot 'enter the body and flesh of the symbols;' he can only come to them from the outside (1984: 110). A man cannot 'enter the body and flesh' of feminine symbols because a man and a woman 'can never occupy each other's place'. Each is unknowable and impenetrable to the other, irreducible to the other.

We must therefore stop thinking of the alliance, of the coupling of woman with man or of the infinite with the finite, as a coupling in which two, always become one – become one, moreover, by being absorbed in him. It is no better if woman absorbs and obliterates man, the Mother-God the Father-God, or the infinite the finite, than than if the same thing happens the other way around. Each must be allowed to exist, each must be allowed to coexist with the other, in their difference. Therefore, says Irigaray, we must think of the alliance as a joining of two beings or entities which are different and irreducible to each other, each of whom has his/her own place in the world. In the Holy of Holies, God spoke to Moses from between the cherubs, which, according to Raphael Patai, were male and female. 'So here,' says Irigaray, 'there are two angels who face each other to guard the presence of God . . . They face each other on the ark of the covenant. Beneath them the tables of the Law, and between them, between their wings, the imperceptible, invisible divine presence' (1983: 56). The presence of God issues from between two angels coming to an encounter with each other from opposite directions. God comes in the interval between two angels who can face each other or turn their backs on each other, because each has its own place, its own envelope. For life, for love, for fecundity, for the presence of God, says Irigaray, 'there have to be at least two' (1984: 70). Two, neither of whom swallows up the other because each is separate from the other and distinct from the other. Two, who are separated from each other by an interval, by a limit, and by the fact that 'each is a place' and has a place. But two who also know how to meet, for neither can be fecund or generative alone. There has to be a link as well as a separation between the Father and the Mother, between man and woman, finite and infinite, body and spirit and all the other supposedly opposite terms of 'male stream thought'. For life, for love, for fecundity, for the presence of God to be possible, pairs of 'opposites' have to coexist, both separate and interdependent.

To develop a both/and logic in which men and women (who also figure as paradigmatic opposites) can coexist in their separation and interdependence, without one excluding the other or swallowing the other up, Irigaray uses a few simple but far reaching images of the feminine and maternal-feminine body.

First, she argues, human bodies are envelopes, material limits, boundaries which give each person her/his place. 'The Universe contains all bodies . . . but each has a place, this place-here which only envelopes him/her, which is the first envelope of his/her body, his/her corporeal identity, his/her limit in relation to other bodies' (1984: 43). Living bodies don't merge like amoeba or or ingest each other. Even within the mother's body, 'in that first envelope, the child remains whole and the mother whole' (1981: 20). Even in the mother's body, there is an interval between bodies, in this case the interval described by the amniotic fluid. At their closest, bodies are like two lips, or two hands held against each other in prayer: 'strangers to dichotomic oppositions. Gathered one against the other, but without any possible suture' (1984: 24). Holiness means separation, and God as an ethical principle may be understood as 'intervening so that there may be a reciprocal limitation of envelopes' (1984: 94). To live, bodies have to be separate from each other; they have to be finite and delimited. To swallow up a body, to obliterate its separateness, is to kill it. In the first instance, therefore, ethics means that 'we must constitute a possible place of habitation for each sex, each body, each flesh' (1984: 24).

But secondly, this envelope which is the mother's body is always ajar – there are always entrances and exits, openings through which the other (the man, the child) enters and leaves. Where men have conceived of enveloping forms as closed, constricting surrounds – complete circles, closed totalities, fenced rectangular or triangular surfaces, swallowing abyssal maws – Irigaray emphasizes that the openings of the feminine body are thresholds through which the other – the man, the child – enter to be enveloped, contained for a while, before they leave, separating themselves again from her. No constriction here or compulsion, no permanent possession and no ingestion. Only openings, thresholds through which separate entities can come together, be together for a while and separate again.

Thirdly, as finite and delimited 'places', human bodies are always in at least two places or positions at once. One place is that of their own enveloping body; the other is that of the other body or place which envelops them. Within her body, the child or the man are

The Logic of Both/And

bodily envelopes which are also wholly or partially enveloped by her. Her bodily envelope in turn is or can be enveloped by the man or the child who embrace her. And everyone's bodily envelope is also wholly or partially enveloped by the envelopes which contain them all – a cave, a house, a valley, a location. Since places too are a kind of envelope, which envelop other envelopes and are enveloped by other envelopes (or places) in their turn, there are enveloped and enveloping envelopes to infinity, constant reversals of the relation of enveloper to enveloped, and constant adjustments of bodies to what they envelop and to what envelops them.

Reversals of the relation of enveloper to enveloped are possible because both possibilities are 'inscribed in the same horizon'. For instance, the hand that I feel from within can also be felt from outside by another hand, and the hand which opens my body onto the world is also part of the world which it touches. 'My movements are incorporated into the universe which they interrogate' (1984: 151). Here there is no subject confronting an object. The relationship between my envelope and someone else's or between my body and the world is one of mutuality – I and someone else, my body and the world, can each 'put the other inside-outside, outside-inside', just as each can mutually affect the other, affirm the other, allow the other to affirm him/her/itself and give the other presence. These possibilities coexist in the same orbit, without necessarily being mirror-images or repetitions or inversions of each other. And they coexist not merely as fixed and static possibilities, like two parts of a jigsaw puzzle, but in continual dynamic interchange, 'in a sort of continual coming and going, from one body to another' (1981: 49).

For, finally, relations between envelopes are fluid, and this in two senses. First, relations between masculine and feminine envelopes are fluid in the sense that men and women join by merging fluids. The threshold between bodies is 'muquous': 'a flux brings the banks together. Who has given this liquid? One bank or the other? Both? Then who is one or the other? No-one? Yet it (the flux) exists. From where? From both. It flows between. Without being held or retained in a source. The source derives from the two who embrace' (1982: 18). Fluids thus permit bodies to join without disintegrating and without losing their boundaries by constituting 'a third term' which both preserves and traverses the interval between bodies, and more important still, allows all three moments – the two bodies and that which flows between – to go on existing simultaneously. In other words, here there is no excluded middle. If anything, the

middle is supplementary to the two sides; related to the two sides simultaneously, produced by the two sides simultaneously, that which manifests itself between is something else again, something not identical with either.
The behaviour of envelopes is fluid too in the sense that they are in perpetual motion. 'Everything is always in movement and in becoming' (1984: 28). Life is growth and change: the constant alternation and interaction of opposites. Like the immemorial waters, therefore, 'as long as we are incarnated, we cannot outstrip a certain rythm of growth. We have to ceaselessly accelerate and break. Both. With and without the world. Both. With and without the other. Both' (1984: 76). In life, everything is constantly being generated and regenerated, including our selves, so that 'at each instant, we are a "recoil" of ourselves, in perpetual growth' (1984: 34). At each instant, we and the world are the same and different, changed and continuing, because in life nothing is stable or finished or complete. For Irigaray, *in-fini* means not 'in the finite' or 'non-finite' but un-finished.[11]

Theorizing Both/And

Irigaray (like other French feminists) has been accused of (biological) 'essentialism' and on the face of it, she does seem to be easy game – until we remember that all Theory is essentialist in one way or another, including historicist theory. It is as essentialist to say, as historicism does that 'there is no permanent, a-historical, unchanging truth' or that 'the history of man is the history of changing cultures and changing human subjectivations' as it is to say 'Man is this or that' 'Woman is this or that'. To say that the unchanging truth is that truth changes, or that truth is always relative to economic and social circumstances, or that the truth is that women have always been excluded and oppressed by the patriarchy, is essentialist too. Theory is always essentialist in one way or another because it always tells us what makes something – history, culture, man, woman, literature – what they really and fundamentally are or have been, what we must look for if we want to talk about them, and how we must therefore approach them.

The question, therefore, is not whether Irigaray is being essentialist, but what a particular form of essentialism can do for intellectual work and historical scholarship. Feminists agree that it has always been the male body and male experience which have been projected onto God and the universe as image, story and concept, and that to see things anew in a more constructive and affirmative way, we need a mythology and conceptuality which draws on the female body and female experience. So the question we need to address is how Irigaray's imaginary of the feminine and maternal-feminine body can help us to develop an other theoretical imaginary, a theoretical imaginary in which both/and can coexist.

Let us begin with Irigaray's image of the body as a partly open envelope which is both enveloped and enveloping, and with her assertion that we need to think of the masculine and the feminine as 'mutually enveloping each other' rather than as 'destroying each other's envelopes'. What happens to the relation of person to society, of text to cultural con-text, or of parole to langue if we think of them in these terms? When we thought of such categories as destroying each other's envelopes, we got marxism, where the individual is absorbed into the collective; we got deconstruction, where opposites dissolve into each other; and we got poststructuralism and postmarxism, where language speaks through people's utterances, and persons or texts are conceived as sites traversed by social practices and cultural ideologies. When envelopes are destroyed, we are either left with indeterminacy, undecidability and nothingness, as in deconstruction, or, as in poststructuralism and postmarxism, the collective term – society, culture, language – overruns the singular term – utterance, text, person – and obliterates it as a distinct and different entity.

If, on the other hand, each utterance, text and person is thought to have an envelope, a material identity and boundary which limits it in relation to other entities and which allows it both to contain other entities and to be contained by them, we have a different scenario altogether. We have a scenario in which the utterance and the language, the text and the context, self and others, the person and the culture each remain more or less intact. 'The child remains whole and the mother whole.' The utterance is contained within a language, the text is enveloped by con-texts, the person is enveloped by others – family, group, class or whatever – as well as by his/her location, language, culture and socio-historical environment, but without being overrun by any of them. For the utterance, the text and the person also envelop some determinate portion of language, context and culture in such a way as to set them off from the collective whole, and to give them a different boundary, a different delimitation, and a different import. The finite mind envelops what it knows without knowing all that there is to know. The finite life envelops some portion of experience, not all possible experience. The finite text, the finite utterance, envelops what it speaks, separating what it speaks from all the other texts and utterances in language, even while it is enveloped by other texts and other utterances. A finite person can be a distinct entity with a distinct and finite collection of words, thoughts and actions, and with a distinct and finite place which sets her/him off from others even within the same family or group or gender, even while being enveloped by others, and by a space which contains them all.

Thus, even if everyone and everything has an envelope, each envelope is delimited differently, each is 'qualitatively different' (1984: 87). And, at the same time, no envelope exists without the other(s). No envelope is independent of the other(s). Each envelope is both separate and interdependent. Both unique and shared. Both/And. Irigaray's image of bodies as enveloping and enveloped envelopes allows us to think of opposite terms – self, other; text, context; utterance, language; individual, group; nature, culture; or whatever – both as distinct from each other in such a way that each makes its own finite and determinate kind of sense and as imbricated in each other in such a way that each is unthinkable without the other.

At the same time, because envelopes are also ajar, because they can be entered and exited, elements of one can enter another, reversibly. A word coined in an utterance can exit the utterance to enter language and leave it again, or vice versa. A social practice or cultural ideology can exit the anonymous collective to enter a singular person's body and mind, and leave them again. Nature can interrupt culture and culture nature. Elements of one language or culture or text can pass into another language or culture or text and leave them again, and so on. And in the process of this 'continual coming and going from one body to another', each changes the other. Each transforms the other because each is imbricated in the other in such a way that 'each becomes the cause of the other by giving the other the possibility of being a cause of itself' (1984: 87). Each becomes what it is by virtue of the other, in interchange with the other, by adapting to the other and by reconfiguring both itself and the other. The relationship between self and others, utterance and language, individual and society, nature and culture, and all the other abstract dualisms of male-stream thought becomes one of

The Logic of Both/And

mutuality and interdependence, with each constantly flowing into the other and changing what both are by virtue of this two-way flow. Neither term of any dualism therefore remains constantly the same. People and things, nature and culture, selves and others, languages and utterances, are constantly in the making and in the unmaking.

And what about Irigaray's image of the presence speaking in the interval between angels who come to an encounter with each other from opposite directions? What about her image of the flux between two banks? What happens to such traditional dichotomies as idea and reality, ignorance and knowledge, mortal and immortal, good and evil, or individual and collective if we think of them in these terms? For centuries, our thinking and our utopias have tried to accord or reconcile such dichotomies by purifying good from evil or knowledge from ignorance, by trying to make ideas correspond to reality or reality to ideas, by subordinating man to God or God to man, or by seeking a 'higher term' to sublate and *aufheb* oppositions. In each case, one term has been encouraged to swallow or master another – we speak, for instance, of knowledge conquering ignorance, or of good overcoming evil, or of revolution requiring the dictatorship of one set of people over another. Alternatively, we have left both terms of the opposition in place and found ourselves confronting impossible paradoxes and double-binds, as contrary terms face each other without a decidable victory of one over the other across an excluded middle (see Chapter 3).

A different logic would ensue, however, if we thought of opposite terms not only as unable to usurp each others' place, but also as facing each other across an interval which is fluidly 'full' rather than cavernously empty. Instead of trying to accord or reconcile dichotomies, we would allow both terms of the opposition to remain as markers, each in its own place, each facing the other from opposite banks. And we would begin to think about the different ways in which things dispose themselves in the intervals between them.

This would mean, first of all, thinking of the utterance, the mind, the text, human groups and human thought as somewhere between such opposites as change and the unchanging, ignorance and knowledge, good and evil, matter and spirit, singularity and commonality. One salutary effect of this kind of logic would be to eliminate the a priori one-sidedness of so much of our theory and critical practice. Why, for instance, do we have to speak of literary works either as unique products of towering genius, as Romanticism and the New Criticism did, or as mere effects and products of hegemonic cultures, as poststructuralism and post-marxism do? Why not somewhere in between? Why not in movement from one to the other? Why not sometimes more this, sometimes more that? Why do we have to think of persons either as docile bodies or as rugged individualists, agents or patients, saints or sinners, conforming or resisting? Why not somewhere in between? Why not in movement from one to the other? Why not now one, now the other? Why not one text or genre or person or group or period more this and another more that?

Secondly, if we thought of the flux in the interval between opposites as 'bringing the banks together' in such a way as to constitute a 'third term' which is composed of both and identical with neither, we would think of delimited entities as a mixture of opposites. This possibility is familiar to us from deconstruction where, for instance, the *pharmakon*'s unstable mixture of medecines and poisons dissolves opposite categories into undecidability and from (de)construction where the double-bind of being 'both my mother and my father' either remains unresolved or is solved by appropriating the (m)other and murdering the father in a reiteration of the classical either/or solution of male-stream thought. But as Irigaray might say, both these solutions flee the both/and complexity of life. For while mixtures of opposites may confound or deconstruct categories of thought, they do not deconstruct any living child. The living child is necessarily both/and. 'Yet it exists. From where? From both.'

In the logic of both/and, 'I am my mother and my father' means that I, who am distinct from both my mother and my father, am at the same time composed of both, interdependently. Composed of both, 'I' am both finite and unfinished, both good and evil, both ignorant and knowledgeable, both beautiful and ugly, both mind and body, both flesh and spirit, both mortal and immortal – 'accelerating and breaking. Both. With and without the world. Both. With and without the other. Both.' And composed of both, 'I' constantly navigate between and by both. In the logic of both/and, 'I am my father and my mother' means that the texts, cultures and social worlds that we create between us can be – at the same time and at different times – both nurturing and destructive, both medicine and poison, both material and ideational, both beautiful and ugly, both known and unknown,

The Logic of Both/And

both continuous and discontinuous, both life-giving and death-bringing, in always different proportions and different ways. The text and the world 'actually live' because they combine opposites. In this logic where both the middle and the extremes exist together – where the child does not obliterate his parents or the flux drown the banks – the middle can be placed or described in relation to the extremes. There is therefore nothing undecidable or indeterminate about particular mixes. Both/Ands are specific, capable of clear formulation, incapable of univocal resolution. And people (men?) are cutting through them to make decisions or take sides – either/or – all the time. The logic which is capable of speaking both/and is therefore neither an expression of ambivalence nor another attempt to reconcile or escape binary oppositions. For the logic of both/and sees logically incompatible dimensions as inescapably bound up together, correlatively conjoined. It sees them as different, linked and unsuturable faces, moments or aspects of the same issue, the same subject, the same body or the same situation, which people and texts are constantly navigating as best they can – as women constantly navigate between the incompatible claims of sameness and otherness, motherhood and selfhood, home and work, husband and children, family and friends. The logic of both/and therefore invites us to abandon the superficial complexity of Hegelian and post-Hegelian language and logic, which have led us to one-sided, oversimplified characterizations of persons, culture and history or to the night where all cows are black. In contrast, the relatively simple theoretical recognition that both/and are combined in most persons, groups, places, texts, situations and things leads to much more complex analysis by requiring us to try to understand how each person, group, place, text, situation or thing combines and navigates the opposites of male-stream thought. And this, in turn, reopens the ethical and political question as a question of navigating opposites in a both/and world where things are in flux and where the same things and the same people can be – both at the same time in the same circumstances and at different times in different circumstances – both good and bad. Undecidability and either/or are both, in their different ways, evasions of this real ethical, political and spiritual difficulty. For it is into a world where opposites combine, where things are in flux, and where the same things can be good and bad, that our actions, that our politics, that ethics, that God, have to come. Or as Irigaray puts it: 'God has to be raised up through us, between us . . . (1984: 124).

Irigaray's image of the flux flowing, growing, and taking form, between two banks or two lips or two unsuturable hands also gives us a different way of conceiving human agency and human labour. Male-stream images of work have assumed an instrument which elevates, divides and penetrates things, or they have assumed a tool – or mind or will – which cuts into things, separates things and imprints things with its marks. By the same token, male-stream images of agency have been images of acting on people or things, of striking a blow and leaving an imprint, of cutting a path through obstacles or difficulties and of getting everything under control. When male-stream agency tries to build a world in which man can feel at home, home turns out to be a place where everything depends entirely on such agency, where everything will have been made and controlled by man. For better and for worse, this is certainly one way in which we work and act.

But there is also another way: here work is a matter of offering the conditions in which things can happen and where people or ideas can grow both with me and without me, and agency is a matter of acting as the hands or lips or banks which enable something else to flow, and grow and take form. To put raw food in a pot on a flame is to arrange the conditions in which the food can cook 'by itself', both with and without the cook. When we create electricity or 'harness' atomic particles to human ends or even grow food in the ground, we try to construct or modify circumstances to provide the conditions which make possible the reactions we want. When we carry a child, we provide the conditions in which the child can do its own growing, both with us and without us. To 'have' an idea, is to allow it to expand and develop and take form in the mind. In this kind of human agency, unlike the other, we are never quite 'in control' of it all. The food can burn or fail to cook properly despite our best efforts. The atoms can surprise us and do something they were definitely not supposed to do. The thought can take some unexpected turns or fall still-born from the mind. The conditions we provide for the child, like the circumstances we provide for small and large people to learn or teach or work or live in, can prove wholly or partially inadequate. In this kind of agency, we are not 'passive' or 'receptive' as opposed to 'active' and 'assertive'. In this kind of agency, we do, but only our part.

And finally, what are the epistemological implications of

The Logic of Both/And

both/and? What are the implications of those images of 'movements incorporated into the universe which they interrogate' and of those bodies which can each 'put the other inside-outside, outside-inside?' The first image is not new with Irigaray at all – as I am about to explain, it describes one of the major epistemological problems of our time. The second image will give us the seeds of an answer.

If the movements of our bodies, of our minds and of our instruments are always already part of the matter they interrogate, then our thinking and our instruments of thought, our presence and our acts are always also part of the matter we perceive, part of our knowledge and part of our results. As Dorothy E. Smith has put it: 'The only way of knowing a socially constructed world is knowing it from within. We can never stand outside it' (1987: 93). The sociologist works in the same medium that she studies; she is 'on the same plane' as her material. Quantum physics came to much the same conclusion about our relation to the physical world in the '30s and '40s. It concluded that scientists can never stand outside the physical world because bodies, minds, and scientific apparatuses operate in the same medium as atoms, quanta, and whatever else the universe is composed of. They too live and breath and think and work in the medium they study. Semiosis also is something which can only be known 'from within', something which we cannot ever stand outside. In reading and writing texts, we too inhabit and act in the same medium that we study.

This continuity between subject and object has created difficulties not only for traditional epistemology which holds that 'objective knowledge' is possible, but also for poststructuralism and quantum physics. The basic problem is this: if we inhabit the medium we study, if we cannot get outside it, and if our movements are continually affecting and changing what we study, how can we know 'it', i.e. that which is other than ourselves?

Geertz and the New Historicists have tried to solve this problem by resorting to 'thick description'. This reintroduces the artificial, formal barrier between subject and object, between the knower and the known, or between the social text and its reader/anthropologist which has characterized traditional epistemology in a slightly different form. 'Thick description' reintroduces this purely formal barrier by trying (and failing) yet again to describe the object as an object 'out there' while trying (and failing) yet again to neutralize the subject-observer by meditating on his role. This does not solve the epistemological problem of how we can really know 'it' and often convinces us that we cannot. It could be argued, however, that the problem lies elsewhere – in the objectivist assumption that knowledge is only knowledge if it is entirely separate from and unaffected by the interests or concerns of any singular knower. As Dorothy Smith observes, 'being interested in knowing something does not invalidate what is known' (1987: 88).

The same problem takes a different and less commonly recognized form in the marxist paradigm, which reproduces the objectivist impasse in aggravated form by equating what is constructed as being entirely separate from any singular knower with the 'objective' social world, or its aliases – 'the symbolic order', social formations, and discursive and disciplinary practices which function independently of any singular person and so on. This aggravates the problem by turning the objectivist construction of knowledge into a stick to beat ourselves with. The barrier erected between knower and known to make knowledge 'objective' by excluding the knower, also creates the 'other' as that which is on the other side of the barrier, like the object out there entirely separate from the knower. When objectivist epistemology is problematized, and it becomes uncertain that one can know anything objectively, this also makes the other unknowable.

Poststructuralism's reaction to the inscription of subjects in the same horizon as what they study has been no more satisfactory. Like quantum physics, poststructuralism responded by removing the artifical barrier between knower and known, and assuming a simple continuity between them: what is inside the subject is the same as what is outside the subject. We have already considered the shortcomings of assuming a likeness between inside and outside (Chapter 2) and of destroying envelopes (see above). But there is another problem too: assuming a simple continuity between knower and known makes all knowledge either completely 'subjective' or completely 'objective'. In other words, either what is 'outside' (objective in traditional terminology) is also inside the subject, in which case we are spoken more than we speak and the subject as a separate and different singularity 'is' not; or what is inside the subject is also what is outside the subject, in which case the subject's constructions determine what is seen and known, and 'objective' reality 'is' not. And if objective reality is not because it cannot be spoken by human language or human constructions, all knowledge becomes fictional. Each of these solutions obliterates its other: if the world speaks the subject, the subject is not, and if the subject speaks the world, the world is not.

Operating within the either/or logic of binary oppositions, one can attack this difficulty by arguing that one's epistemology gives one two options – either to obliterate the subject or to obliterate the world – and that one can alternate between them. Borrowing from Bohr's 'complementary sets' Lacan therefore argued for an oscillation or alternation between subject and world. In quantum physics, when one considers matter as particles, the properties of matter as waves fade from view, and vice versa; one cannot see both at the same time. Similarly, in Lacan, when I see myself in the other – in the 'symbolic order' or in my imaginary identifications with others – 'I', the real subject, fade from view, and vice versa. I cannot see both, occupy both places, at the same time. 'I' must obliterate the other, or the other must obliterate me. Either/Or. This 'solution' gives me both options, but as two sets or systems (the system of the 'Real' subject and the system of the 'real' symbolic order, or the system of waves and system of particles) which are 'split' from each other. Neither of them can speak the other or come to the place of the other, and only one of them can be seen at any time. Since in male-stream thinking a system can only be true if it explains everything in a non-contradictory and all-inclusive manner, this inability of either set to include the other means that both fall back into untruth and fictionality again. Bohr argued that both the wave and the particle theories are fictional constructs of physicists' minds; poststructuralism has argued that we are spoken by fictions, and that all subject(ive) constructions are fictional too.

Within Irigaray's both/and logic, there are 'complementary sets' too, but these do not relate like two mismatched halves of different globes, only one of which is visible at any time. For Irigaray's complementary sets are envelopes each of which can 'put the other outside-inside, inside-outside'. As envelopes, 'complementary sets' – subject and world, or subject and subject or subject and text – are discontinuous and separate from each other. Each occupies her/its/his own place within her/its/his own boundary. Each exists separately from the other – even when the other is not looking. But when they join, each can envelop some part of the other. To know the world or the other as a bounded entity knowing another bounded entity is the act of letting the other 'inside' as something determinate and different from the subject's own insides. The other (the person, the world, the text) appears outside inside me, and inside me as

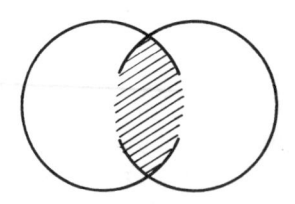

Figure 1

being outside. To let the other inside me is therefore also to create a space where both I and the other coexist, and to constitute a third entity, which is composed of both myself and the other without being wholly identical with either, and without obliterating either. The epistemological consequences of this can be envisioned in terms of the overlap between two partly open circles (Figure 1).

The shaded area where each circle envelops the other is the area knowledge, and like anything that flows between two sides, it is a fluid mixture of opposites. Neither 'subjective' nor 'objective', knowledge is a determinate and dynamically changing mixture of both. Both 'subject' and 'object' are visible and present at once. What we know is a composite of both self and other, or of both subject and subject, or of both person and world. Each has her/his/its part in the mix. For knowledge, for life, for fecundity, there have always to be two – two who can join, but who are never identical with each other. Each can 'put the other outside-inside, inside-outside' – knowledge can be approached through either envelope. But these alternations are not simple inversions of each other. 'I' do not necessarily figure in your knowledge or in a text or in the collective 'world' or in a photograph as 'I' or you, the text, the world or the photograph figure in me.

For the circles also exceed each other – the white areas in the drawing represent the part of each which remains beyond the other's ken, the part which bounces back with something unanticipated in my work on the world: 'the universe and thought' says Irigaray, 'are always bigger than he is at any moment x' (1984: 87). For Irigaray, no subject, no human construct, no science can master or should try to encompass everything that there is to know. 'I love a part' says Irigaray, 'but you want to keep guard on the whole' (1980: 17). Loving a part does not mean being content with knowledge that is relative; it means accepting that, like everyone and everything which is alive, knowledge is in-finite – unfinished, incomplete, always 'in movement and becoming'. Loving a part, and a mixed part at that, does not mean either that one cannot really know the other at all; it means allowing the other – the world, the other person, the text – to exist both with me and without me, both in what I know and as what I don't know, and leaving space for both/and.

The drawing is static, like this page; the logic of both/and is not. The fluidity of everything 'in movement and becoming' is one of its most important features, because 'the fluid eludes "thou art that"' (1985: 117). This is what subverts stable master theories, recurrences of the same a priori structures and conclusions, and fixed systems, and makes it possible to speak singularity. The marxist paradigm and its offshoots – structuralism, poststructuralism, postmarxism – have been unable to speak singularity because, like mass production and the management and education theories which grow out of it, they have assumed that people and things are infinitely substitutable for each other. They have assumed that one-mass made object, one mass-trained person, one docile body, is just like another, and that as long as a given function or structure (of administration or production, a given lesson plan, a given syllabus, a given disciplinary practice, a given discursive formation) recurs, it does not matter who performs the function or even, increasingly, what product is being produced. To understand and control the structure and its functions, to 'impose a dead grid on the living' (1984: 167) is therefore all that is necessary for knowledge and for success.

But 'life', says Irigaray, 'is never identical with itself' (1980: 47). Love, writing, teething, teaching, morning, meals never return in the exact same way twice. One 'Thou' is never precisely the same 'that' as another. For the woman giving birth, each time is different; each child is different; each moment of each child's growing up is different; and no child can take another's place. One friend, one lover, one manager, one Chair, is not just the same as another, and it is not a matter of indifference to us who occupies which place. And we all know with half our minds, that no institution, no state apparatus, no law, no book, no department, and no teaching plan is going to be any better than the singular people and singular dynamics involved. People come and people go, interactions change, and companies or institutions see the moment of their greatness flicker. In practice, people are not just so many clones. Each person is a world and has a world. Each situation has a dynamics of its own.

To speak both this singularity and the determinate and changing separation and interdependence of different people and situations at finite and determinate historical junctures, we need 'a speech which has nothing universal about it' (1984: 167), a speech which looks beyond potted formulas and stable, predetermined organizing structures. We need a language which is constantly adapting itself, reinventing itself, constantly making and unmaking itself to speak the both/and complexity of life: 'Same am forever, and at the same time, always different. And thus come and go, change and remain, continue and return, without any circle. Exposed and open in this endless becoming. And without one ever prevailing over the other. For they do not separate. Which is not to say that they are to be confused with one other.'

5
Factitive Fictions and Possible Worlds

> Mixture, not homogeneity, governs textual matters.
>
> Thomas Pavel

Postmodern and objectivist theories share a traditional but unhelpful assumption about fictions. They assume that fictions and the real occupy different and antithetical spaces, disposed one above or over the other. For both objectivist and postmodern theory, fictions are fashioned and feigned symbolic constructs which are essentially 'at variance with fact' (*OED*) and 'not real' (*Littré*). And for both kinds of theory, language is either factual in the sense that it is a true and adequate duplication of reality, or fictional in that it does not speak the real. The difference between objectivist and postmodern theories here is largely a matter of where the line between fact and fiction is drawn. Objectivist theories generally hold that the line falls between different ways of employing language, and that they can determine which discourses are factual and which are fictional. Postmodern theory, on the other hand, places all discourse in the fictional camp by drawing its fiction/fact line between all of language and all of reality. It preserves the space of 'reality' as discourse's antithetical other by marking it either as absence, indeterminacy and lack or as that which can be created by language and transformed by praxis.[1] Neither the objectivist nor the postmodern argument therefore takes us beyond the alternative fact *or* fiction, because neither takes us beyond the correspondence theory of truth, which holds that discourse has either to duplicate reality or not, and that discourse is fictional when it does not.

But matters are not so clear cut. For, like language, theory-fictions allow us to orientate ourselves in actuality and to work effectively in the actual world, even though they do not duplicate actuality, and often precisely *because* they do not do so. As Vaihinger pointed out, 'devoid of reality' does not mean 'devoid of utility' (1924: 22). Even objectivist epistemology would not claim that the perfect circle or absolutely straight line or negative numbers or two-dimensional geometric structures correspond to anything in nature, and the same can be said for temporal indices like 24 hours, or directional indices like North and South, or up and down. For Newton, gravitational force was a fiction, as waves and particles are for physicists now. And I am told that Ptolamaic astronomy is still being used in navigation today. Vaihinger and Nelson Goodman have both observed that scientists often choose an 'amenable and illuminating lie' over an awkward truth or over one which does not fit comfortably with other principles, and that the simplicity, cogency, compactness, comprehensivenss and organizing power of a theory are generally more important than its truth to reality. And Horkheimer showed that societies too have functioned perfectly well on the basis of the most erroneous ideas, concluding, not unjustifiably, that it is more important for the functioning of societies that they have organizing ideas, than that these be right or true.

Clearly, one can orientate oneself in the physical world, organize societies and operate within them, calculate and predict the behaviour of real objects, and even discover new things (the planet Pluto) on the basis of theory-fictions or fictional versions of the world. And the factitiousness and fictiveness of facts, their dependence on the theory-fictions which construct them, do not necessarily prevent them from functioning in the ways that we expect facts to function in the actual world.

Postmodern theory can no more account for the ability of theory-fictions to speak the real in these ways than objectivist theories can explain how known falsehoods can give true results. Nelson Goodman, however, has tried to do so, by arguing that 'we have to make what we find'. Giving as his example the attempt to make out a stereo system in a crowded room, and the fact that someone from the jungle would not have the means to figure out what that group of disparate boxes is, Goodman argues that 'finding what is already there may turn out to be very much a matter of making' (1984: 35). We have to have constructed a world-version or theory-fiction which includes the possibility of stereo systems or of the Great Dipper or of an extra planet before we can discover them in reality. Since we cannot find anything that we do not also make, we cannot know 'reality' except in terms of the plurality of often incompatible world-versions or theory-fictions we invent, which is to say that we cannot know it 'in itself' at all. But at the same time, 'while we make world-versions, we can hardly make versions true' (1984: 34). Words do not create reality in the sense that they can summon up a nonexistent beefsteak or turn back the tide, as poor King Canute tried to use them to do. Even if world-versions are fictional in the sense that they do not duplicate reality and do not adequately correspond to the real, they must nevertheless 'fit' or at least intersect with something beyond themselves to provide knowledge of any kind. For clearly, 'though we make worlds by making versions, we no more make a world by putting symbols together at random than a carpenter makes a chair by putting pieces of wood together at random' (1978: 94). If we make or adopt a theory-fiction-world in which words create reality and in which we are spoken more than we speak, we do not do so arbitrarily; we do so because this enables us to find and speak a phenomenon of language, or facet of actuality, or manner of acting and being acted upon, that could not otherwise be found or spoken, which 'fits' a world in which we live.

If theory-fictions can thus speak the real, however inadequately and incompletely, if wrong theories can give right results, and if we can also find what we make, then our constructs transgress and collapse the fact/fiction line, whether this is drawn between different uses of language or between all of language and all of reality. And in this case, if we want to go on speaking in terms of fact and fiction, we must follow Hume and Fielding and Jeremy Bentham in describing accounts of reality as uncertain 'mixtures of fact and fiction' or of 'falsehood and truth'. But we cannot rest here, for this description of world-versions only reawakens the desire to distinguish fact from fiction and falsehood from truth, this time on the basis of criteria more certain than those which failed before. And this only sets off the circular process again which brings us back to the same place. For as we all know, truths and falsehoods, facts and fictions, and criteria themselves have the unfortunate and extremely irritating habit of changing their status, despite our best efforts to get them fixed. What is pure invention or myth at one moment (man on the moon, Oedipus) becomes physical or psychological fact at another; what is certainly right at one moment (the world is a great clock, the death of God) becomes wrong or mythical at another; what is a certain way of distinguishing fiction from fact at one moment (observation and experiment) becomes uncertain at another; and we are left wondering, rather patronizingly, how anyone could have suspended disbelief and lent so much credence to world-views, world-versions and methods of distinguishing fact from fiction so patently inadequate or false.

To understand how fictions, whether theoretical or literary, speak the real, we need to abandon the correspondence theory of truth, and we need to stop placing fiction in a space where it jostles with unreality, fantasy, falsehood, dream, illusion and play as reality's antithetical other. Instead of forever defining fictions on the basis of their coincidence or lack of coincidence with objective truth and reality, we need to begin to think about fiction in a completely different way – as an elaboration of possible worlds.

Possible worlds can be given a respectable historical genealogy. The idea that unrealized possibilities exist in worlds of their own can be traced back to presocratic philosophers like the Atomists or Parmenides (Rescher, 1969: ch. 4). The idea that poetic imitations are imitations of the possible rather than of the actual could be attributed to Aristotle, who insisted in Chapter IX of his *Poetics* that 'it is not the function of the poet to relate what has happened, but what may happen – what is possible either in the way of likelihood or inevitability'. After that, any history of possible worlds would have to go through 'scientific' positings of the actual plurality of worlds from the Renaissance on (see Guthke, 1990) and through Leibnitz, who is too often only remembered today from Voltaire's withering satire in *Candide* of the suggestion that ours is the best of all possible worlds.

The idea has been attracted renewed attention since the 1950s and 1960s, when physicists working both on relativity theory and on quantum mechanics began to posit the existence of other possible worlds which connect to our own.[2] Possible worlds here are parallel and alternative versions of our world, where the individuals, temporalities, causalities or outcomes of situations, decisions or actions are, in some respects, different. In relativity theory, other possible worlds are conceived as existing side-by-side with our universe, in quantum theory, as occupying the same space in a ghostly manner. Interest in possible worlds was also given a boost in the 1960s and '70s by attempts to write computer programs which could simulate reality.

Modal philosophers like Saul Kripke, Jaakko Hintikka, David Lewis, Alvin Platinga, M. J. Cresswell and Nicholas Rescher, spent the 1970s and 1980s reworking traditional logic to accomodate the existence of other possible worlds, as well as thinking about the nature of possibility.[3] As Rescher has pointed out, among modal philosophers, there are nominalists who attribute the existence of possibility to language, conceptualists who attribute it to the mind, conceptual realists who attribute it to the mind of God, and realists who posit the realm of possibility as existing independently of human language and thought (1979: 180-2). Of late some literary theorists – most notably Thomas Pavel, Floyd Merrell, Umberto Eco and Doreen Maitre – have begun to explore literary fictions as possible worlds. Pavel brings structuralist assumptions to his analysis, Eco formalist ones, Merrell poststructuralist ones, and Maitre basically empirical-positivist ones.

This broad spectrum of positions on the nature and configurations of possibility testifies to the flexibility of the idea that fictions are elaborations of possible worlds, and to its potential applicability to theories, genres and fictional works of the most diverse kinds. But it also means that Possible Worlds Theory is at present still plagued by imports from traditional logic and extant literary theory – imports such as the law of non-contradiction, the correspondence theory of truth, the two-tier model of real infra-structure and fictional superstructures, and the notion that we need fixed typological models and invariant across the worlds assertions – all assumptions which severely and unnecessarily limit our ability to use possible worlds to think otherwise than we thought before.

In what follows, I will therefore be using extant work in Possible Worlds Theory eclectically, to foreground some of the ways in which it seems to me that reading literary-fictions and theory-fictions as possible worlds can take us beyond traditional assumptions about fictions and beyond some of the impasses into which these assumptions have led us – although some unquestioned and unhelpful traditional assumptions may still be creeping into my account, which others will be able to eliminate. In what follows, I will also be eschewing fixed invariant models, in favour of a variety of I hope suggestive, preliminary and *possible* 'orientations' for thought and research, supplemented by some examples of how they might be used. Possible Worlds Theory is an area of Theory in which a great deal remains to be done.

Accessible Worlds

Possibility is the way things may be or might be – what could be the case, or could have been the case, or might yet be the case, without ever necessarily being the case. The possible is what might exist, be done, be said, be thought or happen; it is another way things could occur, or another way things could be thought or spoken or done. For Possible Worlds theorists, possibility is ubiquitous and not necessarily or even primarily allied to myth and dream and illusion; for 'the rational guidance of human affairs [also] involves a constant recourse to possibilities' (Rescher, 1975: 1). For instance, we resort to possibilities whenever we construct hypotheses, deliberate about alternatives, make plans, anticipate the consequences of actions, perform thought experiments, ponder the cause of effects or the effect of causes, make choices and lie. We also rely on the possible whenever we are critical, for as Merrell says, 'to be critical of a given aspect of a particular 'real world' as it is ordinarily conceived and perceived is to be aware that . . . it could equally have been in part something other than it is' (1983: x). And we resort to possibilities in our most serious and rational thinking, according to Possible Worlds theorists, not only because the actual world is fluid and constantly susceptible to alteration, but also because it is always incompletely known: 'Given that we are so often ignorant of what *is*, we need a rich sense of what *might be*. In matters of practice, we need to consider alternatives where knowledge is denied us. In matters of theory, we need to consider hypotheses where facts are unknown' (Bradley and Schwarz, 1979: 1–2).

As Fabrizio Mandadori and Adam Morton have observed, possibility is also embedded in ordinary language and in our most ordinary thought processes. For instance, from the word 'breaks', we make 'can break' 'might break' 'may break', 'would break if . . . ', 'breakable' and so on – all of which indicate the possibility of breaking. Similarly, we can be watching a game and thinking that X might win, that X might yet be able to win, that X might have won if . . . or that X might have won in a different way if . . . – again indicating the way any actual state of affairs is surrounded by different possibilities, any one of which, had it become actual, would have changed the way things actually are.

One of the most interesting things about possibility from this everyday point of view is our ordinary capacity to elaborate possibilities. We are forever driving along in a car or waiting in line or peeling carrots and thinking about what we might do or about what might have happened – let us say at the week-end. And when we do so, we often develop the possible situation we're thinking about, imagining it and working it through in great detail. We envision precisely what might happen on our date, or what might have happened on our last date if we had said or done something differently. And we can envision different possible scenarios for the same situation, different ways the date might go, different things that might have been said or done by us or by others. Similarly in conversation. In the midst of a discussion of what is actually the case – the state of our bank account, for instance – we begin to talk about what we might do to rectify our finances, to earn more money or to economize our expenditures. We elaborate various possibilities, and even envision taking holidays or buying things with the money we might earn or save, before switching back to the contemplation of our actual bank account.

The possible scenarios[4] we thus elaborate are fictions, but fictions with some important characteristics which the traditional view of fiction does not permit us to think.

First, the possible scenarios we thus construct have a different ontological status from that which we traditionally attribute to fictions when we confuse them with falsehood and illusion as reality's antithetical other. For possibilities are both real and unreal, both extant and non-existent, both 'objective' and 'subjective', and possible scenarios are both believed and not believed, both made and found, both self-contained and umbilically linked to actuality. Possibility is a both/and category.

In their different terminologies, theorists have begun to signal the same doubleness in the status and reception of literary fictions. For instance, Michael Riffaterre recently observed that 'narratology seems to have neglected the constant coincidence between textual features declaring the fictionality of a story and a reassertion of the truth of that story' (1990: 30). In other words, like possible scenarios, fictional narratives are marked as both real and unreal, both to be believed and not to be believed, both to be taken as true and not to be mistaken for truth. Similarly, coming at it from modal logic, John Woods has argued that fictional sentences are 'mixed', by which he means that, unlike non-fictional sentences which are by definition either true or false, a fictional statement such as 'Holmes lived in London' is simultaneously both true and false (1974: 129). It could be argued that the 'as if' character of fictions derives from this positing of fictional statements as simultaneously true and false, extant and non-existent.

Floyd Merrell, Kendall Walton, Thomas Pavel and Doreen Maitre have described the same both/and quality in the reception of fictional worlds. For Maitre, in the 'experience of possible worlds, there seem to be two states of the self which need to be sustained simultaneously . . . one needs to be an *actual* spectator in order at the same time to be an *imaginative* participant' (1983: 46). For imaginative participation is the curious situation of both 'losing oneself' in a possible world, and leaving its states of affairs unchanged because one has *not* lost oneself and knows that one is not 'really' a participant. Merrell, in turn, describes reading or viewing as a matter of being simultaneously 'inside' two different frames, one actual and one fictional, and thus of both 'mediately and intermittently conceiving/perceiving-imagining a fiction *as* a fiction from 'within' one frame and relating that fiction to objects, acts and events in the 'real world' from 'within' another frame' (1983: 24). When a child screams at a monster in a film, it is because something has gone wrong: instead remaining in the both/and situation of occupying two frames, 'the fictional world becomes his one and only "real world"' (25). Maitre and Merrell have difficulty in dealing with these both/ands in the reception of possible worlds, because traditional logic does not permit a person to be actual and not actual at the same time, or to be in two places, so to speak, at once. To accomodate the law of non contradiction, Merrell therefore resorts to the argument that we are not 'really' in two frames at the same time – we 'oscillate' between between actual and fictional frames, but so fast that we are not 'aware' of the oscillation.

Of course, we do move between actual and possible fictional worlds with great ease. For – and this is my second point – possible scenarios and actual events do not occupy different and antithetical spaces, disposed one above the other, with one reflecting, duplicating or coinciding with the other. Nor do we have to 'travel' to them, as Pavel suggests. If anything, we step in and out of them. For possible scenarios and actual events coexist beside each other and envelop each other. On the one hand, we embed actual circumstances in our possible scenarios, just as we recognize the actual situations whose possibilities are being elaborated in novels or television dramas. Possible scenarios envelop actual situations. And on the other hand, in the actual world, we are constantly moving in and out of possible worlds. We slip in and out of possible scenarios in our conversations, in and out of books or television melodramas when the telephone rings or when we go to get a beer, and in and out of the theories we use when we turn our attention to something else. The actual world envelops possible worlds. Indexes of fictionality in fictional worlds and switches in and out of fictional scenarios (as in *Tom Jones*, for instance, where the 'history' is constantly being interrupted by narratorial interventions and essays) are negotiated with similar ease. We switch between possible worlds and actual worlds continually, without missing a beat, not only because, in the language of modal philosophers, possible worlds are worlds which are *accessible* from actual ones, but also because actual worlds are accessible from possible ones.

For while possible scenarios do not coincide with reality or reflect what is actually the case, they are nevertheless umbilically linked to actuality. For instance, they explore and elaborate some aspects of actual situations we face (say the possible motives or consequences of other peoples' actions); or they hold aspects of actuality up to scrutiny by considering them in relation to other ways things might be. We govern our lives, our behaviour towards others, and our interpretations of words and texts as much by what we think may be possible in a given case as by what we know to be actual, and we are constantly side-stepping possible misinterpretations or possibly unpleasant situations or trying to bring possible situations about. Possible scenarios not only grow out of actuality; they also feed back into actuality and work there in praxis because they can be acted upon.

Because the actual envelops and is enveloped by possible scenarios, because we are always moving in and out of some possible worlds and side-stepping others, and because what is merely possible at one moment (a scenario, a hurricane) can become actual at another, the line between fictioned possibilities and the actual world, never more than a trace, is always unstable, and often 'fuzzy' and 'confused' as well (Merrell, 1983: 36, 39). And even without taking into account the further complications introduced by different historical frames of reference and historical changes in the actual world, it must be said that 'it is not possible to say categorically what is and is not possible of the actual world' (Maitre, 1983: 53) and that we are constantly being surprised. The possible and the actual are constantly flowing into each other, altering their contours and changing places.

Moreover, as we saw, even in our everyday elaborations of possibility, we can conceive several different possible scenarios for the same event, and each possible scenario or possible world is different in at least some respect from every other. For thirdly, possibilities are all, in some major or minor particulars diverse, from one another. Consequently, while any possible fictional world or scenario may be linked to actuality and to other possible fictional worlds or scenarios (literary, theoretical, ideological, scientific, political or whatever) in diverse ways, it is not identical with any other.

Looking at possible worlds from within the marxist paradigm, we would have to say that our notions of what is and is not possible are determined by language and ideology, or by the state of the economy and the conflicts of human groups. Within the Possible Worlds paradigm, both ideology and determinism can be approached in a different way. The key difference here is that Possible Worlds theorists view the actual as only one possibility among a host of other possibilities, all a little diverse from each other. The actual – which of course has to be possible or it could not be actual – is the possibility which turns out to be the case, the thing of all the things which might have happened which really comes to pass. But at any moment and in any situation, multiple possibilities coexist, any one of which could become actual. The actual is therefore the outcome not only of an interplay of possibilities but also of multiple local choices amongst them. The way this changes such heretofore deterministic notions as 'programming' or historical 'evolution' becomes clearer from the work of François Jacob, a notable biologist.

As Jacob explains, in modern biology, every living organism represents the expression of a program coded in its chromosomes. But it does not follow that the genetic program is exactly copied out in every generation. For one thing, in sexual reproduction, every program is formed by the reassortment of two different programs. And for another, 'every genetic program – every individual – becomes different from all the others in the population with the exception of identical twins' because every child 'is merely one out of a large crowd of possible children, any one of whom might have been conceived on the same occasion if another of the millions of sperm cells emitted by the father had happened to fertilize the egg cell of the mother – an egg cell which is itself one of many' (1982: 8). Adaptation to the environment is, therefore, not the only, or even invariably a necessary, component in genetic evolution. Changes in the gene pool can also be produced, for instance, by chance events at the reproductive level, by 'genetic drift', gene fixation, indirect selection due to genetic linkage, or the differential growth of organs, and these can give rise to structures which may be of no direct or immediate use at all. Moreover, such historical or 'evolutionary' changes occur within and despite constraints imposed by such things as the genetic body plan of related species, the mechanical properties of their building materials, and the rules governing embryonic development.

Of course, the actual outcome of the historical evolutionary process to date is not materially changed by any of this. What *is* radically changed is the way we describe the historical process and our freedom to act in it – as can be seen by translating Jacob's account of programming and evolution back into more familiar social or theoretical terms.

First, the systems of constraint – the 'disciplines', the design and the necessity – which we call determinism figure here only as the actual outcome and potential source of a host of variations and differences, which are themselves undetermined and essentially unpredictable or, in traditional terminology, relatively 'free'. Always transient, the code, the program, the material and structural constraints at work at any point in history, function as 'diversity-generating devices', and are themselves only an outcome of diversity and of a host of local selections among alternative possibilities. Thus 'the world as we see it today . . . might well have been different; and it might even not have existed at all' (14) and the world as we see it tomorrow may be any number of different ways.

For, secondly, at each historical moment, in each local situation, however trivial, actuality is changed a little. It is changed everywhere at every instant by which possibilities among hosts of others becomes actual – for example, by which possible unions and mutations and erasures of which codes actually come about; by whether a possible hurricane becomes actual in some location; or in even more everyday terms, by which choice is made, which thought is thought, which words are spoken, which acts are performed in which situation and in relation to whom, by each of us. This will not impress those who dream of remaking all of actuality in their image, and it rather lacks mastery and pazzaz. But it does mean that everyone and everything is continually making a difference of some kind somewhere in actuality, whether they know it or not, and that no-one can therefore be dismissed as irrelevant, marginal or exempt from responsibility for what somewhere is.

Thirdly, adaptation to environment, economic or cultural/ideological/linguistic, ceases to be the only explanatory factor. Developments 'inside' a gene pool or 'inside' a given pool of language or ideas need not always create or correspond to some development 'outside' them, and possibilities can be fixed and chosen and developed which are not proximately or immediately either useful or adaptive. To borrow a radical example from Michael Murrin, 'Jerusalem was a tomb for more prophets than Christ' (1969: 26). As Clement of Alexandria and Origen among others understood and Socrates, Galileo and Trotsky discovered, positing a world which contradicts the world inhabited by the multitude has never been either safe or 'adaptive' behaviour, and it does not always meet with success, even beyond the tomb.[5]

Finally, in the Possible Worlds paradigm, ideology (if indeed we wish to retain this concept) can no longer figure merely as a set of fixed, invariant and supposedly 'true' (but really false) propositions about the way things are. In Possible Worlds terms, we might think of disciplines and ideologies as so many attempts to legitimize, institutionalize and regulate possibilities – for instance, the possibility of revolution and of the classless society, the possibility of equal opportunity and of the American Dream, or in the workplace, the possibilities of success, recognition, promotion or financial reward. Theories and ideologies tell us what we can consider possible, or how certain things can become possible for us, as well as what we may consider true of actuality. And disciplines not only hold the stick of surveillance and punishment; they also hold out the carrot of possibility and promise. Viewed conservatively, ideologies, theories and disciplines, whether linguistic, literary, social, political or scientific, could therefore be viewed as so many attempts to 'fix the limits of what is considered as possible' (Jacob, 1982: 9).

But this notion of theories and ideologies as incorporating possibilities and delineating the limits of possibility can also be used in other ways. For instance, the theories and ideologies current at any historical moment could be viewed as so many fields of possibility, in which alternatives thinkable and speakable within their perimeters are debated (as well as overlooked), and in which the possibilities which are actually admitted and taken to be 'true' emerge from interplay and selection. This would give us a much fuller and less monolithic picture of the 'forces' at work at any historical moment, and a different, less rigid and necessitarian, way of understanding historical occurrences and recurrences.

Such an understanding of historical occurrence and recurrence is intimated, for example, by Maureen Quilligan's description of the way changing attitudes to language produce or preclude the possibility of allegory:

> It is possible to write and read allegory intelligently only in those cultural contexts which grant to language a significance beyond that belonging to a merely arbitrary system of signs ... Its existence assumes an attitude in which abstract nouns not only name universals that are real, but in which the abstract names themselves are perceived to be as real and as powerful as the things named. Language itself must be felt to have a potency as solidly meaningful as physical fact before the allegorist can begin. (1979: 156, 157)

It is important to note that the availability in culture of this 'suprarealist' attitude to language does not mean that allegory *has* to occur, only that 'allegory is, if not the dominant form of literature, at least a possible alternative' (157). During the centuries from late antiquity, through the Middle Ages to the 17th century when this attitude to language was available, allegory was not the only mode of writing. But from the 17th century, when it was unavailable – when 'words lost the battle with things' and when following Locke, linguistic signs were considered merely arbitrary or treated as a neutral dress of thought – allegory as narrative all but disappeared, to return in the 20th century in such works as *Gravity's Rainbow* with the formalist and postmodern return to language as the real source of meanings.

This is an interesting beginning. But I think we would also wish to go beyond this sort of description of conditions of possibility, if only to explore how theories or ideological fields can also give rise to possibilities which challenge, transform or displace the limits they have fixed.

To briefly suggest some ways in which aspects of this orientation to possible worlds might apply in the analysis of fictions, I am going to interrupt the theoretical analysis with a partial illustration; and to insist on the diversity of possible scenarios, begin by recounting three abduction scenes, one from *Evalina*, one from *Emmeline*, and one from Mary Brunton's novel *Self-Control*, all of which portray women escaping abduction in different ways.

Evalina (1778) stresses the heroine's fear and emotion, and her difficulty, once in Sir Clement Willoughby's chariot, in preventing him from making love to her. Evalina pleads with Willoughby, breaks from him forcibly, puts her head out of the window, calls for the coachman to stop, and looks around for other people on the street who might help her. And to some extent this succeeds. Finding that she is not going to be easy meat, Willoughby declares 'I will not compel you', directs the coachman to take her home, and on his knees 'pleads' for forgiveness 'with so much submission' that she promises not to complain of him to anyone (99, 100). The implication, however, is that if Willoughby submits, it is due less to Evalina's ability to compel Willoughby not to compel her, than to the fact that Willoughby has been made aware that Evalina is in some sense under Lord Orville's protection.

In *Emmeline*, pleading and remonstrating fail, and there are no male protectors waiting in the wings. But Emmeline, normally the most rational and level-headed of heroines, succeeds in routing her abductor, Delamere, by giving way to an excess of sensibility. Weakened by terror and excessive weeping, 'her whole frame sinking under the fatigue she had undergone both of body and of mind' she sinks into insensibility, revives, develops a fever, becomes delirious, and in short convinces Delamere that her 'perturbation of spirit' has put her life in danger. Confronted by her limp, bloodless and fever-wracked body, Delamere's sexual passion (not surprisingly!) subsides, to be replaced by an 'agony of fear' that she is dying. Emmeline plays on this fear:

> 'Delamere' said she, in a low and tremulous voice, 'Delamere, why all this? I believe you have destroyed me; my head is so extremely painful. Oh! Delamere – this is cruel – very cruel.' (154)

Emmeline uses her prostration to compel Delamere not to compel her and to reverse the power-relations between them. By the end of the scene, Delamere is ready to submit to her in all things:

> 'Emmeline! I . . . entreat that you would quiet your too delicate mind and dispose of *me* as you please. Since you cannot resolve to be mine now, I will learn to submit . . . Tell me only that you pardon what is past, and you shall go to Mrs. Stafford's or whithersoever you will.' (158)

Like Evalina and Emmeline, Laura in Mary Brunton's *Self-Control* (1810) has been tricked into travelling alone in a man's chariot, but where Evalina is frantic with fear, Laura is not:

'Do not fear to trust yourself with me.' [says Warren, her abductor] 'Fear *you*' repeated Laura with involuntary disdain. 'No, but I am at a loss to guess what has encouraged you to make me the companion of so silly a frolic.' (113)

Where Emmeline used prostration to keep her would-be lover at a distance, Laura uses disdain, 'sternness of manner', 'smiles of calm contempt' and contumely. She keeps her cool and bides her time till she can act. And then she seizes the reins with a force that makes the horses rear, springs out of the carriage and walks back to town, 'leaving her inammorato in the utmost astonishment at her self-possession, as well as rage at her disdainful treatment' (114).

Because such scenes have been approached with traditional assumptions about fiction and reality, they have been dismissed as fantastic, melodramatic or simply as conventional. Abduction is treated as a recurrent topos in 18th-century novels, and usually as a topos which is traced back to Richardson's novel, *Clarissa*. Subsequent novelists are assumed to be repeating and imitating a purely formal and fictional device which he invented. For obviously such scenes do not 'reflect reality'.

But if we think of fictional scenes as possible scenarios, we can approach them differently. First, since possible scenarios elaborate ways things might go in an actual situation, we have to ask whether an actuality was enveloped in such scenes. And it turns out that women actually did get abducted in the 17th and 18th centuries, and that there was an actual risk of being bundled off in some so-called gentleman's carriage and 'ruined'. It is hard to tell from the evidence we have in diaries and letters how frequently this occurred, since abductions mostly occasioned comment when there was something extraordinary about them – for instance, when it was an heiress who was abducted, when the abductors were teenagers, or when the abducted young woman happened to be rescued by Sheridan and the Prince of Wales. But abduction for the purpose of what was euphemistically called 'seduction' was something that might actually happen to women. It could be described as the 18th century version of date rape: an extreme instance of the exercise of male force against a woman, on the part of a man who is well known to her.

The bare bones of this actual situation are embedded in each of the scenes I have described: in each case, the abductor is well known to the heroine, in each case the heroine is carried off in a carriage, in each case there is a marked exercise of male force, and in each case what is at issue is whether the heroine is going to be forced to have sexual relations against her will. But viewing fictions as possible scenarios does not commit us to saying that the scenes I have described are therefore 'true to reality'. They are not. Burney, Smith and Brunton are not reflecting the way things actually are, but exploring possible ways in which women, once abducted, might resist, might turn the tables on their abductors, and might succeed in saving themselves in the end. In Hanna More's words, they are 'furnishing [women] with a stock of ideas and principles and qualifications and habits, ready to be applied and appropriated, as occasion may demand'. In other words, they are elaborating possibilities of evasion and resistance, which feed back into actuality not only by underscoring the clear and present danger of being abducted, but also by helping women to consider what they might do if they were.

If they were. This is important. For the 'actuality' enveloped in possible scenarios is not to be conceived as we conceive of 'reality' – it is not some seamless, invariable and solidly present surface waiting, immobile, to be reflected in fiction. For actual women in an actual world, abduction, like date rape, is itself only a possibility, something that might happen to us – until, heaven forfend!, it does actually happen to us. It is a real possibility, perhaps, but a possibility nevertheless. Possible scenarios might therefore be described as elaborations of possible responses to a possible situation which in actuality has been faced by some and might very possibly also have to be faced by others.

Of course, what Burney, Smith and Brunton suggest women might do once abducted seems fantastic to us today – we now delineate an entirely different range of possible scenarios relating to rape, from submission to counselling to mace; 18th century possibilities are clearly elaborated from within a different mind-set than our own. But it is worth noticing that, just as possible scenarios can envelop actual events without reflecting the way things are, so the possibilities developed in these scenarios can envelop cultural assumptions or mind-sets, without duplicating them.

The scenario in *Evalina* envelops the 18th-century fiction that women lack both reason and power, and are therefore gormless and helpless without male guidance and protection. It was this fiction which made fathers, husbands and brothers womens' 'natural protectors', and at the same time, the legal governors of their lives and property. Burney severs Evalina from all such natural and legal protectors by making her an orphan and by separating her from her guardian. And she explores not only the possibility that delicately nurtured Evalina can, after all, deal with adverse circumstances on her own, but also the possibility in a tight spot of using or threatening to use other men than one's 'natural' and 'legal' protectors to frighten off the wolf.

Sensibility was another supposedly feminine and feminizing characteristic, and one likewise associated with helplessness – one has only to think of all those 18th-century portrayals of women with flowing unbound hair, on their knees, weeping, pleading and distraught, or of the total ineffectiveness of Mackenzie's *Man of Feeling*. What Charlotte Smith was exploring in the second scene I described, however, was the possibility that an excess of sensibility, turned on at the right time and in the right way, might work *for* a woman and not against her. The extreme prostration brought on by the constantly demonstrated excess of such sensibility might not only put one's would-be lover off his sexual stride, but also leave him in an 'agony of fear' that he will find himself being held culpable for murder.

Another of the sticks that 18th-century men liked to beat women with was the argument that women are better formed by nature than men for the perfection of virtue – this justified expecting perfectly conformable behaviour of women, while leaving men their pardonable and far more pleasurable vices. According to Adam Smith, 'self-command' was the virtue from which all other virtues derive, and Mary Brunton's heroine in *Self-Control* is a model of self-command. But Laura is not conformable. For what is being explored is the possibility that women can use self-command and superior virtue to control men and take command of their own fate. Laura's righteous superiority renders her abductor impotent, and her self-control enables her to control the situation (and every other in her world). It gives her the self-possession to bide her time until she can act decisively.

In each scenario, therefore, the possibility of escaping abduction and rape envelops oft repeated and widely held assumptions about women. But in no case does the scenario duplicate or confirm these assumptions. On the contrary, what is being explored is the possibility that the mind-set of the time offers possible ways in which women might take back the sort of control over their bodies and their fates which the mind-set denied them. What is being explored is the possibility that women might be otherwise than helpless, powerless and conformable, and the possibility of reversing the actual power-relations between men and women so that, for a change, *he* might submit to *her*, rather than she to him. Such scenarios not only imagine diverse ways in which women might perhaps escape abduction and ruin; they also signal the possibility of at least local success in turning the tables on men, and they provide quite diverse images of a possible world in which women might no longer be entirely helpless and conformable, and men might no longer be able to have things all their own way.

But it must also be said that reversing the power-relations between the sexes was not the only set of possibilities 18th-century women explored. Another set of possibilities explored in diverse ways by other women-writers, and in some cases by the same writers I have discussed, is that self-determining women might share power with men. Many 18th-century fictional scenarios, for instance, explored the possibility that women had – or could have with adequate education, suitable opportunity or financial independence – the qualities of mind and character upon which men based their superiority and their right to rule over women. Prime among these was the sovereign light of reason (women being supposed to lack reason), and there are hosts of different scenarios in 18th-century womens' writings elaborating the possibility that women would prove capable of rationally governing their own lives and those of others. Likewise, there are hosts of scenarios (associated for example with the 'companionate marriage' or with parent-daughter relationships) appropriating for women the Rights of Man as these had emerged in the course of a succession of revolutions from the 17th-century on, most notably the rights to liberty and equality. And these too were not the only possibilities being explored. When one begins to consider the wealth of different possibilities for women which were being elaborated in different ways – not only in novels, but in educational treatises, conduct books, essays and the rest – it becomes apparent that blanket terms like ideology or world-view and simple propositional statements about their contents can only be proffered *sous rature*.

Theories may be described in much the same sorts of ways. Like literary fictions, theory-fictions envelop some aspects of the actual text or the actual world. Can we say that sexuality plays no part in human development or the economy in the government of our lives in society? Can we say that some workers did not want

Factitive Fictions and Possible Worlds 131

to overthrow the machine and liberate themselves from machine owners in 19th-century England or that kings and governments have not in actuality been overthrown? Can we say that texts do not intertextually allude to, repeat and change other texts, or that language has no impact on what may be said? Such elements of the actual world are embedded in diverse theories, as the actuality that women did get abducted is embedded in the diverse literary scenarios I described. Like literary fictions, theory-fictions are accessible from the actual text and the actual world.

But theory-fictions do not therefore reflect the way things really are, or even the way they must be. They are elaborations of possible worlds – worlds in which human sexuality or economic factors or the structures of language or 'gravitational force' are thematized and explored. They are worlds in which the different possible manifestations or workings of such factors are imagined and instantiated in tremendous detail. Theory-fictions provide diverse and complex elaborations of the ways things might be in a world where language, or human sexuality or molecules or gravity were all, just as the literary fictions I described provide diverse and complex elaborations of the way things might be in a world where women were not helpless and men did not have things all their own way. The worlds constructed by theories are therefore fictional in the first sense I described: they are both real and unreal, both extant and non-existent, both made and related to some actuality.

And this relation to actuality runs both ways: we not only move from the actual world or actual text to elaborating possible constructions, but from the possible constructions we elaborate to actual texts and the actual world. Theory-fictions give us that 'preconception of what is possible' by which we orientate ourselves in the maze of actual material and determine what is worth looking at and how. Each of our theory-fictions teaches us to look at the same texts or the same phenomena with a different set of possibilities in mind, offering us different possible ways of working on the text or on the world.

It is because they are elaborations of merely possible worlds, worlds which depart from the way things actually are in both senses of the word depart, that theory-fictions both 'work' in some respects and invariably fail to work in others, and that they can invariably both be 'proved' to be 'true' and falsified. It is also because they are elaborations of merely possible worlds, that our theory-fictions are so good at suggesting how things might be otherwise – otherwise than we thought them and otherwise than they actually are. From this point of view, theory-fictions show us where actuality might open onto as yet unrealized possibilities, and how what might be has transformed, does transform and can again transform what is.

Compossible Worlds

So far, I have been considering one broad 'orientation' to possible worlds, an orientation in which alternative possible worlds and the actual world are viewed as coexisting side-by-side in such a way that each is 'accessible' from the other. In that orientation, different possible worlds and the actual world were basically conceived as occupying different spaces, although, as we saw, each also 'enveloped' some part of the other and each 'flowed' into others. But this is not the only way of disposing possible worlds in relation to each other and in relation to the actual world. And to make that point, it is worth venturing (and I say venturing advisedly) on another very different disposition of possible worlds, a disposition I will call 'compossibility'.[6]

When they are disposed compossibly, different possible worlds and the actual world occupy the same space – they are possible at once and together. Possible worlds exist within the actual world and the actual word in a 'ghostly' or less immediately perceptible manner. The literality of the word and the materiality of the event partly conceal the possible worlds which are spoken along with the word and which can be lived along with the event. But the word, the text and the world are as they are by virtue of this compossibility of different worlds superimposed on one other and mutually responding (co-responding) to one another. And compossibility is as fully active in any part – of the world, of language – as it is in the whole.

To find current examples of compossibility one has to look to science but history offers manifold and more fully developed examples of it in the type of fiction we call allegory. As Carolynn Van Dyke has pointed out, 'agreement about the identity of allegory extends only to cursory definitions; beyond that disparities proliferate' (1985: 17). And as far as I can tell, the same may be said about many-worlds in quantum mechanics, so we are on shaky ground on both counts. But it seems to me that certain claims which are being made both about allegory and about many-worlds in quantum physics do cooperate in interesting ways to

Factitive Fictions and Possible Worlds

affirm and describe compossibility. And it is these which I will be pursuing.

As Fred Alan Wolf has explained: 'In the new physics, a thing is represented by all of its possibilities, even those that may be remote . . . To know an atom is to know all of its electrons' possible locations in space' (1988: 61, 65). Each of these possible locations inhabits a separate world. In each world only a single possibility or a single viewpoint appears, seeming to exist as if the others were not really present; but the atom has all its possibilities simultaneously because different worlds are superimposed on each other like so many transparencies. Since objects in each layer pass through other layers 'like ghosts in the night', fading in and out continually, a pattern emerges from this superimposition which we call reality: 'many, many possibilities combine, creating what appears to be one gigantic reality. But this reality is just a combination of other flimsier realities' (1988: 42). Or to put it differently, a pattern emerges which is not contained in any single layer. But this pattern is not static. It is more like a wave continually breaking up and branching off as different possibilities are pursued, than it is like a state. For the possibilities in the different worlds interact and interfere with each other, and at each interaction or interference, the worlds split and recombine again into one reality, an other reality which has branched off from conditions before.

Allegory too operates simultaneously with 'parallel levels' (Van Dyke, 1985: 22) which are separate and distinct. As Wimsatt has said and others have confirmed, 'even though the metaphorical meanings [of literal actions] are quite clear, there remain two distinct levels' (1970: 25). The word 'levels' may, however, be misleading if it makes us think of tiers disposed one above the other and viewed laterally like geological strata. The locus classicus for describing the simultaneity in allegorical texts is, of course, Dante's letter to Can Grande della Scala, and it is worth looking at it again:

> One must realize that the meaning of the work is not simple, but is rather to be called polysemous, that is having many meanings. The first meaning is the one obtained through the letter; the second is the one obtained through the things signified by the letter. The first is called literal, the second allegorical or moral or anagogical. In order that this manner of treatment may appear more clearly, it may be applied to the following verses: 'When Israel went out of Egypt, the house of Jacob from a people

of strange language, Judah was his sanctuary and Israel his dominion.' For if we look to the letter alone, the departure of the children of Israel from Egypt in the time of Moses is indicated to us; if to the allegory, our redemption accomplished by Christ is indicated to us; if to the moral sense, the conversion of the soul from the woe and misery of sin to a state of grace is indicated to us; if to the anagogical sense, the departure of the consecrated soul from the slavery of this corruption to the liberty of eternal glory is indicated. And though these mystic senses may be called by various names, they can all generally be spoken of as allegorical, since they are diverse from the literal or historical. (Gilbert, 1962: 202)

Dante does not speak of levels or tiers, but rather of a coexistence in the space occupied by the literal words and the literal action of other – distinct and diverse – 'mystic' or less evident configurations of meaning. As Maureen Quilligan has said, 'the 'other' named by the term *allos* in the word allegory is not some other hovering above the words of the text, but the possibility of an otherness, a polysemy, inherent in the very words on the page' (1979: 26). Literal and allegorical meanings, however diverse, all inhabit and show themselves through the same physical letters.[7] If there is any stratification here, it involves looking down through the 'letteral' surface of the word to superimposed layers of meaning. And this 'shifts emphasis away from our traditional insistence on allegory's distinction between the word said and the meaning meant, to the simultaneity of the process of signifying multiple meanings' (Quilligan, 1979: 26).

These multiple simultaneous meanings are not, however, just layers of meaning. As Dante's explanation indicates, the diverse meanings which inhere in the biblical verse 'When Israel went out of Egypt . . . ' belong to different worlds: an historical world where the actant is the children of Israel; a quite other historical world in which the actant is Christian man; and two worlds, one moral and one spiritual, one ever-present and one always future, where the actant is the soul. The action indicated by the verse – the action of being redeemed from a state of bondage – occurs in all these worlds at once, albeit at different times (past, present and future) and in somewhat different ways. And while it remains possible to treat each world as though the others were not really present and to read the verse as relating only to it, it is the compossibility of these diverse worlds in the same verse, and the much more complex plotting of their interactions, which makes the verse itself what it is – the pattern and nub of a cosmic event.

For allegorical language 'mirrors' the world not like a modern mirror, which only provides a reversed reflection of the surfaces of things, but like a hologram (or microcosm) where every part re-presents in small all the manifold dimensions which make up the whole. In the Middle Ages, the word mirror was used in psychological, political, psychological and literary contexts, for Summas and manuals or guide books – texts both compendious and exemplary, which rendered in a small compass the larger cosmic and eternal patterns obscured by the cluttered world which superficially appears (Wimsatt, 1970: 28ff). And it was because it functioned as a hologrammic mirror that all allegorical language could be as redemptive as the verse which Dante chose to exemplify it. For allegorical language was able to release people from bondage to the literal body of the world and the word by leading them into those other, equally 'real,' compossible worlds, which co-operate and co-respond in the making of the actual world and the actual word and become intelligible through them. Allegorical language envelops and is enveloped by an actuality in which 'the event of existing embraces depths of ultimacy or of reality within the very *immediacies* of experience being lived and observed, literally as a dimension of what is observable and knowable, however elusive or unmanageable' (Meland, 1976: 43). And as Murrin has pointed out, allegory was therefore 'not a process of mere interpretation such as we practice in our schools today; it was a revelation' (1969: 53).

Language could work in this revelatory and redemptive way because the signifieds inhering in signifiers and in some cases, the very form of the letters and sound-images themselves, were not considered to be arbitrary or fortuitous. They were guaranteed by God.[8] The sign was a sacred portal to all the compossible worlds it indicated through its literal and 'mystic senses,' through its previous uses, through its sounds and its letters, and through its etymology. This simultaneous enclosure of worlds within the sign and opening out of the sign onto worlds explains that feature of allegory of which Paul de Man made so much: its tautological self-reflexivity. For on the one hand, as R. W. Frank Jr., Morton Bloomfield and Maureen Quilligan have pointed out, allegories are at pains to return readers from the imaginary action to the multiple compossible significances of the action which are embedded in the literal words used to describe it. It is in the literal – or the 'letteral'

– word that the 'other-speech' and other worlds of allegory are to be found. And on the other hand, 'the plots of all allegorical narratives unfold as investigations into the literal truth inherent in individual words, considered in the context of their whole history as words' (Quilligan, 1979: 33). Or as Barney and Van Dyke have put it, the allegorical action offers its own – narrative – commentaries on key words.[9]

These narrative commentaries are not, however, only a matter of 'interpretation' or of epistemological exploration, as following De Man we seem to be assuming. They are also demonstrations that the compossible worlds (physical, moral, spiritual etc.) to which a word's meanings belong can all be lived. Allegorical characters – themselves simultaneously inhabitants of more than one merely literal and physical world in the manner of 'microcosms' rather than 'personnifications' – live out the worlds which unfold from an individual word in the physical text. They demonstrate how one lives at the same time both in the actual world and in an ethical (or unethical) kingdom where moral and epistemological decisions are constantly being made, how one lives the actual world *as* an ethical kingdom. They demonstrate at the same time how one lives the actual world compossibly as an actual physical world and as an actual spiritual world in which the soul can be saved, how actual events can be experienced as stations in a spiritual adventure. And in so doing, they also show the consequences of choices in compossible worlds, the ways in which a choice or action in one world interferes with conditions in all the others, causing the reality composed of all the worlds to branch off in a new direction and altering the pattern of compossibilities.

Actual historical events therefore figure differently when possible worlds and the actual world are compossible than they do when possible worlds are only accessible from each other and from actuality. As numerous scholars have shown, actual historical people and events are enveloped in allegories, just as they are enveloped in other fictions – Charlemagne's wars in *Orlando Furioso*; the first Crusade in *Jerussaleme Liberata*; John of Gaunt's relationship to his wife, Blanche, in Chaucer's *Book of the Duchess*; political events under Richard the Second in the 'Fable of the Mice' in *Piers Ploughman*; an actual Beatrice in *The Divine Comedy* and so on. But they are enveloped in a different way. Actual historical moments are so overladen with all their significances and consequences in the other, compossible worlds in which they participate that actual moments of national or personal history become as polysemous and as hologrammatic as the sign itself. Like the letteral surface of the word, the literal occurrence in national or personal history becomes a sign, a portal, to the worlds – ethical, political, spiritual and cosmological – which co-respond in its making and show themselves through it.[10]

There is, moreover, in allegorical texts not only a compossibility of worlds in the space of the same word and the same event, but also a simultaneity and compossibility of different historical moments. Murrin has compared the temporal compossibilities in allegorical texts to looking at the stars and seeing a pattern made by lights emitted at a variety of different points in time and at a variety of different temporal distances from us. For in allegories, together with the actual historical event, 'all the happenings in time are simultaneously present and can be seen to manifest an ordered pattern' (Murrin, 1969: 110). Murrin points out, for instance, that in Book I of *The Faerie Queene*, Spenser is 'bringing together elements from four or five different periods of human history' (109), and others have explored the complex temporal superimpositions created by the 'typological' relation of one allegorical text to other earlier texts (most often the Bible or Virgil) and to the historical actions enveloped by them. Murrin suggests that this simultaneity, superimposition and compossibility of different times, past, present and future, is the God's-eye view of time, and that 'when the poet runs together different periods of history . . . he is imitating divine judgement, by seeing history from a point of view outside time . . .' (112).

We should notice too that compossibility of worlds and compossibility of historical times is not necessarily restricted only to those works which we officially classify as 'allegory'. The ethical, political, metaphysical and cosmological worlds onto which a play like *King Lear*, for instance, opens, certainly do not need to be restated – though it might perhaps be said that critics have tended to focus on one or other of these worlds, rather than on the more complex patterns created by their co-existence, interferences and corespondences. Nor is it necessary to demonstrate again how the action in *King Lear* unfolds as a commentary on the meanings of the polysemous word 'Not(h)ing' or how we are constantly brought back from the play's imaginary action to the language which is used to speak it. But it may be worth remarking that, like the works we consider allegories, *King Lear* also envelops an actual historical event: the advent of a King, James I, who believed firmly in the Divine Right of Kings and in keeping 'the name and th'addition to a king,' but who left the actual 'sway and execution' of governance to machiavellian courtiers, while he went hunting, amused himself with flattering courtiers and with his fool, Archie Armstrong, and prided himself on his 'wit'. As a popular ballad had it: 'Little Cecil trips up and down/He rules both Court and Crown.'[11] This historical event is so overladen with its significances and implications in all the compossible worlds, ethical, political, metaphysical and cosmological, opened by the play, that to our modern eyes, instead of expanding into the pattern and nub of a cosmic event, it shrinks to a mere 'allusion' or to a piece of scholarly marginalia which is peripheral to the 'real' global and cosmological significance of the play. We treat the presence of an actual historical Beatrice or an actual historical John of Gaunt in works which we categorize as allegories in much the same inverted sort of way.

It may also be worth noting the compossibility of different historical times in Shakespeare's play. For the superimposition of times in *King Lear* goes beyond the obvious superimposition of current events onto the earlier historical pretext of an old King Leir who divided out his kingdom among rival daughter-dependents. For instance, when it places Lear on the heath in a situation where the meanest wretch can 'beard me to my face', the action also superimposes two times and two kings, one present and one past, onto yet another king and yet another past – a past in James I's own life when, as James VI of Scotland, he was, in his own words, 'a king without state, without honour, without order, where beardless boys would brave us to our face'.[12] In so doing, the action also looks forward (with the same 'prophetic' power that the Fool in the play claims for himself and that allegories speak by their 'God's-eye' view of time) to that time later in the century when another Stuart monarch who believed in the Divine Right of kings would again find himself wandering the heaths of Scotland, a king without a state and without honour, seeking shelter and friends.

Theory-fictions could be spoken in terms of compossibility too. This is not, however, our current practice. For even when we follow Northrop Frye or Paul de Man in saying that 'all commentary is allegorical interpretation', we exclude compossibilities or deconstruct them.

On the one hand, rather than think in terms of the compossibility of diverse worlds of meaning, we think in terms of the substitution of an other, newer or heretofore concealed, interpretation for a literal interpretation or for one already in place. And rather than think in terms of the compossibility of different historical moments in the same text, we either think in terms of the correspondence of each text to 'its' own particular historical moment, or in terms of a displacement of past concerns and meanings by present ones. As Susan Sonntag has put it: 'Interpretation presupposes a discrepancy between the clear meaning of the text and the demands of (later) readers . . . . Interpretation is a radical strategy for conserving an old text, which is thought too precious to repudiate, by revamping it' (1989: 546).

Yet against this, it could also be argued that allegorical interpretations of the text and the world are accepted *as* interpretations of that text and that world only inasmuch as they appear to be compossible with the literal text or the physical world. The theory-fiction which interpreted the behaviour of electrons allegorically in terms of the way planets circle around the sun – was dismissed when it was found incompossible with the manifest behaviour of electrons. The theory-fiction which interpreted society and history allegorically in terms of the development of living beings from infancy through maturity to the decline of senility and old age – was dismissed when it was no longer thought to be compossible with the actual course of events. And theory-fictions which interpret Shakespeare's politics allegorically in terms of their conformity to a depersonalized, mechanical, and apparently unchanging Ideological State Apparatus called 'Monarchy' – still try to demonstrate the compossibility of this reading with the actual texts of Shakespeare's plays. The 'truth' of theory-fictions may turn out to be very much a matter of compossibility.

On the other hand, when we do work with the simultaneity of polysemous meanings in the same word, we implicitly or explicitly draw on the correspondence theory of truth and on the law of non-contradiction to deconstruct the compossibility of diverse meanings. We say that a word which figures as an intertextual *Mittelpunkt* for diverse meanings expounded in diverse contexts has no 'proper' meaning of its own – and therefore, that the word has no meaning at all. We pretend that it is only proper for each word to correspond monogamously to one meaning, and that its polygamous compossible meanings dissolve its capacity to function as a word. Thus despite our avowed political desire for spaces where 'incommensurabilities' can coexist, and despite our practice of reading interpretative strategies as allegories of political action, we effectively preclude the compossibility of incommensurabilities. And we recreate the sign as a space of rivalry and conflict, where it is always and again a matter of one meaning *or* another, this allegorical interpretation *or* that, them *or* us.

As Derrida's (de)constructive use of language and recent theory of 'translation'[13] demonstrate, however, there is no binding reason why compossible meanings should deconstruct a word, rather than construct it. And despite the rivalry among universes of discourse, it might also be said that new compossibilities are being created de facto all the time by the simultaneous presence in language and culture of diverse theory-fictional worlds relating to the same actual entities. Actual beings – the actual child or the actual woman, for instance – could be described as polysemous cyphers, overladen with all their meanings in compossible worlds: worlds of fashion, marketing and entertainment, as well as worlds of psychology, sociology, medicine, politics, education, literature and law. Actual texts could be said to become weighty, portentous and culturally significant through the accumulated weight of superimposed allegorizations. And since, as Goodman points out, 'we have no ready rules for transforming physics, biology and psychology into one another and no way at all of transforming any of these into Van Gogh's vision or Van Gogh's into Canaletto's' (1978: 3), we could think of ourselves as placed at the nub of a variety of compossible, but often incompatible worlds which we negotiate either by means of a de facto acceptance of both/and or, if we get worried about the law of non- contradiction, by means of what Goodman, like Merrell, would call 'judicious vacillation' (1984: 32).

Simulated Worlds

Simulations inscribe a wholly different orientation towards possible worlds, an orientation which affects us in the postmodern world even more directly than the others. Computerized and non-computerized simulations are now to be found in aerospace programs and in government offices, in businesses and in schools, in video games and in some books for children. Since the 1960s and '70s, they have been used for research in the physical and social sciences, and for planning in industry, in the economy, in

Factitive Fictions and Possible Worlds 141

local government, in international relations and in the military-industrial complex. Simulations are also used for the training of pilots, astronauts, managers, salespeople, accountants, policemen, social workers and teachers, and for teaching a variety of subjects in the classroom. Simulations are most familiar to most of us, however, as a favoured source of pleasure and play in arcades, in fantasy parks, and in the home.

Simulated worlds do not, as we sometimes imagine, reflect or duplicate reality. Instead, they 'model' some problem, or system or sector in the actual world – for instance, the conditions of a plane in flight, life among hunter-gatherers, a boxing match, the behaviour of a complex transportation system, American pioneers journeying by wagon across dangerous and hostile territory, a decision-making process, or the poverty trap in the ghetto. To 'model' a delimited portion of some actuality is to work with probabilities and possibilities and to develop a theory about the variables involved and about the different possible (mathematical or logical) interrelationships amongst them. As Maidment put it, 'when one designs a simulation, he is actually stating a theory in very concrete terms' (1973: 11).

A particular simulation-model is therefore never anything but one tentative, possible construction of the data. Textbooks on simulation repeatedly emphasize that the 'same' problem or system might be modeled in completely different ways and that the most complex and highly refined models are inexact, simplified, merely approximative and potentially misleading. They also indicate that the status of the model always remains provisional and experimental. 'Built by educated guesses, analytical techniques, cut and try and other iterative procedures' (Colella *et al.*, 1974: 41), simulation models are never made and fixed once and for all. They are remade over and over again through trial and error, by repeated comparison of the information derived from the model with the performance of its counterpart in actuality and by adjustments of the model in the light of discrepancies. The 'process of elaboration and enrichment [therefore] involves a constant interaction and feedback process between the real world situation and the model . . . . As each version of the model is tested and attempts to validate it are made, a new version is produced that leads to retesting and revalidation' (Shannon, 1975: 20). When modelers stop at one version of the model, it is not because that version is considered 'true' to reality or wholly representative of the problem or system under study.

Modelers only stop at a version which is judged 'acceptable' (at least for the time being) because feedback from the actual world and from users or participants confirms that insights gained from working with the model are now satisfactory enough for the purpose at hand.[14] This looping, iterative disposition of world-model and actual world differentiates simulated worlds from accessible or compossible worlds, since, as Singer succinctly observes, it means that 'reality is neither in the world nor in the model, but in the process of working back and forth between the world and the model' (in Shannon, 1975: 180). Modelers insist that 'we understand reality only to the extent that we can model it' (Holstein, 1974: 1) and that we learn about the world in the looping and iterative process of trying to model it.

Simulated worlds differ from accessible and compossible worlds too in that they are worlds which actively explore alternative, and often incompatible or contradictory, possibilities. If simulations always model some actual problem or system by 'substituting for the real signs of the real,' they do not do so, as Baudrillard supposed, to 'double things with their own proper scenario' and to dissimulate one by means of the other until reality 'itself' all but disappears (Baudrillard, 1981: 11, 24). To argue this is to conflate simulations with simulacra, and all kinds of different information technologies with each other.[15] Simulations substitute signs of the real for the real to ask and try to answer a variety of 'what if' questions. They manipulate signs to experiment with different possibilities and different options – for instance, to see what might happen if this or that policy were implemented, if this or that variable were changed, if this or that piece of equipment were used in this or that way. In simulations, models are set in motion to explore the possible consequences of alternative assumptions or decisions, the possible behaviour of a piece of equipment in alternative possible circumstances or environments, the possible reactions produced by this or that action in human interactions and such. Simulations are experiments with alternative possibilities in situations where 'to actually test and evaluate various policies is too expensive . . . [or] risky' or just plain impossible, and where decisions have to be taken despite 'complexity and incomplete information' (Abt, 1970: 11).

Different types of simulation model actuality differently. I am only going to be looking here at dynamic, stochastic, interactive simulations, of the type known in the '70s as 'simulation games' and now referred to as 'interactive fictions'. Translated into video games

Factitive Fictions and Possible Worlds 143

and chidrens' books, such simulations are beginning to fashion the imaginary (assumptions?) of many of our children, students and young people. Although they are generally disparaged in the professional literature on simulation and dismissed for being 'fantasy' worlds, these simulated fictional worlds are modeled according to the same principles as simulations used for research, planning, training and teaching. This should give us pause, not only because it once again puts in question the boundary between fiction and non-fiction, but also because the modeling principles involved radically revise assumptions about the construction of reality derived from the marxist paradigm which we are still trying to teach the next generation.

Interactive simulations can be run with pencils, paper and a couple books as well as through a computer, but even non-computerized simulated worlds – like the cultish *Dungeons and Dragons* simulation fiction, which I am going to be using as an example – bear the unmistakable imprint of their origin in computer programs and computer languages. This means not only that computer-think is no longer confined to interaction with the machine, but also that it is beginning to have an impact on the shape and function of the book.

Interactive simulated worlds model actuality in a writing space and as a writing space which is at once both linear and non-linear, both determined and undetermined, both changing and fixed. Governed both by rule and by chance, such worlds are (at their best) infinitely various and infinitely repeatable because the same world plays out different possibilities each time.

Considered statically, an interactive simulated world exists in two modes simultaneously: one spatial, 'logical' (though the logic is not the traditional logic of non-contradiction) and non-linear; the other linear, temporal and causal.

The author of the simulated world designs his world diagrammatically as what Bolter calls 'a structure of possibilities' (1991: 119) by working with what is described metaphorically in the literature as a pattern of 'nodes' and 'branches'. Nodes are events, scenes, episodes, obstacles, encounters – fragments of text; branches are possible links between one node and any number of others. The author of a simulated world writes a number of nodes – possible events or scenes, which are not only different from each other, but often mutually-contradictory as well. For instance, in one node a character may be killed by a monster, in another that same character may defeat the monster in battle and live on, in another s/he may be saved by a magic spell, in yet another s/he may have an illuminating conversation with a mage, in yet another s/he may be injured by falling into a pit and so on. The author also provides a number of possible links between nodes: for instance, the conversation with the mage might lead to the episode in which our hero falls into a pit, to the episode in which s/he is killed by the monster, to the episode in which s/he defeats the monster *and* to the episode in which s/he is saved by a magic spell; and/or the episode in which our hero falls into the pit might lead to the episode in which s/he is saved by a magic spell and thence to the conversation with the mage. In the author's design, then, a variety of alternative possible events, a variety of alternative possible relations between events and a variety of alternative possible sequences among events coexist in a spatial, simultaneous and atemporal manner.

The reader-participant does not, however, see these coexisting possibilities; they are hidden inside the program. For the reader-participant, branches are decision points, places in the text where s/he is asked to make a choice which will lead from the episode s/he is 'in' to one of the episodes which branch off from it. For instance, at the end of the episode in which the hero falls into the pit, the reader-participant might be asked whether s/he chooses to talk to the mage or not: if s/he does choose to talk to the mage (option a), s/he might read a story in which s/he is saved by a magic spell; if she does not (option b), s/he might find herself reading a story in which s/he fights a monster in the pit. The reader-participant chooses her/his 'path' through a series of forks and choices. His/her decision about what s/he wants to do, or about what s/he would do in the hero's place, decides the course of the story s/he is reading from screen to screen – and indeed which story s/he is reading, for the stories can be wholly different, and completely incompatible with each other. But whichever story s/he reads, the story, as s/he reads it, is linear and sequential, with one thing following after another in the usual temporal, causally intelligible, narrative manner.[16]

Early translators of computer simulations into books produced what is called (or was called in the '70s) a 'scramble book'. Scramble books (like the 'Make your own Adventure' series, or the earliest *Dungeons and Dragons* adventure modules) basically consist of discontinuous, non-sequential, numbered paragraphs or episodes at the end of each of which the reader is given choices which lead to another numbered paragraph or episode. In scramble books, all possible events, sequences and relations are present simultaneously in the book; but the reader only reads a relatively small number of paragraphs or episodes, hopping and skipping his/her way forwards and backwards through the book, wherever his/her choices lead, to construct his/her 'own' linear story.[17]

A more successful translation consisted of turning computer simulations into *two* books, one of which performed – or helped its reader to perform – the functions of author and computer, while the other informed the choices reader-participants would make in the interactive simulated world.[18] In early *Dungeons and Dragons* books, the Dungeon Master's book provides the text (events or encounters) to be read to player-participants by the reader who performs the function of the computer. It also gives that reader information that the other players do not have and alternative ways s/he can run the action, thus giving the Dungeon Master an overview of the possibilities which reader-participants do not have, and preserving the uncertainty and incomplete information on the basis of which reader-participants have to make their choices at decision points. In *Advanced Dungeons and Dragons*, the Dungeon Master's book is only a Guide: it provides an enormous amount of data about different possible components of the simulated world (monsters, magic weapons and such), far more than would be required for any one story, as well as the rules governing it (I'll come back to that), and it leaves its reader to become the author of the text (events, encounters, obstacles etc.) that participants in the simulated world will hear and respond to. In both cases, the Players' Handbook provides data about a number of types of character who might inhabit the simulated world, and it invites reader-participants to make their choices not as themselves, but as the character they have chosen to act for in the story. This turns readers of the Players' Handbook into authors too, since they are no longer just choosing among a number of pre-determined paths, but speaking, thinking, planning, and acting for their characters. In book form, therefore, the structure derived from the writing space of interactive computer simulations opens onto far more possibilities than even the most complex computer program. For in book form, each instantiation of the simulated world also depends on the unpredictable possibilities derived from the imagination and inventiveness of its reader-writer-participants and from the interaction of their diverse texts. This also makes *Dungeons and Dragons* more attractive to many of our brightest young people than either video games or the traditional book.

Considered dynamically, simulated computer worlds also move in two manners simultaneously: one limited, fixed, rule-bound, repetitive, and pre-determined; the other, open, unfixed, fortuitous, transmutative and unpredictable.

To model a delimited reality is to chop it up into finite 'entities having attributes [which] interact with activities under certain conditions, creating events that change the state of the system'[19] (Shannon, 1975: 109). It is also to program the computer by specifying morphologies and rules. To simulate interactions between persons in a social cybernetics program called Atman,[20] for instance, modelers specified generic behaviour rules for 'selves' and listed human attributes (shyness, sociability, intelligence etc.). They assigned 'selves' moods, needs, intentions, beliefs, hopes, and commitments as well as expectations and a capacity for surprise and disappointment. They also specified for the computer which conditions had to be fulfilled for a 'self' to be suprised or disappointed or believing or hopeful. They developed a 'life trajectory scheme' for 'selves' and sets of everyday routines which could be assigned to subjects automatically on the basis of sex, age, profession, marital status, and number and age of children. They set rules for interactions, biased so that persons in the same social or geographical location (in the same street, shop or place of work) would have the highest probability of interacting, and rules for compatibility according to selve-ish attributes. They associated physical contexts with maps, and listed the 'selves' or types of selves located in each mapped cell. They even introduced the concept of 'looking' into their simulation model and a condition allowing 'selves' to communicate only with persons they were looking at, and assigned them a moving direction and a sitting or standing position in locations. They gave selves a memory – a 'schedule of appointments', one to store information from the past, and one for future events – and an ability to forget. And they produced protocols for each task (analysing situations, interacting with others etc.) which specified not only the preconditions for the applicability of the task, its temporal duration, and its compossibility with other tasks, but also the sequence in which its elements were to be performed. In other words, they produced what sounds like a deterministic, poststructuralist nightmare.

But interactive simulated worlds are not deterministic. For their rules are married to probability distributions. For instance, the computer is told that a self has a 40–60 per cent chance of being surprised or disappointed in such or such conditions, a 60–80 per cent chance of having an intelligence level of whatever, a 20–50 per cent chance of having the property of shyness or sociability, a 50–90 per cent chance of being married, a 60–85 per cent chance of being at work during the day, and so on. And the computer is programmed to take a random sampling from these probability distributions by generating random numbers. The instruction 'Create self' therefore generates a variety of different selves with different attributes in different combinations and in different proportions, who react differently (within certain parameters) to the same situation – this one is shy, married, not surprised under given conditions and has an intelligence of 120, that one is not shy, only moderately surprised, married, and has intelligence of 80 and so on. Stochastic, interactive simulated worlds are worlds where 'randomness [is] needed to portray real life' and where 'variations appear to occur by chance and cannot be predicted' (Banks and Carson, 1984: 122, 22). They are worlds in which it cannot be known with any certainty when the next customer will arrive at a grocery store check out, how long a bank teller will take to complete a transaction, whether the repairman will be able to fix your refridgerator, or how someone will react to any given stimulus. They are worlds in which the same protocols are run through according to the same rules, again and again and again and again in a closed and iterative circuit, but where they play out differently each time.

In *Dungeons and Dragons* (D & D), similarly, there are endless rules. There are classes of characters – fighters, mages, thieves, dwarves, elves etc – each with its special characteristics, and classes of non-player characters run by the Dungeon master, such as monsters, ghouls, dragons and such. Characters have lists of attributes – intelligence, dexterity, charisma, wisdom, strength, constitution – as well as a life span, beliefs, a capacity to learn and acquire experience, memory and a capacity to forget, the capacity to be surprised, skills and property (money, armour, weapon, books, clothes and such). The physical context (the dungeon) is composed of cells, each of which contains treasure, traps and/or monsters. And there are 'combat rules', 'encounter rules', and protocols galore for the interaction of characters and monsters, for the interaction of player-characters, and for the interaction of player-characters and Dungeon Master. This is *not* an easy world to know.[21]

Randomness is introduced into rule in the way it was introduced in games before there were computers to generate random numbers – namely, by throws of the dice. But in *Dungeons and Dragons*, there are six die, all with different numbers of faces (3, 4, 6, 20 etc.) and all for different purposes. Characters are created numerically by throwing the die to determine a numerical quotient for each attribute of the character (intelligence, charisma, constitution, and the rest), with the result not only that no two characters, even in the same class, are ever just the same, but also that chance determines a character's make-up and fate. Throws of the die determine what combination of characteristics (low charisma, high intelligence for example) goes into that character's make up, whether that character has sufficient strength to be a fighter or sufficient wisdom to be a mage, as well as what happens to that character in her/his life trajectory and in her/his encounters in the simulated world. Reader-writer-participants can go on playing the 'same' character story after story, in which case they advance through levels by acquiring numerical experience points which change their vital statistics and preclude them from remaining the 'same'. But how they do so depends in part on what they start with, and they can 'die' at any point as a result of their encounters. Encounters are also decided numerically, by making complicated calculations in which chance and necessity combine. For the chance throw of several die decides whether a character is surprised, or defeated or victorious, or convincing or capable of inspiring loyalty in others – but only after the player-character has decided how s/he is going to act or react to the encounter, and in combination with the numerical givens of that character's attributes, with the numerical probabilities of success or failure determined by that character's weapons and situation in the encounter, and with the numerically measured handicaps or advantages attached to both.[22]

Clark Abt, one of the founders of both of 'serious' and of playful simulation, has pointed out not only that simulated worlds allow reader-writer-players to 'explore the many branchings in the maze of fate' but also that they demand 'an ethic of personal responsibility, in which there are no real excuses except 'bad luck', which is a viable excuse only once in a while' (1970: 7, 6). The two are wholly compatible in a world like that of *Dungeons and Dragons* because 'fate' is a composite of multiple variables interacting as they do by chance, and because 'fate' is always set off by choices – by what a character chooses to do with

Factitive Fictions and Possible Worlds 149

whatever chance gives him/her in the way of capabilities, skills, handicaps, opponents, opportunities and potential disasters. Or, to put it differently, fate and choice interact, as does everything else in this sort of simulated world. It is by interacting with the simulated world and with other player participants, by feedback and by iteration, that reading-writing players 'learn what works and what does not', (Abt, 1970: 7) gain experience points, and change both themselves and their fate. It is by interacting and by experimenting again and again that they learn how to weave constraint and freedom, rule and randomness, potency and impotence into the adventitious destiny which is their story. And it is by interacting with other player-characters both in the actual and in the fictioned world that they construct and try out possibilities in a shared, imaginary simulated world by looping iteratively from their actuality as reader-writer-players sitting around a table to the fictional world they fashion through language and back.

Finally, in interactive simulated worlds, time too does not work precisely as it does elsewhere. Familiar, sequential linear time exists, but doubly – as the 'real time' of actual people sitting in front of their screen or reading-writing their simulated world, and as the time of simulation, measured by the computer or by the Dungeon Master. These two linear times are not the same – in real time, for instance a *D & D* round can take half an hour, an adventure anywhere from 2 hours to a week; but each round only moves the time of the simulated world on by about a minute. Life trajectories in simulated worlds are also quite conventional – selves or characters have a past, a present and a future trajectory, all suitably documented and stored in the computer's memory or, for a *D & D* player, on a sheet of paper. Stories too, as we have seen, are sequential, causally coherent narratives, with their past and present and future. But both are more transient and impermanent than when fixed and monumentalized in the material form of the traditional book. As Zigfeld points out of computerized fictions, 'once authors introduce twenty to thirty branches, there is a practical sense in which the 'work' itself becomes highly variable (construed conservatively) or even indeterminate, because the branching permutations make it unlikely that any two readers would randomnly take the same set of branches. It would even be difficult for a single reader to recreate the experience randomly' (1989: 364). In other words, to find your way back through the same story, you might have to take notes as to where you had been. In book simulations (or indeed stochastic video games), the generation of random numbers prevents any player from running through the same sequence of obstacles or encounters in the same way twice even as the 'same' character – to say nothing of the character or the story's sudden end if the reader-writer player happens to lose the sheet of paper on which her character's (or story's) vital statistics, possessions, past history and future plans are stored.

But there are also respects in which the time of simulated worlds is not linear or conventional at all. One of these has to do with the looping, iterative dynamics of the process by which simulated worlds are both made and run.[23] Another has to do with the way the past and the future are modelled. To build a world on the basis of probability distributions is not the same as using historical information to reconstruct what happened at some particular time in the past. As Shannon explains, 'using raw empirical data from one year would replicate the past. [It] would replicate only the performance of that year and not necessarily tell us anything about the expected performance of the system. The only events possible are those which have transpired' (1975: 28). Simulated worlds do not reproduce what has always already been; they explore once and future possibilities. Even simulated worlds which model the past do not replicate what has transpired, or present events which have transpired as the only events possible. Instead, they model past constraints (of knowledge, or technology, or on behaviour), past rules, and past protocols according to probability distributions, take random samples, and set the past in motion so that it lives again as all its possibilities, as all its might-have-beens-for-someone. In 'Oregon Trail', a computerized simulation of American pioneers going West, for instance, the reader-player learns what it might have been to get a family across difficult territory in a wagon interactively – by playing out constraints, making decisions and taking her/his chances in estimating the amount of provisions required, in fixing broken wheels, in fighting wild animals, in getting the wagon through water and so on. And times intersect, as the reader-player's present becomes the past and as the past takes on in the present configurations it always and never had.

Theory-fictions in literary and cultural studies do not yet work in these sorts of ways.[24]

World-Making

Two final points – one about worlds, the other about reading-possibilities.

Like possibility, 'world' is a both/and category, but it is also an extraordinarily indefinite one. A world envelops everything – and nothing invariable. We use the word world both for 'the universe, all creation, everything' (Oxford dictionary) and for particular parts of it (the Old World and the New, the animal world); both for society (the social world) and for particular spheres or domains of society (the world of letters, sport, art, business, fashion etc.); both for fictions (the world of *Tom Jones*) and for actual 'human affairs, their course and conditions' (Oxford dictionary); both for secular, temporal matters and for 'other-worldly' matters (this world and the next); both for what is concealed within a person (the inner world) and for 'everything that exists outside oneself' (Oxford dictionary); both for what is intelligible (the world of forms, the world of the atom) and for what is material and sensible ('the state or scene of existence'); both for spatial configurations and for temporal ones (the ancient world).[25] The word world indicates whatever is placed within a boundary, but this boundary is indefinite, fuzzy, variable and unfixed. Worlds come in all shapes and sizes, with all sorts of different contents.

The same indefiniteness attaches to the inner constitution of worlds, as Possible Worlds theorists have unwittingly demonstrated. Possible Worlds theorists have depicted worlds as 'complete possible situations, which supply everything that is the case' (Cresswell, 1988: 33) or as 'complete descriptions' of what pertains in a particular fictional world (Vania, 1977: 3). But they have also shown that descriptions of fictional worlds are generally incomplete – 'a text can only be an infinitessimally partial description of its universe' (Pavel, 1986: 65) – leaving much to be filled in by readers or users (Maitre, Merrell). And in reference to any actual world, they have shown that possible worlds do not supply everything that is the case if only because in their construction, they delete some aspects of actuality and supplement others, and give one of a variety of possible compositions, decompositions, sortings, weightings and reorderings to components (Goodman, 1978). Similarly, Possible Worlds theorists have argued that a world is constituted as a world insofar as it is self-consistent and non-contradictory, and they have also shown that worlds, whether literary or scientific, are frequently inconsistent and full of contradictions. As Pavel points out, 'our commitment to coherence is less warranted than it appears' (1986: 50). A world appears, therefore, to be two opposite things at once: both somehow complete, encompassing, delimited and consistent, and somehow selective, incomplete, uncompleted and inconsistent with itself.

Arguing that we have had too much 'unlimited semiosis' recently, and that 'texts are the human way to reduce the world to a manageable format', Umberto Eco insists that we need a fixed definition of what constitutes a possible fictional world and 'rules which allow a contextual disambiguation of the exaggerated fecundity of symbols' (1990: 21)[26] I would respectfully suggest, however, that the temptation to specify what constitutes a world or to determine definitively how all worlds are constructed is something to be resisted. Indefiniteness or minimal specification on the theoretical level can be a strength rather than a weakness, inasmuch as it allows us to provide ourselves with some possible orientations for exploration without pre-determining what we must invariably find. As soon as we specify what is always or necessarily the case in all possible worlds, we in effect give ourselves a typology which not only excludes other possible constructions, but also tends, in practice, to make us blinder and more lazy readers. As Eco says, when one has a set of rules and a fixed typology, 'it is the structure provided by the possible worlds theory that does the work' (1990: 65).

Indefiniteness or minimal a priori specification on the theoretical level is all the more helpful in that, at least in this case, it is perfectly compossible with specificity regarding the construction and constitution of particular fictional or theoretical worlds. One does not have to have a typology of how all worlds work, or of what a world must be to be a world, in order to describe and explore the workings of particular theory-fictional or literary-fictional worlds. For particular fictional worlds, whether literary or theoretical, are made by stipulation, or by what John Woods has called 'elementary say-so' (1974: 133). They are made by saying 'Let there be a world in which a king called Lear divided his kingdom among his daughters' or 'Let there be a world in which everything to do with fashion is contained' or 'Let there be a world of typologies, deep structures and invariable laws'. Fictional worlds are made by describing parameters, by stipulating what does and does not pertain within their boundaries, and by designating the rules or conventions (generic or other) which are in force in their domain.

This does, however, add another dimension of complexity to our consideration of fictional worlds. For in stipulating what does and does not pertain within their boundaries, literary-fictions and theory-fictions also indicate, in one way or another, what is to be taken as actual, and what may be possible, within the worlds they describe. As Pavel has observed, 'most fictions involve mixed systems, containing actual, possible and fictive elements' and may therefore 'be classified as heterogeneous' (1986: 95).

On the one hand, this enables fictional worlds to make *impossibilities* possible or actual within the boundaries of their particular domains. Fictional worlds frequently stipulate that things are actual within their boundaries which are impossible in the actual world – speaking animals, magical objects, humans with super-human powers, or time-travel, for instance. And it has been argued that entire literary genres – fairy stories, ghost stories, science fiction and escapist fiction, for instance – to say nothing of entire political or scientific theories, elaborate worlds which from the point of view of the actual world are impossible. Impossibilities, and even absurdities, are credible within fictional worlds not merely because, as Riffaterre has pointed out, 'verisimilitude' is created by the 'system of representations' and the 'grammar' in force, but also because fictional worlds posit givens which are incontrovertible within their domain. We grant them their *données*, whether these are possible or impossible in other worlds, *as* a possibility in the world they describe, and having granted them that, we grant them also whatever seems to follow from it, however impossible, improbable or incredible elsewhere.

On the other hand, the fact that fictional worlds indicate in one way or another what is actual, what is possible and what is fictive in their domain also allows fictional worlds to thematize, formalize and/or play with the relations of possibility to actuality in a variety of sometimes very elaborate ways. And this engages the reader, too, in reading-possibilities. I am going to take a rather extreme example to make my point.

In the world of Richardson's *Clarissa*, the heroine's abduction by Lovelace is marked as an actual event: 'Clarissa Harlowe is gone off with a man!' (I, 471). This departure is one of a series of actual events within the world of the novel which can be listed very loosely thus: the Harlowes force Solmes on Clarissa, Clarissa corresponds with Lovelace, Lovelace conspires with Joseph Leman, the date of the marriage to Solmes is set, Clarissa meets with Lovelace, Clarissa departs with Lovelace. But Clarissa's actual departure with Lovelace is enveloped in variety of possible constructions which 'explain' the event by placing it in different possible con-texts and which differ, among other things, by which prior events are linked to the departure. Most curiously, these possible constructions of the event are inter-epistolary – they are, for the most part, not confined exclusively to the 'perspective' of one correspondent, but weave back and forth across narrations. If the event is marked as 'actual' by its acceptance as fact by all the reader-writer-character-narrators in the world of the novel, constructions are marked as possible by being weighed and disputed among the correspondents.

One possible construction, for instance, links Clarisssa's departure to the prior meeting with Lovelace in the garden. There are several versions of it, but in the interests of brevity, I will give only two. In version I, it was because she had 'so inconsiderately given in to an interview' that Clarissa put herself 'into the power of [Lovelace's] resolution and out of that of [her] own reason' (I, 485). In this version, Lovelace figures as the powerful villain, and Clarissa as his essentially passive victim, and the story as elaborated follows the archetypal and obviously intertextual pattern of the sexually innocent maiden tempted and seduced by a worldly and wicked rake. In version II, on the other hand, it is because she was overconfident in her own strength and in her own power to prevent Lovelace from 'apprehended rashness' that Clarissa met Lovelace in the garden and 'rushed into real rashness herself' (I, 486). Here Clarissa figures both as the culprit and as the victim of her own act, and the story as elaborated follows the archetypal and obviously intertextual Christian pattern of spiritual autobiography: pride, sin, fall, recognition of sin, repentance.

Another possible construction links the departure to the fact that immediately before it, Clarissa's parents had set a date for the marriage to Solmes. In one version of it, it was because of extreme parental persecution which reached its head in the setting of the wedding date that Clarissa is driven to flee from her home. In this version, Clarissa figures as a victim of the patriarchal family, and the story as elaborated could be described as an early version of Mary Wollstonecraft's 'Subjection of Women'. In another version, the Solmes marriage represents not parental persecution, but the greed, avarice and self-love of a family anxious to increase its wealth and standing in the world, and the story as elaborated engages in contemporary debates, inspired by Mandeville, about whether such vices really produce the wealth, well-being and power of nations.

Another possible construction links the departure to Clarissa's correspondence with Lovelace. Clarissa repeatedly disobeyed her parents, she broke the prohibition against corresponding with Lovelace, and her departure was a direct result of her disobedience. Here again, Clarissa is the victim of her own acts, but this time she transgresses cultural norms of filial duty, maidenly propriety and proper order – what Locke calls 'the law of fashion or opinion' – and the story as elaborated follows the morality book pattern of 'how have I been led from little steps to great steps . . . ' There are other possible constructions too: for instance, the story which links Clarissa's departure to Lovelace's contrivance with Joseph Leman to simulate discovery and pursuit, and which, as elaborated, makes Clarissa figure as the traditional dove in the coils of the traditional serpent, the devil as shape-changer and master of disguise.

There are also prospective constructions of the event which turn out to be fictive. In one of these, Clarissa meets with Lovelace in the garden, effectively prevents him from realizing his threat to visit the house, and persuades him to depart from her for ever; in another, Clarissa meets with Lovelace in the garden and departs with him to the home of some of his female relatives, who will house her and protect her from her immediate family and from the Solmes marriage. These constructions are not less possible than the others; they are marked as fictive in the world of the novel, however, by being unequivocally disproved by actual events. Clarissa does not persuade Lovelace to depart from her; and she does not depart with him for the home of his female relatives.

In the world of *Clarissa*, then, every event is hedged about with possibilities: 'He knows how I am beset. He knows not what may happen. I *might* be ill, or still more closely watched than before. The correspondence *might* be discovered. It *might* be necessary to vary the scheme. I *might* have new doubts. I *might* suggest something more convenient for anything he knew' (I, 461). Instead of the single, certain and actual, underlying causal 'logic of events', which narratologists tend to look for in all narratives (Bal, 1985: 12), there are actual events and a variety of possible logics of events, some of which prove to be fictive.

As a reader, one can combine different possible constructions in different ways – as, indeed, the character-narrators try to do themselves. One can compare possible constructions and try to work out which, or which elements of which, constructions seem most likely or most interesting or most appealing. One can privilege one possible construction over the others, again as the characters in the novel sometimes do – by saying, for instance, that *Clarissa* is a story of pride, sin, fall, recognition of sin and repentance, and never mind the subjection of women. One can give the event other possible constructions which are not elaborated by the character-narrators, simply by introducing a different causal logic: because the Harlowes force Solmes on Clarissa, Clarissa corresponds with Lovelace, and because Clarissa corresponds with Lovelace, Lovelace conspires with Joseph Leman; or alternatively, because Lovelace conspires with Joseph Leman, the date of the marriage to Solmes is set and so on. One can even give the event a perfectly possible postmodern construction: for instance, linking Clarissa's departure to her repeated attempts to delay and defer all action, her own and others', one could elaborate a story about Clarissa's desire for a life without story, a life which would be perfect absence.

But the point is that inasmuch as the world of Clarissa involves actual, possible and fictive elements, reading it involves reading-possibilities. It involves exploring possibilities, judging possibilities, and constructing possibilities within the terms given by the fictional world, as well as measuring what is actual or possible within the fictional world against what is possible in the actual world and in other fictional worlds.

Reader-reception theorists have recognized that many texts are susceptible to different possible readings, but they have tended to limit each possible reading to one 'interpretative community' or 'horizon of expectations'. In this view, only one possible 'schematized view' of the text is actualized by any group of readers. If there is any play of possibilities in the actual process of reading – for instance, in the anticipation of possible outcomes of fictional situations or in trying out different possible coherences to make sense of what is going on – this play of possibility is superceded in the final, actualized reading. This may be an accurate description of the progress of certain texts. And it is certainly an accurate description of current reading practices and of how we are teaching people to read. But it is not the only way we can read.

As I have been trying to suggest, we could think of fictions – both literary and theoretical – as 'provid[ing] sustained explorations of possibility in all its forms' (Maitre, 1983: 17) and read them for the very diverse ways in which they open, propose, dispose and elaborate some of the many possible worlds which intersect with, impinge on or can be reached from our own.

6

The Critic as Translator

> Bilingualism is, for me, the fundamental problem of linguistics.
> Roman Jakobson

On Babel and Ivory Towers

Babel is a name for the plurality which entered the universe-ity upon the collapse of the traditionally bounded, socially and intellectually homogeneous, and at least partially mythical, ivory tower where everyone more or less spoke the same language. Babel is also a name for the re-problematized face of plurality, decentering and difference. In Babel, there is a plurality of languages – but 'one person will not hear (*yeshamah*, also: listen to, understand) the language of an other' (Gen. 11: 7). In Babel, there is discontinuity, dissemination and difference, but also such rivalry, conflict and confusion that it becomes impossible to 'build a city' (11: 8). Translation is an old-new name for ways in which Derrida and others have begun to rethink the work of writing and teaching in the universe-ity to address problems of Babel.

In the heyday of poststructuralist utopianism, plurality was not understood as a problem. Barthes, for instance, described his sexual/textual/social/political ideal as a 'happy Babel' where 'the Biblical myth is reversed, the confusion of tongues is no longer a punishment, and the subject gains access to bliss by the cohabitation of languages working side-by-side' (1975: 3–4). In Barthes' happy Babel, there are 'as many languages as there are desires' (1982: 467) and 'no language has a hold over any other' (1977: 164). No language, or meaning, or ideology, or practice is either dominating or subjected, but all are equally performative and free. Poststructuralism's idealized Babel called for what Lyotard labelled 'a politics of incommensurabilities' (1977: 31): different individuals, groups or meanings were no longer to be viewed as interchangeable with each other or as reducible to the same overarching law or schema which holds for everyone, as in the egalitarian model of the good society; instead, they were to be viewed as discontinuous, irreducible to one another, resistant to any common or unifying measure, and 'at play' in a multi-dimensional space.

In poststructuralism's political imaginary, then, it seemed as if all one had to do to achieve a plural and decentered classless society[1] was struggle to introduce plurality and difference where they had been lacking before. The poststructuralist Writer-Critic could feel that s/he had fought the good fight when s/he had opened closure onto heterogeneity and logocentrism or phallogocentricism onto the play of difference. But once (at least a measure) of plurality and difference had actually penetrated the academy, it became apparent that the 'cohabitation of languages working side by side' was not, in practice, very blissful.

In *Homo Academicus*, published in France in 1984, for instance, Bourdieu shows how the heterogeneity introduced in the '60s by the recruitment of 'outsiders' into a largely homogeneous and self-reproducing teaching body produced an apparently ongoing 'crisis' in the French University. The 'outsiders' in question – provincials, foreigners, intellectuals, left-wingers, innovators, Jews, and children of poor families who had been educated at public expense instead of in elite private schools (no mention of women) – had the impudence to expect the same career structure as those faculty members whose inherited (Roman-Catholic-Parisian-bourgeois) social and cultural privilege, old boy network, and shared behavioural and intellectual norms really entitled them to the highest University posts. That the 'old order' frustrated the newcomers' expectations was one source of conflict, but there were others.

For heterogeneous faculty also meant heterogeneous languages, heterogeneous 'life-styles', heterogeneous politics, heterogeneous intellectual interests and heterogeneous attitudes to the 'real' work of the University. With sociological heterogeneity, says Bourdieu, there also came to 'exist, quite objectively, a plurality of rival principles of hierarchization, and the values which they determine are incommmensurate or even incompatible, because they are associated with mutually conflicting interests' (Bourdieu, 1988: 11). For instance, the principles of hierarchization promoting those whose claim to legitimacy rests on what Bourdieu calls 'academic capital' (the power within the university which comes from having the right background and the right friends, sitting on key committees, administering grants, deciding appointments and promotions, and generally occupying 'strategic positions which give control over the progress of one's competitors') proved to be incommensurable with the principles of hierarchization favouring those trying to promote themselves through 'scientific capital' and through 'intellectual renoun' outside their departments and universities. Since the accumulation of each type of capital became so time-consuming that one could not, or in practice did not, successfully 'do' both administration and research, these principles of hierarchization served the interests of different and conflicting groups. By the same token, the 'innovation and intellectual creativity' which produce non-canonical disciplines and untraditional approaches to canonical disciplines proved to be incompatible with what Bourdieu calls 'the prudence of *academica mediocritas*' which requires 'self-censorship and obligatory reverence towards masters' and gives the 'recognition granted to an institutionalized thought only to those who implicitly accept the limits assigned by the institution' (94, 95).

In France, then, according to Bourdieu, sociological, intellectual and professional heterogeneity only produced conflict within faculties, between Faculties (Law and Medicine being more conservative and less 'intellectual' than the Sciences, for instance) and between different sectors of the University ('central' and 'marginal' institutions).[2] In practice, the introduction of at least some measure of plurality, heterogeneity and difference into the university did not produce a 'happy Babel'. It only made the university a 'site of permanent rivalry for the truth of the social world and of the academic world itself', even as it has made life in the university a 'struggle of each against all, where everyone depends on everyone else, at once his competitor and client, his opponent and judge, for the determination of his own truth and value, that is, of his symbolic life and death' (Bourdieu, 1988: 19, xiv). The Biblical myth was not reversed by 'the cohabitation of languages side by side'.

In the introduction to the English translation of his book, Bourdieu suggests that academics in other countries may also find this a recognizable portrait of their own Universities. And there are certainly those in the States who would agree that, as feminists, minorities, and theorists have come in from the cold, the institutional scene of writing has become a theatre of conflict where incommensurable 'languages', theories and political or instructional agendas struggle for intellectual and institutional supremacy, and where rivals – armed with various kinds of 'correctness' and various kinds of academic censorship – fight to de-legitimize and unseat, or to contain and silence, all those who do not speak or think like themselves. As Kerrigan and Smith succinctly observe, in the academy 'the production of writing becomes patently involved in competition, prestige and territorial impulse, which in turn lends urgency to the "right reading" and the exposure of the "wrong reading"' (1984: xv).

Gerald Graf, however, provides a different analysis of the Babel of languages working side by side on the American university scene. In his view, 'far from being organized on a centralized logocentric model, the American university is itself something of a deconstructionist, proliferating a variety of disciplinary vocabularies that nobody can reduce to the common measure of any metalanguage' (1987: 12–13). Here then, there is no single homogeneous identifiable origin to be disrupted by difference: '"we" as a unified body, doing one kind of thing, do not exist' (251). The American university has almost always already been plural, decentered, heterogeneous; it begins from difference. And it manages its differences quite effectively by administrative means. Using a 'field-coverage model of departmental organization arranged to cover an array of historical and generic literary fields' has enabled departments to 'add' heterogeneous units to 'the aggregate of fields to be covered' without obliging pre-established units or habits to change (1987: 6, 7). This administrative spacing has, according to Graf, enabled the American academy to incorporate innovation and difference, and made 'the modern educational machine friction free', preventing 'conflicts from erupting which would otherwise have to be confronted, debated and worked through' (7). But it has also functioned as a 'principle of systematic non-relationship', (8) isolating languages from each other within departments, 'remov[ing] the need for continued collective discussion' (9), and turning the aggregate of languages in the university as a whole into the sort of 'interdisciplinary chaos which results when it is assumed that something constructive will arise merely by mixing a variety of topics and vocabularies from different departments' (259). In this Babel, then, different languages do not have to hear or understand each other, any more than they really have to fight it out, but the Babble of different tongues leads to chaos and confusion because adding units to an aggregate of units simply doesn't add up to anything at all.

Despite his assertion that administrative spacing has made the university machine virtually 'friction free', Graf structures his history of the American university as a series of oppositions and conflicts: 'classicists versus modern-language-scholars; research investigators versus generalists; historical scholars versus critics; New Humanists versus New Critics; academic critics versus literary journalists and culture critics; critics and scholars versus theorists' (14). 'A university', he says, 'is a curious accretion of historical conflicts that it has systematically forgotten', and 'each of its divisions [into subjects and departments] reflects a history of ideological conflicts' (257–8). According to him, these conflicts have only been concealed by the administrative spacing which has resulted in intellectual chaos and confusion, and Graf argues that we can overcome interlingual chaos and confusion by foregrounding, institutionalizing and debating ideological conflicts in our departments, in our classes and in our curriculae.

I am not concerned here with the accuracy of Graf's or Bourdieu's diagnostics – personally, I find them both recognizable and both useful in different ways. In this regard, I would only note that their work suggests, among other things, that the amount of homogeneity or heterogeneity one perceives in any institution depends at least in part on how close one is standing. From very close up, two New Critics or two groups of humanists can be seen to be very heterogeneous. At some distance, a mixed catalogue of provincials, foreigners, children from poor families, left-wingers and Jews becomes a sociologically homogeneous group. And at a middling distance, it might become apparent that the binary opposition pitting the Academy's Ancients against its Moderns pluralizes into a complex of old and older and new and newer oppositions once one adds to the heterogeneous (and perhaps partly defunct) conflicts among the ancients, the heterogeneous (and perhaps still vital) conflicts within avant-garde turfs, and between turf and turf. But what really interests me here is an unquestioned assumption which Bourdieu and Graf – who are speaking of different university systems and who are in other ways so very different – are certainly not alone in sharing. It is that, sociologically, topographically and intellectually, the university is – must be? – defined by conflict.

In *The Mirror of Production*, Baudrillard argues rather convincingly that the centrality of the category of production in Marxism was an inverted mirror image of the capitalist emphasis on production which it contested. One could argue, along not dissimilar lines, that marxist and liberal-capitalist paradigms also give us different versions of another shared assumption: that society is necessarily – for ever or for now – a battle-field in which different ideas, different individuals and different groups have to fight things out. From this point of view, conflict, competition, revolution and *renversement* might be said to mark differences in the degree of violence, in the sphere of violence, in the overtness of violence and in the code according to which it is permissible, or even lawful, to do violence to others.

To concretize this in very small corner of a vast issue, we might think of critique as one such code in our ordinary academic writing practices. For to different degrees, critique (in all its forms, from the 'critical review' to deconstruction) could be described as a legitimation of violence done to the words and works of others. Critique lives on conflict, and perpetuates it. Inseparable from 'the conflict of interpretations', it figures in the academy as a respectable and lawful weapon in the struggle (debate?) among different ideas, different books, different people and different groups. Critique is, of course, an extremely effective offensive weapon, for words can damn, maim, destroy, disable, obliterate or shoot others down, as well as missiles. Critique also allows one to be heard – indeed, it is often equated with marking one's difference from others. But it is not designed to promote cohabitation or to allow others to be heard. For critique denigrates or silences the other to wrest for the Critic or his group the right to speak the authoritative word about the other's (un)truth. And identified with judgement or with quality-control in the institutional business of the university and in the 'assessment' of others' work, it can serve not only as an instrument of discipline and punishment, but also as a means of putting down (eliminating?) competitors and rivals.[3]

Translation introduces a wholly other response to problems of Babel. Translation is not necessarily uncritical, in the sense of credulous or undiscriminating – as we will see, it has its own ways of dealing with differences and disagreements and its own ways of 'intervening' – but translators are not rivals or combattants or even debaters. As George Steiner has observed, 'translators are men groping towards each other in a common mist' (1975: 62). As we will see too, translation is not a fail-safe device; but it does reposition persons and issues in relation to one another, introduce a different code of writing and speech into the academy, and mark the possibility of a wholly different response to a Babel of languages which, as Derrida has pointed out, is not going to go away.

Some Questions of Translation

The translation here in question is no longer the single, relatively insignificant, merely derivative and wholly marginalized, activity we came to think it in the course of the 19th and earlier 20th century, in the wake of narrow specializations and the cult of 'originality'. If, as Jakobson argues, 'for the linguist, like for the ordinary language user, the meaning of a word is nothing but its translation by another sign which can be substituted for it' (1963: 79), then all forms of understanding, explanation, repetition, interpretation and commentary which involve rewording are translations – as are all forms of code-switching, from the transferral of meanings or terms or paradigms from one discipline to another to the transmutation of linguistic into non-linguistic signs (when a film is made of a book, for instance). In this case, inter-lingual translation – the conversion of signs by means of signs in another language – becomes one variant in a larger field which includes intra-lingual translations and intersemiotic translations of all sorts. Or, since it could be argued that the options, implications and difficulties of translation are most evident in its inter-lingual mode, inter-lingual translation can be treated as a boundary situation, as a test case and as an avenue through which other modes of rewording and re-signing can be rethought.

Translation also ceases to be a single, easily isolated, marginal activity if it is understood as a (con)version of another text. For in this sense, there are obviously different practices of translation. Dryden indicated three: metaphrase, where one converts a text word for word and line by line into an other language; paraphrase, where one does not strictly adhere to the words of the other text, but generally keeps the sense in view; and imitation (in the Horatian sense), where one is not bound either by the words or the sense of the other text, but borrows, adapts and varies 'general hints from the original' as one pleases.[4] Brower suggests that parody, which Dr. Johnson defined as 'a kind of writing in which the words of an author or his thoughts are taken and by a slight change adapted to some new purpose', can also be viewed as a mode of translation (1974: 1, 4; see also Brisset, 1985 and Godard, 1990). The words translation, *traduction* and *Uebersetzung* only commit us, after all, to carrying something across from one language, one text, one form of words to another.[5] We hardly need to be reminded that all the above-mentioned ways of carrying something

The Critic as Translator

across from one language, discipline, culture or text to another have always already been part and parcel of Western poetic, writerly and academic practice. But we do not always remember that translation has always already 'introduce[d] new concepts, new genres, new devices, and [that] the history of translation is [also] the history of . . . the shaping power of one culture upon another' (Bassnett and Lefevere, 1990: ix).

The translation in question, then, is not a single, isolated, marginal and clearly delimited, activity. Indeed, it is hard to know where it begins or ends. Nor is it a simple or a straightforward matter for, as you may have come to expect, translation is – or has become – a both/and category.

Translation is a both/and category most obviously, perhaps, because for translation, there have to be at least two – two languages, two texts, two writers – one of whom allows the other to be heard. Despite the myths we constructed in the 19th and earlier 20th century about the invisibility and instrumentality of the translator's role, there can be no translation without a translator to give signs of/from an other language and an other text. And despite 19th and earlier 20th-century myths about the transparency of the translator's text, the fact remains that when we read a translation, we read one language, one text to hear (listen to, understand) the voice(s) of an other. In translations, one text is not obliterated in/by an other, though the two texts are not, and cannot be the same. The source text lives on both within its own linguistic envelope, and in that of the translating text.

But there are two ways of thinking this survival of one text, one voice, one signature, in another, both of which have been employed by Derrida. In the first, one considers the translating text as a space in which at least two languages, two texts, two writers are bound together. Gary Aylesworth describes one aspect of this binding together of texts when he says that, 'treated deconstructively, translation is not completely distinguishable from its original text and vice versa. Thus translation includes a moment of 'undecidability' of the same order as deconstructive reading' (Silverman and Aylesworth, 1990: 164). In other words, when reading a translating text, one cannot always be sure just whose voice, translator or source writer, one is hearing at any given moment. The more problematical aspects of this binding together of texts (the double-binds) begin to emerge, however, as one tries to resolve those innumerable, local, ethical and political questions, about one's relation to an other and about one's cohabitation with an other in the space of the translating text, which inescapably arise in the process and practice of translation. The *de facto* undecidability of the translating text is neither a solution nor a response to these moral and political questions, since, as we will see, it can mask a variety of different relations within the translator's text between the two cohabiting writers, the two cohabiting texts. If anything, undecidability about who is 'really' speaking in the translator's text re-doubles the bind the translator is in, since it increases her/his response-ibility to, as well as for, the other who is heard and judged through her. The same word *traducere* which gives us *traduction* (translation) can also give us 'traduce'.

The second way of thinking the survival of one text in an other is to think in terms of the relation between two envelopes and two acts of communication. As Barbara Godard explains, translation is then conceived as a relation between two text systems: Author-Text-Receiver and Translator-Text-Receiver. Here, the translator is neither marginalized nor confused with the author. S/he is seen to be no less the producer of an utterance than the author since s/he is the originator of a distinct and separate act of communication; and there is what Meschonnic calls a 'decentering' of the source text as the focus shifts to 'the textual relation between two texts, two language-cultures' (1973: 308). Or, if we put it in terms of recent literary theory, the author ceases to be dead, and there is a decentering of critical Writing as the focus shifts to a more balanced weighting of Writer and Writer, and text and text. For here we have to do with two distinct communication acts, both of which remain in presence like two columns on a page, even while something is carried across from one to the other.

In the two-communications model, moreover, the translator figures both as the receiver and as the sender of a communication (Godard, 1990: 92). And as we learn from Derrida, this is not a minor point. In *'Envois'*, which is among other things a witty parody of Jakobson's communications theory, Derrida illustrates the virtual impossibility of sending (on) a message that one has not first received. Jakobson had argued that the ordinary language user and the academic/linguist are in different positions in relation to senders' messages, because the academic/linguist is not the addressee (*destinataire*) of any messages, but more in the order of a cryptoanalyst, poring over messages flying between senders and addressees to deduce their underlying code. Because 'private property in the domain of language does not exist' (1963: 33), Jakobson saw no difficulty in decrypting messages not destined for or addressed to the cryptoanalyst himself. 'Envois' proves him wrong by offering us a series of 'open' (public) and nevertheless 'private' sendings, which use a variety of devices (gaps, ellipses, undecypherable references etc.) to prevent the reader from occupying the position of receiver or addressee (*destinataire*). Placed exclusively and ineluctably in the position of Jakobson's cryptoanalyst, the reader can only pore over Derrida's sendings, seeking and failing to decypher both the message (what is 'really' going on, what the sender 'really' wants to say) and the code. If messages can thus be sent quite publicly on 'open' postcards without finding a destiny and a destination, it is because to have a destiny and a destination, they have to reach a *destinataire* – someone willing and able to occupy the position of receiver, someone who finds him/herself personally addressed by these specific sendings and who is capable of hearing them and of passing them on. If missives do not necessarily reach their destination, if it is not always their destiny to live on, this is because it is not a foregone conclusion that they will find such a *destinataire*. The picture of Plato standing behind Socrates on the other face of the postcard in '*Envois*' confirms that the one cannot be heard except by virtue of the other. And, setting aside for the moment the temporal and factual reversal here, the picture of Socrates writing down what Plato indicates to him also suggests that even those we think of as 'proper' or 'original' writers ('authors', 'philosophers', originators of systems) are only translators sending (on) messages that they have received from an other.[6] Positioned at once in two related 'text-systems' or communication acts, then, the translator is someone who is capable both of receiving a message from an other and of passing it on through another act of communication. This means that the translator is a 'relay-station' between source text, source language, source writer[7] and others who may become receivers and relay-stations in their turn. From this point of view, questions of translation are also questions of transmission and of tradition; they are questions of our relationship to the past, and questions about what things and how things are to be relayed through writing and teaching across time, across languages, and across cultures.

The positioning of the translator in two related communication acts also means that a translation is what Meschonnic calls 'the writing of a reading-writing, the historical adventure of a subject'

(1973: 307). The historical adventure of the translating subject in the act of writing a reading-writing can be described in diverse ways. It can be described as an event in the singular history of the subject – thus as the process through which the subject learns to hear, to receive and to transmit sendings from others, especially sendings other than those that s/he has always already heard before. As Hillis Miller has pointed out, I may have to 'become the person that letter needs as its receiver, even though that new self is discontinuous with the self I have been up to now' (in Smith and Kerrigan, 1984: 136). And as Derrida suggests in one of his papers about the University, this 'having to become' is crucial to the learning process itself: 'for knowing how to learn, and learning how to know, sight [associated here with 'unveiling differences'], intelligence and memory are not enough. We must also know how to hear and to listen' (1983: 4).

The adventure of the subject in the act of writing a reading-writing can also be described as an adventure with a specific historical moment – thus as that mixture of chance and necessity by which the translator finds a means of transmitting the signs s/he has received from an other in such a way that the other can be heard afresh at her/his date. Lefevere and Bassnett, for instance, point out that 'faithfulness' to the source text involves trying to get one's translation to 'function in the target culture the way the source text functioned in the source culture' (1990: 8). And this means that changes of the source text in translation to make them more receivable at another time and in another place are – and, indeed, have always been – very much on the cards.

But perhaps most interestingly of all, the subject's historic adventure in the act of writing a reading-writing can also be described as an adventure with bilingualism. For, as Douglas Robinson has pointed out, translation is 'a transaction involving three people, two speaking different languages, a third speaking both' (1991: 119). This too is not a minor point. For if subjects are indeed 'spoken' by language and culture, and if (as Frederic Jameson and Milton between them might put it) the prison house of language is cause of all our woe, then subjects who speak/are-spoken-by at least *two* different languages are subjects who are 'never enclosed in the column of one single tongue' (Derrida, 1986d: 17). Bilingual subjects are subjects who can cross over from one language-culture-milieu to an other negotiating (con)versions, subject at once to neither and to both. Can we therefore say that bilingual subjects have escaped the prison house of language, that they have flown the coop?

Here again, we are confronted by a both/and. For translation is – or has become – both possible and impossible, and translators are, as a result, both bound and not bound by the constraints of the particular language-cultures between which they work.

Until recently, translation was thought to be perfectly possible and possible perfectly. Translation 'proper' or proper translation was thought to consist of finding an *equivalent* for the meaning of words in another language. Meaning was viewed as something dissociable from words, and thus as a *tertium comparationis* which 'hovers somewhere between languages in some kind of air bubble and "guarantees" (no less) that a word in the target language is indeed equivalent to a word in the source language' (Lefevere and Bassnett, 1990: 3). Thus, as Steiner has put it in his monumental and invaluable study of translation theory through the ages, translation theory assumed a dichotomy between sense and word (1975: 276). The possibility of translation therefore rested precisely on the arbitrariness of the relation between signifier and signified which we have come to associate with poststructuralism. It was precisely because meaning was *not* necessarily or inevitably bound to particular words that it was possible to convey it in other words.

If Derrida says that 'the philosophical operation . . . defines itself as a project of translation' (1982a: 119), it is to remind us that philosophy has also been implicated in these assumptions about equivalence and language[8] – as indeed have literary criticism, commentary and all forms of *explication de texte*. For despite polite disclaimers in deference to the 'uniqueness' and 'originality' of great works, traditional 'rules of evidence' and claims to 'serve' the literary text rest on the possibility of conveying the truth and meaning of one work in another equivalent form of words. And if we bear in mind that 'there are in one linguistic system perhaps several languages or tongues' (Derrida, 1982a: 100), then intertextual quests in the marxist paradigm for homologies between different texts or different spheres of culture can also be described as projects of translation based on an assumption of equivalence between languages.

Attempts in the '50s to do machine translations based on the equivalence of meanings in different languages helped to send the equivalence theory of translation the way of the correspondence theory of truth. For they confirmed what any translator who has ever scoured the bilingual dictionary, the thesaurus and her own linguistic *combinatoire* in a vain attempt to find an exact equivalent for the meaning(s) of a word or phrase has always already known: that particular meanings are undissociable from particular words or phrases in particular languages. To change the word is to change at least some of the meaning(s). In translation, there may be losses and gains, but no equivalences. Even the English term 'equivalence' and the German term *Aequivalenz* are not equivalent (Tabakowska, 1990: 80). Even 'Yes' in English is not equivalent to 'Oui' in French, if only because French also has the word 'Si'. Moreover, as Jakobson reluctantly observed, even in intra-lingual translation, 'to say synonym is not to say complete equivalence' (1963: 80).

The impossibility of achieving equivalence only increases when one takes the historical and cultural dimensions of words into account: for again, as every translator has discovered, there are innumerable concepts, objects, and nexi of meaning or emotion in one language which lack not only equivalents, but even approximations in another; and 'no two historical epochs, no two social classes, no two localities use words and syntax to signify exactly the same things, to send identical signals of valuation and inference' (Steiner, 1975: 45).

We have come around to think, therefore, that Saussure was right after all: signifieds are, in practice, inseparable from signifiers and from the differential system of a particular language-culture. And theoretically, this has two consequences for translation. It displaces the focus of attention from meaning to words and from the transportation of free-floating signifieds to the particular associations of signifiers and signifieds in the signs with which and between which one is working. If meaning does not hover anywhere except in and around particular signifiers, translation becomes the activity of converting or transforming signifiers. The undissociability of signifiers and signifieds also results in a recognition that 'far from being the most obvious, rudimentary mode of translation, "literalism" . . . is in fact the least attainable'. And this means that if the goal of translation is to produce a 'total counter-part' or 'repetition' of a message or text, this goal cannot be reached. 'No such perfect double exists' (Steiner, 1975: 308, 302).

Translation becomes even more impossible when one adds personal and hermetic factors to the linguistic, historical and cultural ones. There are different ways of describing the personal factor:

one can say like Robinson, that there is an 'idiosomatic' aspect of language use (1991: 10) or like Steiner that each of us has a 'private thesaurus' (1975: 46). One can say like Levinas and Steiner, that 'each communicatory gesture has a private residue' (Steiner, 1975: 46), or like Derrida, that language is a sponge which also encrypts traces of something wholly other than the subjectivated self. But however one puts it, the singularity of the language user is in retreat from translation, if translation is a matter of finding equivalences in the public tongue between two shared and collective symbolic orders. In the hermetic tradition, there is a retreat from translation too, but a retreat of another kind. For here, not everything may be translated. As Steiner says, 'theology and gnosis posit an upper limit' for translation, thinking it 'best to preserve the incomprehensible' (1975: 249).

For all these reasons and in all these ways – linguistic, cultural, historical, personal, hermetic – translation is impossible. But translation is also evidently possible, for as writers and as teachers, as readers and as speakers, we are translating all the time. Indeed, we cannot understand (hear, listen to) or transmit the words of others without translating them. We could regard this as a very sobering double-bind: 'we cannot translate, but we must. It is possible to fail (in an infinite variety of ways), impossible to succeed (in the one true way)' (Robinson, 1991: 167). Bearing this in mind would certainly change the way we receive and assess each others' work; it might even render it unacceptable for anyone to pose as the one who is competent to translate.

Regarded in another way, however, the impossibility of translation is also its value. As Moyal and St. Pierre have suggested, 'what is untranslatable is what makes translation necessary, and what, in making it necessary, makes it impossible' (1985: 3). What is untranslatable is what is really other in the other's language, in the other's culture, in another writer, in another text. What is untranslatable in the other's language and in the other's text is what makes the other singular, different, strange, a stranger to one's own cultural-linguistic household and to one's own frame of reference. And this is precisely what has to be heard (listened to, understood) and valued if we are to learn from one another and carry something back into our own language from our encounter with the other's language and the other's text. To relate to this untranslatability, to defer to it or otherwise re-mark it in one's translations, is one way of recognizing that there is always something outside and beyond one, something that cannot be mastered, annexed or regulated by one's own language, culture, discipline, world-view, code or law. As Goethe said, 'when you translate, go as far as the untranslatable, then you catch sight of the foreign language and the foreign nation for the first time' (in Lefevere, 1977: 9). This is also to refuse the position of master and colonizer, and to treat the stranger as a guest.

The impossibility of succeeding in translating in any one true way also makes translation possible insofar as it leaves us with diverse possible translations and diverse possibilities for translation, none of which is perfect or entirely successful, and all of which are, like languages themselves, inevitably incomplete. And this, in turn, means that there is no single formula for translation, no techne or theory which has only to be mastered to be reapplied time and time again. There are no set or satisfactory answers to questions of translation. There are only incommensurable questions incessantly addressing one as one translates, and a 'kind of impossible and necessary compromise . . . always deprived of insurance' to which 'each man and each woman must commit his/her own singularity, the untranslatable factor of his/her life and death' (Derrida, 1982b: 69).

The possibilities of translation to which we now turn are therefore just that – ways of responding to old-new questions which arise in a singular way, each time for the first time, whenever we give any version of another text.

The Other in Translation

What is at stake in both intra-lingual and inter-lingual translation is the symbolic life or death of another person and another text. And this bears both on the dead and on the living. For translation is not merely a matter of bringing dead writers and forgotten texts from the past back to life by teaching them or re-editing them or writing about them again; nor is it only a matter of giving the dead that renewed interest which enables them to survive the term(s) of their actual life and actual moment and live on. Translation has also become a matter of survival for the living.

Marcelle Marini, for instance, explained in an interview with Alice Jardine and Ann Menke that her university post and feminist seminar in Paris 'would not exist if I had not opened an international exchange between the US, other European countries and France – it's that simple' (1991: 162). For her, like for many other innovative French academics, male as well as female, survival *in* her department and university depends on being heard *outside* them. For Bourdieu, both intra-lingual translation (being repeated, quoted, paraphrased, reviewed, interviewed, (re)published etc. in French) and inter-lingual translation (being repeated etc. in other languages) are crucial indexes of 'scientific capital'. And Derrida remarked to a no doubt sympathetic audience of French-speaking Canadians, that 'today, [when] a book is published in two thousand copies, a book which is not translated remains a quasi-confidential and private document' (1985a: 12). Since English displaced French and Latin as the international *lingua franca*, we English-speakers have become less sensitive to questions of inter-lingual translation than we were before,[9] so it may not be altogether surprising to find that much of the new work on inter-lingual translation in the '80s issues from non-English speaking countries. But I think we all understand the importance of intra-lingal translation for that version of survival known as the academic career.

What is at stake in translation, then, is the economic and/or symbolic survival of other people (or at least of their 'name'); and not merely their survival, but the manner, meaning(s) and credit or discredit with which they survive. And these are questions which open both onto ethics and onto politics.

There has always been an ethics of translation. As long as translation was understood as the process of finding equivalences in one language or form of words for the meanings and truths expressed in another, the ethics of translation consisted of two virtues: fidelity and humility. In seeking to be true to the original, the translator supposedly effaced himself before the text or truth he served, only to be humbled in a different sense by his repeated failures to achieve the perfect equivalence, the perfect truth, he sought. Fidelity therefore also made every translator a sinner against fidelity; or to put it differently, the ethics of fidelity means that every translation invites and justifies flagellation even though – and because – no translation can be what it must be, namely faithful and true. The ethics of fidelity therefore ultimately makes critique, however devastating or destructive, an ethical act, just as it justifies a politics of permanent rivalry for fidelity to the truth of the social world, of the literary text or of the academy itself.

When what is at stake in translation is the symbolic life or death of another person or text, however, the ethics of translation is an ethics of responsibility – translation is a matter of what one person, one text, is doing to or for another. And since the translator occupies two positions at once – inasmuch as s/he is bound up with the other in the translating text, yet also figures as the originator of a separate act of communication – this responsibility points in two directions at once. It is a responsibility towards the other one is translating and a responsibility towards those others addressed by one's translation for whatever one is thereby transmitting to them. The ethics of responsibility is therefore what Robinson calls a 'situational ethics': it is always and only a matter of what my words and my text are doing here and now, in this situation, to and for this and this writer and this or these audiences. It is always and only a matter of how I situate my words – of how I turn them.

For, as Douglas Robinson reminds us, if translations are only versions (*vertere*, turn, *tour*), then every translation also inevitably gives its source text(s) a turn or a twist. Versions are turns one person, one text, plays on another within the undecidability of the translating text, where the translator necessarily speaks for and as another, and they are turns played in and through the turns the translator gives language with each turn of phrase. For, in practice, translators have always had their turn at the original. Even working within the equivalence tradition and producing what readers have naively assumed are accurate translations, translators have silently disambiguated ambiguities, corrected 'errors', grammar or inconsistencies, rearranged sequencing, bowdlerized and abridged. They have also silently changed punctuation (and thus meaning), reduced sentences or whole texts to one of their significations, omitted whatever they disliked and guessed or made up whatever they didn't understand.[10] On occasions, 'out of a very gratifying form of malice', they have also silently rendered the text 'in all its ghastliness' (Robinson, 1991: 173). Even traditional word for word translators therefore give their own turns (*vertere*) to the text they are translating – perverting, subverting, converting, and/or diverting it in any number of ways. And these turns always revert back to the translated text and to its writer's name or fame as its/his/her own proper truth. That all this affects the living as much as the dead is illustrated by Philip Lewis's analysis of what he calls the 'mistranslations' in the English version of Derrida's 'White Mythology' (in Graham, 1985: 46ff). The 'Derrida' we know in England or in America is not just 'Derrida', but also what his inter-lingual and intra-lingual translators (commentators, explicators, imitators, etc.) have made of him; and what they have made of him is different both from 'Derrida' in French and from 'Derrida' for the French. This is not an indictment of Derrida's translators. For if there is no possibility of equivalence between languages, much less between language-cultures, and if a translator can only transmit what s/he hears as s/he hears it, then such turns are inevitable. But to begin from the inevitability of such turns – thus from the inevitability of difference between translated and translating texts – and from the inevitable reversion of versions to the original text and its original signatory, is to begin from the realization that writer and translator, writer and writer, are in fact collaborators. Whatever they write, they write together. As Plato dictates to Socrates on Derrida's postcard, so each translator gives antecedent writers and texts their value, their meaning(s) and their credit.

However, if this is the case, the critic as translator is not another writer's rival for fidelity to the truth, but his/her ally. For each needs the other. The critic as translator is indebted to another writer for the gift of the signs which bring her/him to writing, and the other writer is indebted to the critic as translator for enabling her/his work to live on by making it possible for the signs the writer gave at his/her date, to be heard again at a different time and in a different place. As Derrida says:

> The original is not a plenitude which would come to be translated by accident. The original is in the situation of demand, that is of a lack or exile. The original is indebted *a priori* to the translation. Its survival is a demand and a desire for translation, somewhat like the Babelian demand: translate me . . . If the translation is indebted to the original (this is its task, its debt (*Aufgabe*)) it is because the original is indebted to the coming translation. (1982a: 152–3)

To begin from the impossibility of fidelity in the old sense and from the inevitable difference between translated and translating texts which follows from it, is thus also to begin from the realization that 'translation is writing' not transcription, a 'productive writing called forth by the original text' (Derrida, 1982a: 153). And inasmuch as it is the task of this writing to assure the survival of the original at another time and in another place, this means that the translator is bound to produce such modifications or changes in the original as will permit it to be heard again as something which has bearing on another time and place. To assure the survival of a text is not, therefore, to reproduce it, or to restitute or communicate its meanings; it is rather to ensure

> the growth of the original. Translation augments and modifies the the original, which insofar as it is living on, never ceases to be transformed and to grow. It modifies the original as well as the translating language. This process – transforming the original as well as the translation – is the translating contract between the original and the translating text. (1982a: 122)

Here too, then, the relation between the original and the translating text is one of reciprocity. For the original text to be heard again at another date, the translating text has both to transform the original and to allow the original to transform it. For if the translating text were not to change the original, it would not be heard; and if the translating text did not allow itself to be transformed, the original would also not be heard, because in this case we would only hear what we have always already heard from translating texts before. Translation is therefore not a matter of inserting texts into a predetermined modern or postmodern language, world-view, or frame of reference, but of allowing the texts one is translating to change those languages, world-views or frames of reference.[11] Translation is an agreement that I will change you and you will change me. It founds alliance in a readiness to change and be changed, a readiness to give and be given.

For Derrida, the relation of the translating text to the original is also a relation of supplementarity[12] inasmuch as the original 'calls out, desires, lacks, calls for the complement or the supplement or as Benjamin says, for that which will come along to enrich it' (1982a: 152). But supplementarity is, as we all know, a tricky business. It involves supplying lacks in the other – thus reading out or reading in to another text whatever that text seems to call for here and now to make it useful or interesting or applicable. But supplementarity also involves supplying one text for or as the other, offering one text in place of another. And there are at least two ways of understanding this.

One has to do with what text one supplies *as* the original text. For Derrida, this is a matter of particular moment when it comes to writers like Hegel, Marx, Nietzsche or Heidegger, who have been

The Critic as Translator

heard in different ways: there is a 'left' and a 'right' Hegelianism, there are innumerable versions of Marx, and both Nietzsche and Heidegger were either appropriated by or identified with Nazism. It is worth noting that Derrida was himself imported into England in the wake of Althusser as a marxist or quasi-marxist (see Easthope, 1988), and into America under the auspices of his friends at Yale as an a-political formalist. It would be interesting to know what they are doing with him in Japan.

For Derrida, the problem here has nothing to do with his or Marx's or Nietzsche's meaning or intentions, or with what their texts 'really' convey. The problem is that 'reactive degeneration [can] exploit the same language, the same words, the same utterances, the same rallying cries as the active forces to which it stands opposed' (1982a: 29). Politically and historically, the same texts can be heard, received and implemented in very different ways. This means not only that what we supply *as* the text of Marx or Heidegger or Nietzsche or Derrida (or anyone else) has political and historical import, but also that the political and historical responsibility for that text's import devolves on those receive it, translate it and transmit it *as* the text of Marx, or Heidegger or Nietzsche, or whoever. From this point of view, the way we in-vent a text[13] or give it to be heard by others in and through our translations is also a political and historical intervention (in both senses). But it is also a political and historical intervention which depends on the survival of those prior texts. And this, in turn, means that instead of either critiquing a text or quietly burying it, we can give it the survival which it calls for and which we need it to have, by construing, translating and transmitting it differently. Where Lacoue-Labarthe and Nancy virulently attack Heidegger for his Nazism, therefore, what Derrida supplies as 'Heidegger' in *De l'Esprit* is an other Heidegger and an other text.

But the danger here, which is particularly clear from the last example, is that what we supply as the original text will also be mistaken for it. This is a danger inasmuch as it can lead to the sort of substitutions of one text for another for which the Communist Party in Russia and the *Historikerstreit* in Germany and France were infamous, when they produced versions of their national history in which there had been no gulags, no five-year plan which didn't work, no Jewish question and no holocaust. Allowing one text to be mistaken for another is also a danger inasmuch as allowing the supplement to supplant the original once again obliterates the singularity of the other signatory and the difference of the other text, and papers over the translator's indebtedness to them.

Derrida circumvents these difficulties by invoking the 'untranslatability' which, as we have seen, is also part and parcel of every act of translation. As he puts it, the 'law' of translation is always 'do and do not translate'. Do translate the other writer and the other text, but do not translate their singularity and their difference. Leave these untouched and unexpressed by your language – but also re-mark them *as* untouchable and inexpressible, by hinting darkly at that spectral tracework of affirmations which, as we have seen, sounds through every text.[14] For Derrida, 'Do and do not translate' also seems to mean: translate but be unwilling to translate everything. In the case of Heidegger in *De l'Esprit*, for instance, Derrida's unwillingness to translate manifests itself as an unwillingness to pretend that Heidegger did not identify with the Nazis or to explain this away. The other Heidegger supplied by Derrida is given as a Heidegger who sounds alongside or behind or through the Heidegger who spoke for Nazism, as his possible or spectral double. In the case of Joyce or Ponge, on the other hand, Derrida's refusal to translate takes the form of an unwillingness to encompass the whole of their work or to say what it might all be 'about'; Derrida confines his translations of these writers to phrases or fragments of their name or works. In the case of Benjamin, however, Derrida's refusal to translate is more intimately bound up with his readiness to translate, since Derrida translates Benjamin (in *'Des Tours de Babel'* for instance) in such a way that one cannot begin to fathom Derrida's translation without also going back to read Benjamin. There may therefore be as many possible ways of *not* translating as there are of translating, or indeed of supplementing another's lacks – which is also to say that the 'law' of translation gives no law. It only calls for a purely 'situational ethics' of response-ibility to and for others.

Derrida repeatedly associates the 'law' of translation with Babel's God. At Babel, God deconstructed the tower that people were building to make a great name for themselves and sowed war and confusion by dividing and pluralizing language(s) so that no man could understand another. The two acts belong together not only inasmuch as war, rivalry and confusion grow out of peoples' struggles to make names for themselves,[15] but also inasmuch as the dissemination and dispersal of language *is* the deconstruction of 'the colonial violence or linguistic imperialism' of the column of

The Critic as Translator

any single, universally, dominating ratio or tongue (Derrida, 1987c: 210). From this point of view, (de)construction's deconstructions of the stele, of the *Stand*, of self-identical structures and of the socio-historical cult of man's erections and Works (see Chapter 3) can be regarded as repetitions of God's archetypal Babelian act.

At the same time, in associating the 'law' of translation – 'Translate and do not translate my Name' – with Babel's God, Derrida also indicates that at Babel, God was not only destroying one tower (*tour*) but offering another in its place: the *tours* (turns) and detours (*des tours, détours*) of translation.[16] The command to translate thus becomes a command to repair the damage (*tikkun olam*) created by the deconstruction, by turning one person, one text, one language to another so that each can hear (or understand) each other again. By the same token, the prohibition – do not translate my Name – becomes a command to treat the singularity and otherness of the other as something as untouchable, as inexpressible and as sacred as divinity itself.

For the critic as translator in Babel, then, the 'critical' in 'Critical Theory' comes to mean 'crucial', and this in at least two senses. It is a critical matter for the critic as translator to determine what needs to be translated here now at this date and to give the texts we have inherited those supplements which can make them useful or applicable again. And it has become critical for the critic as translator to promote those turns of one to another and that respect of one for another which are the precondition for co-operation, co-habitation and mutual understanding.

These are political matters as well as ethical ones. Translation is critical in the first regard now that education has become a commodity like any other, teaching a service like any other, the value of which is determined by consumer satisfaction and quantifiable demand. For as Zygmunt Bauman points out, this means that in practice, the market (or he who knows how to manipulate consumer opinion) determines what is good and bad, true and false, in education and in teaching, even as it 'reduces the cultural elite to one of many taste and interest groups vying with each other for the benevolent attention of the consumer' (Bauman, 1987: 158). The critic as translator's response to this situation is to recognize that if s/he does not give meaning and value to the texts we have inherited and to the work of other academics like her/himself, noone else will either. S/he recognizes that by making works of the past 'biodegradable' and by promoting reciprocal invalidation of academic work, critique only plays into the hands of those who are already disdainful of or indifferent to the world of the mind, and who would equate all teaching and education with training in marketable skills. The critic as translator also recognizes that if her/his translations do not enable the works of the past and the current work of the academy to live on as something worth turning to again at this date, they will simply not survive. S/he therefore acts in the knowledge that her/his own survival is both directly and indirectly bound up with that of others, past and present.

Turning one person, one text, one language to another has become critical, too, for another reason, which has to do with the loss of the intellectual's traditional 18th and 19th century social roles. Writers and academics are no longer accepted by society at large as authoritative arbiters of taste, cultural prophets or legistators of truth, even if we still aspire to these roles; and the function of expert, as practised to date, involves a relation to power and subjection which has been rendered thoroughly suspect by poststructuralism and postmarxism. Translation offers writers and teachers in the academy the possibility of another role. I will leave Bauman to make and conclude this argument:

> With pluralism irreversible, a world-scale consensus on worldviews and values is unlikely, and with all extant Weltanschauungen firmly grounded in their respective cultural traditions (more correctly: their respective autonomous institutionalizations of power), communication across traditions becomes the major problem of our time ... The problem calls urgently for specialists in translation between cultural traditions. The problem casts such specialists in a most central place among the experts contemporary life may require. (1987: 143)

Intertranslation

In many areas of the postmodern world, communication across linguistic-cultural traditions is already an established fact. One has only to think of the moves being made to unite Europe, or of the fact that, as Dirk Delabastita reminds us, 'for many cultures in Europe (not to mention in the Third World), a very substantial part, if not most of the mass media messages in circulation have undergone some process of translation' (1990: 97). As he points out, translation

The Critic as Translator 181

processes already 'play a very effective part in both the shaping of cultures and the relations between them' (ibid.). But how do translations 'shape cultures and the relations between them?'

If we were to answer this question from within the marxist paradigm, we might say one (or all) of the following: translation is a way one culture appropriates and/or naturalizes what properly belongs to another; translation is a way one culture depropriates another by depriving it of its own proper meaning(s) and values and turning it into an indeterminate, exotic or inferior 'Other'; translation is a way a dominant culture imposes its products, its values and its hegemony on others; translation is cultural-linguistic manipulation undertaken in the service of power; how a work is translated is a function of the relative weight (prestige, power) of the two cultures involved; how a work is translated is a function of the centrality or marginality of the work in its culture of origin; how a work is translated is a function of the economics and conventions of textual production and reception in the translating culture.

But recent work on translation has been putting in question the assumption about the national self-identity of cultures upon which such arguments rest.

Closest to the marxist paradigm, André Lefevere, for instance, indicates that translations have played an important part in the struggle between rival ideologies or poetics within a national culture. Translators have frequently borrowed the authority of texts belonging to another culture or hidden behind the immunity of 'mere' translators to attack or change features of their own cultures or poetic traditions with which they were dissatisfied. Quoting Hugo – 'to translate a foreign poet is to add to one's poetry; yet this addition does not always please those who profit from it . . . A language into which another idiom is transferred does what it can to resist' – he also points out that translations can be experienced as threats to the identity of a culture (1990: 17).

Working on Czech culture, on the other hand, Vladimír Macura shows that Czechoslovakia's cultural revival at the beginning of the 19th century was almost entirely based on translations of German texts which would have been equally accessible and comprehensible to most Czechs in the original German. The same practice – of translating texts which literate people could also read and understand in their original language – prevailed in Western Europe until the end of the 17th century. Macura therefore argues quite convincingly that, although Czech revivalist translations demonstrate some special features, in fact 'the development of national cultures is marked by periods when the culture as a whole or in part exhibits some typological features of translation, when it takes over cultural phenomena that have originated elsewhere and adopts them' (1990: 70). Also speaking from Central Europe, Piotr Kuhiwczak rebuts critiques of such cultural appropriations, which righteously take the part of the 'supposedly weak and dispossessed', by denying that 'if there is a gain, there must be a concomitant loss'. The history of cultural appropriations in Central Europe, he argues, shows instead that 'a belief in 'dominant' and 'peripheral' cultures is an illusion' and that 'sometimes a political/or cultural appropriation bears more fruit than a rampant nationalist revival' (1990: 119). Both argue, therefore, that at some formative point in its history, every national culture has borrowed heavily from others by appropriative translations, and that this fact deconstructs all nationalist claims to linguistic-cultural supremacy. The existence of appropriative translations in all cultures only goes to show that there is a fundamental lack of self-identity in national cultures, as well as a fundamental interdependence.

'Self-translation' deconstructs cultural self-identity in a different way. Self-translation is a term used for writers who translate their own work into another language-culture. And as Brian Fitch shows through a study of Beckett, who is treated as French literature by the French and as English literature by the English, self-translation puts in question all assumptions about works belonging to an original national language-culture – especially when, like Beckett, the author himself introduces significant variations between his two different linguistic-cultural versions of the 'same' text. For, as Fitch says, this means that the author must be 'seen as having merely suspended his enterprise when he finished his first text; the final realization of his work had thus been suspended and deferred. And it is the second version that will subsequently come to complete his first version' (1985: 117). Written 'across languages', the author's 'original work' thus belongs to neither national language-culture and to both. For it exists only as different-language variants of a non-existent 'original'.

The term 'self-translation' can also (for want of a better term) be extended to cases where a person translates her/his own linguistic-cultural tradition into another linguistic-cultural tradition, whether the practice is inter-or intra-linguistic. Self-translation of this sort characterizes feminisms of different kinds – for instance, when feminists translate inherited female traditions of relationship or community into the masculine language-culture of political theory, or when Irigaray translates 'certain Oriental traditions' which speak of the two sexes as 'giving each other the seeds of life and eternity' into the language-culture of contemporary French philosophy (1984: 180). Self-translation is, of course, also practiced by Derrida when he translates philosophy into poetry (or vice versa) or traditional Jewish thinking into the language-culture of Heidegger and both into the intellectual tradition of the French.

Such self-translations between traditions disrupt the cultural self-identity of both traditions, inasmuch as they produce something which belongs to neither and to both. Local or familial female traditions of relationship or community are no longer the same when they have been analysed, rationalized and projected onto a national political arena, any more than the language-culture of that arena is the same after such translations. By the same token, Derrida's 'JewGreek' is something other than either Jewish tradition or traditional Western philosophy; it changes both. As Brian Fitch puts it in a different context, self-translation 'appears to bring two languages into a condition of reciprocal interference and interplay that has nothing to do with that mere contiguity of languages that obtains between translation and original' (1985: 120).

By putting national cultural self-identity in question in these ways, recent work on translation implies what Zygmunt Bauman provocatively argues: that the concept of bounded, self-identical national cultures belongs on the scrapheap of history, because 'culture' itself has only been an 'episode in history' (1987: 116).

Bauman argues that the word 'culture' was borrowed from the vocabulary of gardening, farming and husbandry (and thus from the designed and supervised cultivation of plants and animals within a relatively bounded space) and reapplied to society during the Enlightenment, when rulers and *philosophes* between them conceived the project of reshaping their dominions under the guidance and control of (their) reason. Differences among people and peoples which had previously been seen as spontaneous manifestations of the diversity of the human race or as part of a pre-ordained divine plan were brought under the aegis of 'culture:' as the French put it, 'one culture in one nation'. Like plants in a garden, people (or peoples) were now supposed to grow healthily and tidily into a single nation as a result of the ministrations of humanly or divinely appointed gardeners. 'Culture' thus presupposed the malleability of human characteristics, the control over a piece of land (kingdom, or nation) by cultivation (education) and management (legislation) of the people growing on its soil, and the coherent ordering, which it has also been used to prove or find.

The concept of 'culture' therefore seems to belong, historically and ideologically, to the era of nation-states, which were (or pretended to be) autonomous and self-regulating. 'Culture' is properly speaking a feature of societies which constitute more or less coherent, more or less self-determining, and more or less self-contained wholes.[17] It belonged to the era when each sovereign state or its means of production could (or could be held to) determine what happened within its own borders, more or less independently of others. And it belonged to an era when the economic and/or cultural development of one country could be thought to emulate – or made to emulate – that of a more 'advanced' country. This no longer seems to be precisely our situation. The process of uniting Europe, growing global economic and ecological interdependence, the rapid inter-national movement of information and cultural commodities, trans-national businesses and the increasing impact of inter-national politics on what happens 'inside' countries, are beginning to crack even superpowers' sense of their own economic, political and cultural autonomy and independence. Nations are becoming turned upon one another. As Bauman puts it, 'ours is the time of "post-culture"' (Bauman, 1987: 156).

Derrida mimes the 'promise' of such post-cultural turnings in his translation of Benjamin's translation of the messianic 'reconciliation of tongues'. But to hear him, we will have to make a short detour.

Benjamin had argued that 'translation ultimately serves the purpose of expressing the central reciprocal relationship between languages' by releasing 'the one true language' or 'language of truth' which underlies all languages and makes each the necessary complement or supplement of the other (1968: 72). Extant languages were (like) broken shards of that one language-vessel which had been confounded and scattered at Babel, and the translator's redemptive task was to repair the vessel by leading us back to the now hidden convergence and harmony of tongues.[18] But Benjamin's descriptions of pure language are ambiguous. For instance, when he says of this pure language that it 'no longer means or expresses anything but is, as expressionless and creative Word, that which is meant in all languages – all information, all sense, all intention finally encounter a stratum in which they are destined to be extinguished' (1968: 80) – it remains unclear (in all language-versions) whether pure language is an expressionless Word which extinguishes meaning, or whether (as he also implies elsewhere in the essay) the Word extinguishes all languages by making them converge on their single, common, underlying meaning or 'intentional object'. In the first case, pure language would be a pure Signifier; in the second, it would be a unity of a Signifier with a heretofore concealed Signified.

For Derrida, the pure and creative Word could not be a unity of Signifier and Signified – first, obviously, because this would take him back to some form of presence, a possibility he still consistently avoids, and secondly, because such a Word would inevitably be a word belonging to one language. The only promises such a Word would offer would be a promise of transnational uniformity (everyone speaking Esperanto) or a promise of the geo-political dominance of a single *lingua franca* (everyone having to do their transactions in Latin, or French or English or Japanese). Derrida's problem was to 'try to ... reconstitute a symbolon, a symbolic alliance or wedding ring between languages' through which one might 'see the coming shape of a possible reconciliation of languages' (1982a: 123) without eliminating linguistic-cultural differences: 'Babel in a single language' (1986a: 54).

Derrida had therefore to focus on the Signifier, but here too there was an obvious problem. For if he were to use the Signifier as he had used it before, to confound meanings and contexts and make the signifier signify Nothing, he would be deconstructing the Word again, not miming a possible reconciliation of languages. However, there were seeds of a solution in an alliance between Jakobson's work on acoustic phonetics and kabbalistic techniques of meditation.

Jakobson had argued not only that there are 'numerous phonological affinities between neighbouring languages, whether they are related or not' (1973: 157) but also that 'the phoneme is the element which is specific to language ... language par excellence, language so called' (1978: 67). Benjamin's kinship between languages could therefore to be sought in sound, and signifying sound *was* pure language. Phonemes (i.e. units of sound which have differentiating and therefore a signifying value in language) also had some other very useful characteristics. For instance, they had 'the paradoxical character of elements which simultaneously signify and yet are devoid of meaning'. In other words, phonemes signify inasmuch as they are part of signifiers (syllables), or stand as signifiers on their own (a phoneme can be a word); but they are devoid of meaning inasmuch as they signify differently in different signifiers, in different codes and in different languages and therefore have no proper meaning of their own.[19] The signifying unit is therefore less as a 'site of original difference' (Andrew Benjamin, 1989: 23) than a site of generation for a multiplicity of different meanings (or languages) from the same intrinsically meaningless unit of sound. It's a case of that which in itself is nothing becoming a host of different somethings.

Jakobson's phonemes had other useful characteristics too. First, 'like a chord in music', phonemes could be decomposed into phonological elements, which were 'mutable' or commutable or con*vert*ible into other phonological elements – i.e., a p could become a v or a b, merge with another element in a signifier or disappear altogether. Secondly, phonemes deconstructed Saussure's opposition between the synchronic and diachronic axes of language, by appearing on both axes simultaneously. And finally, they were firmly associated by Jakobson with telephonic, radio and sound communications of all sorts; phonemes were to language what chemical messages were to DNA and bits to telecommunications.

Kabbalistic (and indeed rabbinical) sources had always already known about converting the phonological elements in signifiers, but unlike Jakobson, they did not make neat binary tables of coded (com)mutations. Their rules of conversion included not only the possibility of homophonies and substitutions, but also the possibility of reversing words, of decomposing and recomposing them, of changing the order of letters, of attaching or detaching letters, and of recombining letters in different ways. Through such permutations and combinations, moreover, the word became 'creative', since by virtue of its *movement*, it produced associations between versions of a word, and insights about the (possible) logic of such associations, which would not have been available without them.[20] Conversion by (re)combination and permutation thus turned different words (and different texts) towards each other in such a way as to make it possible for 'insignificant difference' to become 'a condition of meaning' (Derrida, 1986a: 53). And it allowed the original symbol to 'grow' until 'the whole of the symbolon [becomes] greater than the original itself' (Derrida, 1982a: 123).

Derrida could therefore take a word – let us say, *glas* (which also qualifies as a phoneme) – and make its 'phonic form' (Jakobson, 1963: 162) a symbolon for the reconciliation of languages. Through its acoustic permutations – for instance, *gl*, *glas* pronounced without the s, *glas* pronounced with the s, *clas* pronounced with or without the s, *gal, cal, gel, gle* etc – and acting both as a word and as part of words, *glas* could link He*gel*'s ea*gle* to Genet's e*gla*ntine, and Genet's language of flowers to Hegel's religion of flowers. And/or it could link the flower e*gla*ntine to *galatite*, the '*pierre de lait*, and both to Peter (*pierre*: Peter, stone), the rock of the Church, to the milk (*gla – la – lai*) of the Mother and to the tolling of Church bells (*glas*) as the Mother buries her sons. The sounds of *glas* (*glas* also means sound), could link He*gel*'s *gla*ive to Genet's *gla*vieux, and both to Saussure, for whom *glas* was (merely?) a word. And/or it could link the '*clas*se d'élèves' (class of pupils) in one column of *Glas* to the *élèves* and *relèves* (*élèves* +r) in the other – thus linking questions of *Aufhebung* and elevation to questions of erection (Hegel's or Genet's) and to questions of up-bringing (*on élève les enfants*, one brings up (elevates?) children), and all of these to the son (*fils*) and the thread (*fil*) of filiation. It could also link opposites in double-binds: 'The spear or the acorn (*gland*) in the phoneme, the *glas* in the phenomenon, Panglossia' (Derrida, 1981: 73). Of course, this in no way exhausts the possibilities. For as sound, *gl*as is also the *gl*ue or a*glu*tination of associations which create meaning: 'Association is a sort of gluey contiguity, never a reasoning or an appeal to symbols; chance glue makes meaning (or makes sense), and the progress has the rythm of *little jumps* (*secousses*, also jolts) . . . *little jumps* yield the very rythm of *gl*, the barely strangled putting in (e)motion of the text . . . '[21] (Derrida, 1981: 199). As Derrida points out, such jumps from gl to gl glue things (words, texts, arguments, languages) together interminably and in any of an infinite number of possible ways.[22]

Derrida thus founds the alliance of languages not only in kinships of sound, but also in reciprocal need; for it is by their leaps towards each other, and by their associations with each other, that the languages in *Glas* make (new, more?) sense, and create insights which would be precluded to each alone. Without removing the differences between the languages it turns towards each other, *glas* functions as an 'expressionless and creative Word' which gives rise to 'a whole greater than itself'. With and without Derrida. For while some possible agglutinative movements are suggested or elaborated into arguments or fragments of argument in the text of *Glas*, others are just there to be heard (or not) – to jolt one (or not), to be wondered about (or not), to be made sense of (or not) – by whoever happens on them.

The *glas* (also *gilah*, Heb. revelation, the unspoken word in *glas* and *Glas*) of alliance and reconciliation among languages thus reveals itself performatively and interactively. It depends on the performance by both writer and readers of the 'promise of the reconciliation of tongues'. And this promise inheres in the ability of signifying sounds to cross (one meaning of 'translate') 'a frontier, a country, a house, a threshold . . . every site, every situation in general, from which, practically, pragmatically, alliances and contracts are entered into (*noué*, also joined, knotted), codes and conventions established . . . ' (Derrida, 1986a: 54). The promise of a reconciliation of tongues, households and countries lies in the ability of the word to act as a 'pass-word' (*mot de passe*) or as a *passepartout* (pass-key, frame, and literally, pass-through-everything, pass everywhere).[23]

Where critique perpetuates the conflict and struggle which perpetuate it, intertranslation builds alliances. Through intertranslation, the word can cross those national(ist), cultural, linguistic, ideological and disciplinary frontiers which were once drawn by conflict and war and preserved (in the name of some imagined superiority) by deafness, denigration of others, and the policing of boundaries. Through intertranslation, the word can weave back and forth across frontiers, building bridges between linguistic-cultural households and helping them to join in building something which none could say or do alone. Critique belonged to the era of 'culture' and of more or less autonomous nation-states. It was a choice weapon of struggle in the era when, in various arenas, nation-states, individuals, groups and ideas fought each other for cultural, political and economic supremacy and for the right to impose one truth, one culture, one politics on all. Intertranslation, on the other hand, marks the threshold of a post-cultural era, when nations begin to need each other to survive physically, economically, ecologically, and culturally, and when the challenge is to create workable alliances and modes of co-operation among different ideological, cultural and national traditions.

In Derrida, the word not only allies different linguistic-cultural households by crossing threshholds and frontiers; it also allies different times (*gal-cal-calendar*). The *glas* in *Glas* links Hegel's 19th-century German philosophy (which narrates an evolutionary history of man from ancient times), Genet's 20th-century French world of thieves, Jewish culture in Algeria before independence, Saussure's Switzerland, and more. It links modern French, Old German, Modern German, Old French, Latin and Hebrew, all of which belong (in different ways) to different historical moments. And by miming the reconciliation of tongues in and through pure sound, it also links the messianic end of time to its (supposedly) anasemic (preverbal, preconceptual) beginnings.

Does this mean that the Word 'does not know precisely what time is?' (Derrida, 1981: 149). What is time for the mutations, (con)versions, translations of words?

The Times of Translation

For a couple of centuries, of course, the answer was evolution. Like culture, or under the impact of culture, language developed through mutations and conversions of sound and sense from primitive beginnings to more and more advanced and 'civilized' forms, leaving earlier stages behind (or sublating them) as it moved on. There was a before and after in language and of languages, a before and after in culture and of cultures. Time was a line composed of discrete points (dates, periods, eras) connected by relations of cause and effect, where nothing ever happened twice. Everything could therefore be situated in time once and for all. Everything could be dated, given its own place in an ineluctable order of succession, explained in relation to what had come before and after – even 'timeless' works in 'immortal' language. And everything dated accordingly. For the present (any present) was always at the end of a line which stretched backwards in time, measuring the present's growing distance from every past. And the present's face was always turned towards a future which stretched forwards to an (often utopian) end of the line after which there would be no after.

For the translator, therefore, time was a problem of distance. The function of his translation was to bridge distances – the distance between his present and every past, or the distance between his present and the future. He could carry his contemporaries back into the wonders (or the horrors) of an irrevocably vanished past – Bolingbroke in the 18th century described this as 'transport[ing] the attentive reader back to the very time' and enabling him to 'live with the men who lived before [him] and inhabit countries

[he] never saw;' (II: 186) we speak of it as 'reconstructing' the past. Alternatively, the translator could convert the past into the terms of his present – Dr. Johnson used the 18th-century idea that underlying human nature was the same in all times and places; we use contemporary methods in demographics, or paleontology, or contemporary politico-social thematics. Or, the translator could concentrate on the line itself: he could retrace the mutations and conversions which had led by a necessary chain of cause and effect to his present, or he could follow the same line onwards towards some utopian or cataclysmic end of days. But however he sought to resolve his problem, the translator was always engaging time as distance, and trying to overcome its fastnesses and its remotenesses.

Most of the assumptions about linear time on which the translator's work rested have now been discredited. Despite (or perhaps because of) a healthy political and economic market in futures, it is now denied that history moves in a straight line from a primitive origin through more and more advanced states to some foreseeable telos or end. We have deconstructed origins and we no longer imagine that we can see or control a line to the future. Causal determination has been put in question too. As Ernest Gellner, for instance, stated in 1971, 'nothing is less obvious than the relations between events which 'really came to pass', and the obviousness [of such relations] to contemporaries who participate in these events is an illusion'. Historical narratives which 'consider that the relations between events stand to reason' must be characterized as 'childish' (in École Pratique, 1972: 27, 20). Reinventing the generic affinity between history and story which was a commonplace from the Greeks until the 18th century, postmodernism has also discredited the 'truth' and validity of the *grands* and *petits recits* of conventional, causal, linear, historical scholarship. And reviving a once ignored tradition of 'critical history' which goes back at least to Bayle in the 17th-century, poststructuralism has also deconstructed the possibility of reliably reconstructing the past on the basis of any 'evidence' whatsoever.[24]

What then remains of linear time and of the translator's role within it? Very little. A linguering feeling of distances to be bridged; the same points (dates, periods, and eras) now wholly discontinuous, merely successive, and swollen into more or less coherent (or more or less plural) socio-politico-culturo-ideological structures; and the inevitability of converting the past we have irrevocably left behind into terms dictated by our present.

The question which begs to be asked, therefore, is what time would be like if we also abandoned these last residues of linear time, and started thinking about what time might mean to translation from somewhere else. At present, there are still only piece-meal ventures into an other imaginary of time. In this regard, we seem to be in a situation where, as Gellner puts it, 'new options do not present themselves . . . according to an agenda or 'catastrophically', but in little packets' before we have the means, or the techniques or the technology to implement them (in École Pratique, 1972: 36). The four little packets and pockets of new thinking about time, which I'm going to invoke quite briefly before signing off, are therefore still inconclusive, uncoordinated and incomplete. They are possibilities still seeking methods or means of translation into discourses about language, history, and text. But they open onto wholly other, far less deterministic, non-linear configurations of time.

Drawing on analyses of the interplay of programming and unpredictable variation in physics and biology,[25] Derrida argues that 'unexpectability conditions the very structure of an event' (1984b: 6). The determinate and apparently necessary pattern in time we call a date or historical moment, he suggests, is constituted by whatever happens to (be)fall together at that time and in that place. A date, a structure, a social system, an experience is everything that befalls, and in befalling, falls into a pattern. As Derrida says, 'we can note the incidence in a system of coincidences of that which is prone to fall (well or badly) *with* something else, that is, at the same time or in the same place as something else' (1984b: 6). Historical 'conjunctures' are thus co-incidences of happenings, things which come about together at a certain date.

Any historical conjuncture is therefore doubly heterogeneous. It is heterogeneous inasmuch as 'several singular events can be conjoined, allied, concentrated in the same date' (1986a: 24–5). And it is heterogeneous inasmuch as what befalls is always a co-incidence of 'significant and insignificant chance' (1984b: 6). For 'one and the 'same' date [also] commemorates heterogeneous events, which are all of a sudden each other's neighbours, though one knows that they remain and must remain infinitely strangers to one another' (1986a: 25). The mere fact that things befall together does not yet mean that they have any necessary relationship to each other, or that there is any significance in their befalling. Yet at the same time, the mere fact that certain events have fallen to the lot of a particular day, or year, or person or society, constitutes their 'destiny' or necessity. That is the way things are, or have come to be – necessarily; and the way things are or have come to be in my life or my world can be appropriated as 'my' lot, 'my' destiny, 'my' necessity or 'my luck' (*mes chances*). Since what befalls falls out as it does by a mixture of chance and necessity, such destinies or lots are also always subject to chance perturbations, to interruptions or deviations, by chance, mischance (*méchance*) or design. My luck or ill-luck (*chance, méchance*) in what has befallen can thus also be my chance or opportunity (*chance*).

If historical moments are understood in this way, then historical time(s) can no longer be translated into the language of determinism or into the fixed language of structures. The element of chance and unpredictability has to be factored in. And historical time(s) have to be translated in terms of the 'interfacing of necessity and chance' in every juncture, and in terms of the way 'competition between randomness and code disrupts the very systematicity of the system while it also, however, regulates the restless, unstable interplay of the system' (1984b: 6, 2).[26]

Derrida foregrounds the moment of chance, perhaps to counterbalance the prevalent determinism. But work on Chaos, which began in the '70s and grows out of computer simulations, works with the intricate interrelationships between order and chaos in complex, dynamic non-linear systems with feed-back loops. Nature is one such non-linear system; society is another; and chaos theory has been used successfully to explore such repeating irregularities as weather patterns, population patterns, epidemic patterns, economic patterns, and more.

Chaotic dynamics take us back to a cyclical notion of time, since non-linear systems with feed-back loops repeat themselves. But they never repeat exactly. Through repetition, a tiny difference in one variable quickly becomes an overwhelming difference in the system as a whole, and a minute difference in initial conditions can produce versions of the 'original' conditions which grow further and further apart with each different recurrence until all resemblance – and in some cases cases, all semblance of order – disappears. By the same token, 'windows' of order can suddenly appear in the midst of the most chaotic disorder. Katherine Hayles warns us quite rightly that 'different orientations' to Chaos 'lead to different kinds of conclusions', and that the significance(s) and implications of Chaos are far from settled[27] (1990: 10, 15). But work so far does seem to suggest a degree of freedom, chance and unpredictability in the cycles of even the most deterministic systems which was unthinkable before. It shows that an apparently deterministic system can 'create' not only different versions of itself, but versions which are wholly other than itself, and that 'trends' which appear and are unquestionably 'real', can also disappear as quickly as they came. Work on Chaos also offers translators a multitude of new imaginaries for what Gleich calls 'flow' – 'the evolution of shape in space and the evolution of shape in time' (1987: 195).[28]

Both Hayles and Gleich underline Chaos's debts to the past. Gleich observes that 'the emergence of Chaos as an entity unto itself was a story not only of new theories and new discoveries, but also of the belated understanding of old ideas' (1987: 182). And Hayles, who traces Chaos back to Hesiod, suggests that 'the older resonances do not disappear . . . as new meanings compete with traditional understandings within the sign of chaos . . . ' (1990: 8–9). The same could be said about all the 'new' theories in this book. As we saw, the plural and decentered subject, (de)construction's fable of man, the logic of both/and, possible worlds, and translation are all both new discoveries and belated understandings of old ideas. This suggests, at least to me, that as we abandon the linear imaginary of time, we are also abandoning the assumption that as time moves on, the past is inevitably left behind. For we are no longer just 'liberating subjugated knowledges', as Foucault recommended, and finding in history information and thematics we never sought to develop before – to do this is still to leave the past where it was, behind us, on the line of time. We are beginning, instead, to look to our diverse pasts and to our diverse traditions as to treasure houses, for what they can give, rather than take, from us. We are beginning to value what was once merely 'ancient history' for what we can remember of it and translate into old-new forms. And we are beginning to join with our once denigrated pasts in creating theories where new meanings resonate with old ideas. For the dates of the past, we are beginning to substitute dates with the past. The past is therefore, in a sense, no longer past.

It might be objected that without linear time to give us a clear sense of the pastness of the past and a clear line on the future, we will find ourselves living a Babel of times in an eternal present. It might be objected that we already live time that way in the hyperreality of postculture as a media event, and that this is something to be resisted, not encouraged by the university. I have no good answer to that. But there is also a sense in which the past only ever exists in the memory of living people, and in which our translations and our transmissions of it give us our memories. And there is also a sense in which the future only ever exists in the present, as a possible world which we stipulate through our language and our desire. If this places the burden of the past and future squarely on the shoulders of the present, it may be no bad thing. For once we conceive the past and the future as functions of what we say and do in the present, we can no longer defer responsibility for the one, and excuse the means we use to bring about the other. Without linear time, everything always depends, again and again, on whatever we happen to say and do, you and I, here and now.

Notes

Chapter 1: Critical Theory and the Marxist Paradigm

1. The question here is not one of political affiliation. It is possible to work within the marxist paradigm without being politically marxist. The New Historicism is an ambiguous case in point (see next note) inasmuch as there are many non-marxist practicing New Historicists. Russian, Prague and Israeli formalism is another case in point inasmuch as such formalism seems to represent a flight from politics. See Ehrlich (1955), Galan (1985) and Feldman (1985).
2. Some New Historicists have recently begun to situate the New Historicism in relation to marxism. But its practitioners have, for the most part, emphasized their difference and their newness, and focussed on the diversity of political affiliation rather than on methodological congruity. Compare, for instance, Howard (1986) and Montrose (1986) with Veeser (1989). For a critique of New Historicist claims to newness, see the essays by Brook Thomas and Frank Lentricchia in Veeser (1989).
3. More traditional marxisms have also been trying to appropriate formalist and poststructuralist theory for marxism. For England, see Williams (1977) and Bennett (1979); for America, see Ryan (1982), Norris (1985) and Frow (1986). These are all attempts to mesh critical traditions which are assumed to be fundamentally different. I would argue, however, that marxism is only bringing its own rebellious sons back into the fold.
4. The theory of reflection is a theory of mimesis, though in traditional marxism it was treated as epistemology and science, and the connection was not really made. It is being made now, and it is worth keeping the connection in mind as a sub-text, for instance when considering Lacoue-Labarthe's extensive rethinking of mimesis. See 'Man the Producer and the Poet', Chapter 3.
5. Althusser himself, of course, was not a proponent of the economist theory of reflection, though he did for a long time retain the notion of the determination in the last instance by the economic sphere. He was among those (who include the Frankfurt School and Gramsci) who began to invert the economist position (see below). In *Pour Marx*, Althusser began by insisting on 'the relative autonomy of the superstructure' and its 'specific efficacity'. Later, in his essay on Ideological State Apparatuses (in *Lenin and Other Essays*), he argued that ideology can produce State Apparatuses and functions.
6. Some of those who invert the base-determines-superstructure argument claim that this inversion corresponds to the most recent phase of capitalist development in which the media and information services generally play a dominant role. In other words, the

inversion is presented as a necessary extension of marxist thinking to a new phase of capitalism. This line of thought apppears at least as early as Henri Lefebvre and the Situationists in France (see Lefebvre 1968 (reprinted) or Guy Debord's *Société du Spectacle*). However, despite this historical specification, the inversion is imposed methodologically on earlier phases of capitalism, on feudal societies, and on all texts of culture without difference, thus undoing the historical distinction and turning the inversion into a paradigmatic constant.

7. See for instance, Macherey (1978); Balibar and Macherey (1981) and Williams' essay 'Base and Superstructure in Marxist Cultural Theory' in Williams (1980). For a critical discussion of this idea and its journey from France to England, see Kavanagh (1982).
8. For differences between Febvrian and poststructuralist views of this, see Bannet (1989b).
9. This move should not be associated exclusively with Althusser, Foucault and Cultural Materialism. See, for instance, Horkheimer's 'Authority in the Family' in Horkheimer (1972) and Horkheimer and Adorno's *Dialectic of the Enlightenment*.
10. See for instance, Bennett (1989) and Denning (1987).
11. 'Only in association with others has each invidividual the means of cultivating his talents in all directions. Only in a community, therefore, is personal freedom possible ... In a genuine community, individuals gain their freedom in and through their association' (Marx, 1970b: 83, 84).
12. Ideology has a long history in marxist discourse. For more recent uses, see Eagleton (1976a and 1976b). Narrative and unconscious structures move from the structuralist work of Lévi-Strauss, Propp and Greimas to poststructuralism. See esp. Foucault (1973), Lyotard (1984), and White (in Cohen). For *mentalité*, see Vovelle in Jones (1982), and for collective representations, Chartier (1988). For 'cognitive mapping', see Jameson in Nelson and Grossberg (1988), and for interpretative communities, Culler (1975) and Fish (1980).
13. In current debates, great emphasis is placed on the difference between speaking of classes (which are identified according to their position in the relations of production) and speaking of marginal groups or of subjects occupying different subject-positions and belonging to several groups at the same time. This distinction is significant for arguments about where the proper agent of revolution is to be sought, and it is also often used for labelling – for instance, if you speak of class as well as of a marginal group like women, you are a marxist feminist; if you are concerned only with gender, you are not identified as a marxist. I would argue, however, that the distinction between class and marginal group is a distinction made by theologians who belong to the same Church and espouse the same fundamental tenets, for the debate is about where the subject of revolution is to be sought, not about seeking it, or about how groupings are to be identified, not about whether people should be thought about largely/exclusively in collective configurations.

14. For Lukacs, see Tavor (1982); for Foucault, Foucault (1977) and (1980); and for Spivak, 'Feminism and Critical Theory' in Spivak (1988).
15. For some social applications of this idea, see LaCapra, 'Rethinking intellectual history and reading texts', reprinted in LaCapra and Kaplan (1983), LaCapra (1987) and Iser in Cohen (1989) – Iser here picks up Bloch's idea about the utopian function of art.
16. See, for instance, Aronowitz (1981) and his 'Postmodernism and Politics' in Ross (1988).
17. For some recent thinking about history within the marxist paradigm, see Armstrong (1988), Attridge (1987), Hobsbawm (1983), Eagleton (1985), Ross (1988), Simpson (1988), Terdiman (1985).
18. Chartier seems to be reviving the *Annales* school concept of intelligibility, and trying to combine it with more recent notions of narrativity, as well as with deconstructive notions of the trace. Although not precisely a postmarxist, Hayden White is also now emphasizing the links between narrative and reality. Compare his 'The Historical Text as a Literary Artefact' in White (1978) with his '"Figuring the nature of time deceased"' in Cohen (1989).
19. There are some intriguing parallels between the notion of self-government by the people and control from below on the one hand and Bakunin's anarchist program on the other. It was Bakunin's argument, against Marx's 'authoritarian 'communism' and 'state socialism', that 'groups of human beings' need to 'federate spontaneously, freely, from below upwards, by their own movement and conformably to their real interests, but never after a plan traced in advance and imposed on the "ignorant masses" by some superior intellectuals'. See Michael Bakunin, *Marxism, Freedom and the State* (London: Freedom Press, MCML) 19.
20. Quoted in 'Soviets abandon communist tenets', *The State*, July 27, 1991.

Chapter 2: Limits of the Marxist Paradigm

1. For recent work on the subject, see esp. Jay (1990), Heller (1986), Nealy (1988) and K. Silverman (1983).
2. Ryan makes a not dissimilar point about the dialectic: 'It is in the different modes in which philosophy is used that political values make themselves evident. The dialectic was conservative when it sanctified existing institutions, denied democracy, and foreclosed further knowledge. The radical use of the method takes different forms altogether. It promotes a sense that the social world is in movement, that previous conclusions are merely starting points, and that much remains not only to be known but also made' (64).
3. This argument has recently been taken up again by a whole group of historians and anthropologists who argue that marxism itself shares the capitalist assumptions of the society in which it emerged, and

that it is therefore inadequate as a means of describing pre-capitalist societies. See, for instance, Baudrillard (1975) and Jones (1982).
4. Laclau and Mouffe have tried to resolve this difficulty by giving plural and decentered subjects a capacity for negotiation and alliance which they lack in Foucault, and by conceiving of politics as the democratic negotiation by shape-changing groups of their goals and principles of action. In other words, they try to prevent the formation of any unconscious and anonymous subjecting principle by bringing the principle which will govern the different statements made, the different truths asserted and the (political) behaviour which is permitted or proscribed under the conscious control of a common strategy differentially applied by (the leaders of?) a variety of counter-hegemonic groups. While this does not resolve the problem – since an episteme or discursive formation by definition operates behind or beyond consciously determined strategies – it does bring Foucault's grass-roots maoist politics safely back into a more traditional Marxist mould.
5. This shared assumption erases the sort of distinction one might otherwise wish to make between Pico's or Aquinas's bounded cosmos with its well-defined grid of modes of being, and the more 'open' and fluid cosmos supposedly underlying current thinking, by constructing different grids (hegemonic and institutional this time) and by paradoxically making the 'open' universe even more constraining than the closed one.

Chapter 3: The Other Body of Man in Derrida, Levinas, Lacoue-Labarthe, Nancy and Borch-Jakobsen

1. There are continuities between (de)construction and deconstruction, but these will not be stressed in this chapter. I am using Lacoue-Labarthe's term, (de)construction, even though it is not in widespread use, to mark, by the almost silent difference created by the introduction of brackets, the 'tonal' difference of affirmation. I am also going to be using the terms man and he in this chapter for two reasons: first, (de)construction consistently uses the masculine to represent the self and the feminine to represent the 'other', and if one is to understand anything at all about its work, one needs to keep these two distinct; and secondly, because as some French feminists have pointed out, (de)construction does obliterate real women.
2. For Levinas's impact on the 1968 generation of French intellectuals, see Friedlander (1990); for differences between Levinas and Derrida prior to this, see Robert Bernasconi, 'The trace of Levinas in Derrida' in Wood and Bernasconi (1985).
3. See also Derrida's *Glas* (1974), *Parages, La Verité en Peinture*, and *Psyche. Invention de l'autre*, where the same point is made.
4. Derrida's use of the feminine is at least in part an outcome of French feminist work in the '70s, when Cixous and Kristeva were

exploring the potential bisexuality of writing and the potential bisexuality of a subject who recognizes him/herself in both sexes, or who is prepared to change sex by changing her/his relation to language and power. But as Derrida has made very clear, he is not interested in feminism as such, and not making a feminist point. He seems to have been taking advantage of figures which he found ready to hand in some French feminism (as he took advantage of figures in Lacanian psychoanalysis), grafting them on to a much more ancient body of texts, and re-marking them for his own purposes. Some French feminists seem to accept his concept of bisexuality (See, for instance, Jardine and Menke, 1991) but other French feminists have not been slow in countering his position – Irigaray's response will be discussed in the next chapter. Unlike French feminists, American feminists tend to see Derrida as practising a feminist critique. See, for instance, Jardine (1985) and Nancy J. Holland, 'Heidegger and Derrida Redux' in Silverman and Ihde (1985). However, (de)construction's relation to French feminism in particular and to feminism in general is extremely complex, and cannot be covered here.

5. *Survivre* has been translated 'Living On', which obscures its other meaning. See 'Living On. Border lines' in G. Hartman *et al., Deconstruction and Criticism* (New York: The Seabury Press, 1979).

6. For Derrida's simultaneous use of multiple languages, see the discussion of translation in Chapter 6.

7. According to Gershom Sholem, in mystical ecstasy, Kabbalists of the Abulafia school encountered a double of themselves confronting and addressing them. See *Major Trends in Jewish Mysticism* (New York: Schocken, 1954) pp. 141–2.

8. See also Rodolphe Gashé, 'Quasi-Metaphoricity and the Question of Being' in Silverman and Ihde (1985). For another approach to allegory, see 'Compossible Worlds' in Chapter 5.

9. As Meschonnnic points out, 'the prophet is not a seer. Biblical metalanguage itself distinguishes the seer, *roé*, from the prophet, *navi*, the one who makes come (*celui qui fait venir*)'. See Meschonnic, 1973: 268.

10. In Christianity, the line between good and evil falls broadly between the spirit (good) and the flesh (evil). In Chassidism, the line between good and evil falls between the Godly soul with its vessels (language, the human mind and body, the physical world etc) and the *sitra achera*, the other ungodly side with *its* vessels (language, the human mind and body, the physical world etc.). These sides are inverted duplicates of each other: 'The Almighty has created one thing opposite the other' (Eccl. 7: 14). The separation *from* the other side is holiness.

11. If language, the work and the signatory are imagined as having both a manifest and an encrypted level, they could also be compared to a double-circuit or two-track recording (*double-bande*), where one circuit runs, like the Freudian unconscious, 'beneath' the other, and conveys its insistent message against and through the other.

12. Derrida's essay, 'Facteur de la Verité' in *La Carte Postale* could/should be read as a rewrite of Lacoue-Labarthe and Nancy's *Le Titre de la Lettre (une lecture de Lacan,)* the thesis of which they expounded in one of Derrida's seminars.
13. This has been obscured in English inasmuch as Derrida's essay, '*La Loi du Genre*' has been translated 'The Law of Genre' (*Critical Inquiry*, Fall 1980).
14. One could also read (de)construction as suggesting that Derrida, Lacoue-Labarthe, Nancy, Levinas and their surrounding group of minor prophets are the ones to give the law to others. In this reading, the miming of the prophetic encounter with Godliness in Derrida's texts would serve as legitimization for the new Testament or testimony he is giving us, and converts (those who turn, and affirm in response to his texts) to his teaching (*Tora*) would constitute a class of followers who had only to hear him (or what speaks only through him and his group) and to obey (imitate, imitatio Dei). However, since this is a distinctly less charitable reading, I have preferred the other.
15. For other ways Derrida evades appropriation, see Wood (1989).
16. 'I want to write it down and I am not allowed to do it, I do not want to write it down, and cannot entirely desist; so I write and I pause, and I allude to it again in later passages, and this is my procedure'. Abulafia, quoted in Scholem, op. cit., 127.
17. For a treatment of the signature which confines it to the order of the father, see Peggy Kamuf, *Signature Pieces: the institution of authorship* (Ithaca: Cornell University Press, 1988)
18. Such double entente and double-speak could also be described as 'JewGreek' – inasmuch as it inscribes both Jew and Greek in the same word or text and also marks the distance or difference between their two ways of hearing or understanding the 'same' things.
19. These stereophonic bands or columns are graphically represented on the page in *Glas, feu la cendre* and '*Survivre*'. The syncopation of these two bands or columns is represented by the echoing or bouncing back and forth of words and themes between them.
20. It is noteworthy too that Derrida's work of the '80s periodically takes the socio-historical dimension on board as his earlier work did not. See, for instance, *Shibboleth* and *Les Sauvages dans la Cité* or his series of essays on the university.

Chapter 4: The Logic of Both/And

1. It has been pointed out to me that Barbara Christian's statement may be an expression of the relation of black women to black men. I have, however, found the same sentiment expressed by diverse feminists in the sense I am using it, in relation to men in general – but nowhere so powerfully and so succinctly.
2. For a survey of the various feminisms and their interrelations, see

Tong (1989), Todd (1988), Moi (1987), Greene and Kahn (1985), Offen (1988), and Macia-Lees *et al.* (1989).

3. Gayle Greene and Coppelia Kahn have put it this way: 'If feminist scholars are concerned with challenging and changing the ideology which has subjugated women, then they must beware of borrowing analytical categories from them'. Catherine Clement has argued that 'one would have to cut through all the heavy layers of ideology . . . And that is precisely what feminist action is all about: to change the imaginary in order then to be able to act in the real, to change the very form of language, which by its structure and history, has been subject to a law that is patrilinear and masculine'. In Marks and Courtivron (1980) 131. See also Gross (1987) and Hawkesworth (1989).

4. For a convenient summary of different approaches to motherhood, see Van Buren (1989).

5. See for instance King (1988), de Lattes and Weinerman (1986); and Smith and Valenze (1988).

6. He is also probably Western, white and middle or upper-class.

7. See also Greene and Kahn (1985), Kuykendell (1988), Zagarell (1988) Chodorow (1978), Ferguson (1986), Freeland (1986) and Gilligan (1982).

8. See Valverde (1989), Alcoff (1988), Hawkesworth (1989), Harding (1986), Farell Smith (1986), Scott (1988). Examples could be multiplied.

9. From about 1980 on, Irigaray seems to have been obsessed by Derrida's fable. She returns to different aspects of it, directly and indirectly, in different ways, in different writings, from 1980 to 1985. Few of these writings have been translated yet or commented in English. For an exception see the translation of a chapter from *Ethique de la différence sexuelle* and Andrea Nye's article 'The Hidden Host: Irigaray and Diotima at Plato's Symposium', both in *Hypatia*, Vol. 3, No. 3 (Winter 1989) and Fuss's article in the same place.

10. For Irigaray's miming use of deconstruction to establish a place for the feminine, see Gross (1987) and Godard (1990).

11. The concept of infinity as the uncompletable or untraversable goes back to Aristotle, Kant and most particularly to Gödel. See Moore (1990).

Chapter 5: Factitive Fictions and Possible Worlds

1. See my 'Pluralist Theory-Fictions and Fictional Politics' in *Philosophy and Literature*, April 1989, pp. 28–41.

2. See for instance, Bryce DeWitt and Neill Graham, *The Many Worlds Interpretation of Quantum Mechanics* (N.J: Princeton University Press, 1973); Fred Alan Wolf, *Parallel Universes* (N.Y.: Simon & Schuster, 1988); and Alastair I. M. Rae, *Quantum Physics: Illusion/Reality?* (Cambridge: Cambridge University Press, 1986).

3. There is a suggestion that modal philosophers were also or rather reacting to the computer. According to Holstein (1974), modal attempts to describe world states were required to permit the mechanical derivation of subsequent world states in problem-solving programs where the computer was used to assist in human decision making. The establishment of world-states and rules of transformation was a preliminary to programs which could explore the different possible consequences of decisions or the different possible future states devolving from a present world state.

4. I am using the word scenario rather than the modal philosophers' word 'state of affairs' to indicate a small part of a possible world, because it seems to me that the term 'state of affairs' is static and non-fluid, and because it involves narratologists in efforts to provide models for ways in which one 'state of affairs' can turn into an other which don't seem very useful in this context.

5. Brian Stock has likewise shown that 'changes in medieval modes of discourse . . . often took place independently of or in opposition to real or perceived social forces; that is to say, texts that people enacted were interdependent with, but not functionally supportive of the social material out of which they were constructed' (1990: 35).

6. This term is used by modal philosophers to describe features of a single world which can be present together according to the law of non-contradiction. I am not going to be using it in this sense, but it's a word too wonderful to resist.

7. The distinction between literal and figurative meanings of a word is now considered ideological and historical (see Andrew Benjamin (1989) and Eco (1990) for instance) and problematized. For the argument here, however, I don't think it ultimately matters which meaning is designated 'literal' or even if the hierarchy between literal and figurative is retained. Dante clearly does see some sort of hierarchy in the word, and it is useful to start from there for heuristic purposes. But in principle, any meaning could be designated as the literal one (Platonically, for instance, the most abstract or ideal meaning might be the literal – i.e. the primary and most fundamental or concrete – meaning). And in principle, one could also do without a literal/figurative hierarchy altogether, inasmuch as different possible meanings (or, as we will see, worlds) coexist polysemously and interact within the purely *letteral* configuration of the word. I wonder too whether, for an ancient Egyptian, for instance, the word *Ra* meant sun first and God second, or God first and sun second, or whether it just meant *both* without any particular precedence.

8. This is why God's word is the model for all allegory, and why God can be described by Donne as both a 'literal' and an allegorical God: 'My God, my God, thou art a direct God, may I not say a literal God, a God that would be understood literally and according to the plain sense of all that thou sayest. But thou art . . . a figurative, a metaphorical God too: a God in whose words there is such a height of figures, such voyages, such peregrinations to fetch remote and

precious metaphors, such extensions, such spreadings, such curtains of allegories, such third heavens of hyberboles . . . Oh, what words but thine can express the inexpressible texture and composition of thy word' (Expostulation 19, 1623).

9. Rifaterre (1990) has argued the same about 19th century realist novels.

10. Again, God's works provide the model here: 'Neither art thou thus a figurative, a metaphorical God, in thy word only, but in thy works too. The style of the works, the phrase of thine actions is metaphorical. The institution of thy whole worship in the Old Law was a continual allegory'. John Donne, Expostulation 19, 1623.

11. According to a letter dated January 26, 1604, two years before *King Lear* was performed, from a Mr. Chamberlain to a Mr. Winwood: 'The king finds that felicity in the hunting life that he hath written to the council that it is the only means to maintain his health which being the health and welfare of us all, he desires them to take the charge and burden of affairs and foresee that he may not be interrupted or troubled with too much business'. The Venetian ambassador substantiates this in 1607 in a passage curiously reminiscent of the play: 'The king is sufficiently tall, of noble presence, his physical constitution robust, and he is at pains to preserve it by taking much exercise at the chase, which he passionately loves and uses not only as a recreation, but as a medicine. For this he throws off all business which he leaves to his Council and his Ministers. And so one may truly say that he is sovereign in name and appearance rather than in substance and effect'. Respectively in William Harris, *An Historical and Critical Account of the Life and Writings of James I* (London, 1772) p. 80 and in Robert Ashton, *James I by his Contemporaries* (London, 1969), pp. 8–9. Goneril mentions Lear's hunting.

12. This remark was made by James at the famous Hampton Court Conference of 1604. In Willson's *Life and Reign of King James I* (Oxford, 1927), pl. 171.

13. For Derrida's theory of translation, see Chapter 6.

14. Many textbooks also emphasize that construction of the model deconstructs the boundary between art and science, inasmuch as it is both an interdisciplinary science, which borrows from statistics, probability theory, systems analysis, etc., and a creative art, much like the playwright's work with dramatic scenarios. See, for instance, Abt (1970); Shannon (1975) and Banks & Carson (1984).

15. I would argue that Baudrillard's argument is more applicable to television and film technologies than to simulations as such, despite the fact that his book is called *Simulations and Simulacra*. Work on the impact of the new information technologies among literary and cultural theorists has only just begun, and there is a perhaps inevitable tendency to generalize for the whole field. But information technologies are various and it does make a difference, for instance, if we are talking about television and film, which are produced once, fixed and finalized, and, as Baudrillard says, emitted

to an essentially passive audience; or about information network systems which allow people to communicate with each other and to actively exchange messages in an impermanent and erasable manner; or about something like the Perseus project, which is creating a hypertext which will permit students of Greek literature or culture to move on the computer screen between a Greek play, a Platonic dialogue, a dictionary, a picture of the Parthenon, or whatever, at will; or about simulations. It also makes a difference which sort of simulations we are talking about, and whether they are used as part of television and film technology or not (like cartoons, for instance). For interesting recent work on information technologies, see Bachelard (1988); Poster (1990); and Paulson (1988).

16. Both Zigfeld (1989) and Bolter (1991) explore the implications for our future sense of textuality of the fact that the 'work' here 'consists of the path(s) that readers take through the product' and of the fact that 'once authors introduce twenty to thirty branches, there is a practical sense in which the 'work' itself becomes highly variable (construed conservatively) or even indeterminate, because the branching permutations make it unlikely that any two readers would randomly take the same set of branches' (Zigfeld, 1989: 364). Both also emphasize how this sort of computer writing changes the relationship of author and reader. Bolter (1991) and Poster (1990) explore the relations between this kind of structure and literary (Borges) or poststructuralist texts (primarily Derrida, though I think an argument could also be made for Barthes' latest texts – *Roland Barthes par Roland Barthes*, for instance). As I understand it, video games work on a similar principle of 'if/then' – if the character the player is controlling chooses (a) to kick rather than (b) to duck, then the 'enemy' the computer is controlling does (c) rather than (d). But in video games the whole thing is complicated by a variety of other factors, including randomization, which I will be discussing further on.

17. This did not prove very gripping, even for children: in its own way, it is as limiting as the conventional story, and it 'varies' or 'personalizes' the adventure as machine embroidered monograms personalize mass produced towels. Bolter and Zigfeld predict great things for 'high' literature written in this sort of form with computers, arguing that the problem so far has been the inferior, adventure story material. I am wondering, however, if the problem is really only one of content.

18. Something similar was done in non-computerized instructional simulations. Here the teacher or leader was given a manual showing how to run the simulation, while participants were given manuals with the information they needed to act out their roles in the simulation.

19. Symbolic logic (and perhaps the formalist narratology which imitates it) influenced early programmers. See Bolter (1984) and Holstein (1974).

20. See Holstein, 1974. I am using texts on simulation from the same era

as *Dungeons and Dragons*. The first version of this simulation game came out in 1973, and it has been revised several times since then. 'Advanced' versions have also been produced in several versions. This, as I have suggested above is characteristic of all simulation models.

21. Indeed, it is so complex, complicated, and dependent on charts and data that the *Dungeons and Dragons* books can never be put aside. The reader is told at the beginning of the books that s/he must read the book linearly all the way through in the traditional way to learn the world. But playing involves turning the book into a reference book – and literally looking back at it all the time. The reading-writing of the game is performed with participants sitting around a table, each armed with pencil, paper, a map (divided into cells) and the players' or dungeon master's book. Players need the Handbook every time they create a new character or need to refresh their memory about their character skills or spells, or want to purchase anything (since the book contains the objects they may purchase and their prices). Dungeons Master need their Guide for the rules, protocols and potential components of the game even when they don't need it to give them the game's actual text. Players need pencil and paper to keep lists of their characters' properties and to create a 'memory' by listing possessions, wealth, encounters, and the various numerical statuses of the character and they have to draw maps to keep track of where they are in the dungeon. Dungeon Masters need pencil and paper to keep track of everything, and in Advanced games, to fashion a dungeon and project a possible adventure.
22. It's actually even more complicated than this, since the calculation has to take account of the same features in the character that is being combatted or encountered.
23. See 'The Times of Translation' in Chapter 6.
24. There may, however, be some beginnings in Derrida – see next chapter.
25. There is also a long history of treating literary fictions as worlds in German literary theory.
26. For instance: 'a fictional possible world is a series of linguistic descriptions that readers are supposed to interpret as referring to a possible state of affairs where if p is true then non-p is false . . . this state of affairs is made up of individuals endowed with properties. These properties are ruled by certain laws, so that certain properties can be mutually contradictory and a given property X can entail the property Y' (1990: 66).

Chapter 6: The Critic as Translator

1. See 'History: Utopian and Scientific', in Chapter 1.
2. Bourdieu calls 'marginal' institutions like *École Pratique des Haute Etudes*, the CNRS and the *College de France* which have largely been taken over by untraditional faculty, and teach or research

untraditional subjects in untraditional ways. He shows how the Sorbonne (a bastion of traditionalism, according to him) and Senior faculty belonging to the 'old order' have used administrative means ('faculty governance') to marginalize such institutions, for instance by preventing them from awarding the highest French academic degree, by limiting their access to students and the career benefits they can give students, or by excluding their research findings from the national curriculum and state university examinations. But the terms 'marginal' and 'central' here describe relative positions *within* the University system as a whole, as one might say (though this is not at all an exact comparison) that in the States Ivy League universities are 'central' and other universities are marginal. The *Ecole Pratique*, the CNRS and the *College de France* remain prestigious and important institutions, and despite their difference from the Sorbonne, they are far from being outside the system. This is why I have described dissenting intellectuals who are members of such institutions as 'both inside and outside the pale' (Bannet, 1989: 229).

3. For other discussions of conflict and competition, see James A. Sosnoski, 'A Mindless Man-Driven Theory Machine' and Gayle Greene's response in Kauffman (ed.) 1989; and Valerie Miner and Helen E. Longina, *Competition: A feminist taboo* (N.Y.: The Feminist Press at the City University of New York, 1987).

4. For the relation of imitation to translation in the Renaissance, see Theo Hermans, 'Images of Translation' in Hermans (ed) 1985.

5. According to Robinson, translation is always a crossing: a carrying over (*translatio*), a leading over (*traduction, traduccion*), a setting over (*Uebersetzen*) (1991: 195). According to Steiner, Romance languages derive their term for translation from a mis-translation of the Latin word *traducere*, which means to introduce, to lead into (1975: 295).

6. For the differences between translation theory and Reader Reception Theory, see Samuel Weber, 'Caught in the Act of Reading', in *Glyph Textual Studies* I, 1986.

7. I am borrowing these terms from the technical vocabulary of translators who refer to the language from which they are translating as the Source Language and the language into which they are translating as the Target Language.

8. For the implications of this view of translation for philosophy, see Andrew Benjamin, 1990.

9. From this point of view, it is noteworthy that Jardine and Menke chose to interview (in French) and translate into English only interviews with women 'whose work is perceived in the US as "French Feminism"' and that they therefore excluded women like Christine Delphy and Michèle Le Doeuff, whose work is 'not sufficiently translated' (4). This is not a reflection on Jardine and Menke, who, after all, had to make some sort of selection; it *is* a reflection on the role translation plays in determining who exists for us, and a reflection on how easy it is to overlook this fact when one is speaking and writing in a dominant language.

Notes to pp. 174–187

10. For other deformations in translation, see Antoine Berman, 'La Traduction comme épreuve de l'étranger' (1985)
11. Hölderlin is considered the prime model of such translation. See Benjamin's 'The Task of the Translator', in *Illuminations*; Lacoue-Labarthe's *Hölderlin, L'Antigone de Sophocle* (Paris: Christan Bourgois, 1978) and 'La Césure du Speculatif' in the same volume; and also Kerkhoff (1985), Brisset (1985), and Johnson (1985).
12. For the argument that the relation here is one of complementarity merely, see Joseph Graham, 'Around and About Babel' in Silverman and Aylesworth (eds) 1990. For the supplementary structure of translation, see Derrida (1985a), esp. the section called 'Theologie de la Traduction' and Lewis in Graham (1985).
13. See 'Man's Spectral Double' in Chapter 3.
14. See 'Double Speak and Undecidability' in Chapter 3.
15. See (de)construction's arguments about rivalry in 'Psyche-ology and Psychology' in Chapter 3.
16. As Graham has noted, Derrida's title *'Des Tours de Babel'* can be translated: Of the Towers of Babel, From the Towers of Babel, Of the Turns of Babel, From the Turns of Babel, Some Tropes of Babel, or Detours (*des tours, détours*) of Babel (1985: 206). Since *de* is a genitive which can point in either direction, and since Derrida also identifies the word Babel with God (*El*) (in *Ulysses Gramophone*), the same title could also mean: Of turns (or turnings) from God, Detours from God, God's turns (or tricks), God's turnings, and God's detours. It may also be worth noting that another traditional name of God is *Hashem* (the Name) and Derrida insists that it is the people of Shem (name, Semites) who build a tower at Babel to make a name (*shem*) for themselves (instead of for him).
17. See 'Society as a Whole' in Chapter 1.
18. For the history of this idea in translation studies, see Steiner, *After Babel*.
19. Jakobson's example is the French nasal a phoneme, which can inflect the present participle (*cach-ant*), act as an independent word (*an*, year) or form part of words (*entrer, vent, sang, cancan*) without having anything to do with their meanings (1978: 61).
20. 'Now begin to combine a few or many letters, to permute and to combine them until thy heart be warm. Then be mindful of their movements, of what thou canst bring forth by moving them. And . . . when thou seest that by combinations of letters thou canst grasp new things which by human tradition or by thyself thou wouldst not be able to know and when thou art thus prepared to receive the influx of divine power which flows into thee . . . feel thyself like an envoy whom the king and his ministers are to send on a mission . . . ' (Abulafia, in Scholem, 1941: 136).
21. 'The method which Abulafia and his followers call *dilug* and *kefitsah*, "jumping" or "skipping" viz., from one conception to another. In fact this is nothing else than a very remarkable method of using associations as a way of meditation . . . The "jumping" unites elements of free and guided association and is said to assure quite

extraordinary results as far as the "widening of the consciousness of the initiate is concerned"' (Scholem, 1941: 135–6).

22. For *Glas*, see especially Gregory Ulmer's brilliant essay, 'Sounding the Unconscious' in Leavey, 1986.

23. This seems like another perestroika-style utopia, especially when one thinks of the sort of problems being created now when people *passe-partout* across national frontiers. But I think Derrida would distinguish between a utopia and a promise – a promise, he insists, is always performative. We could think of the symbolon of the reconciliation of tongues, therefore, not as something present or as something which the present must lead to in the course of history, but as a dimension of promise in the present – a possibility opened or reopened by the present – which could only become real if it were to be acted on (performed), thus if the promise were to be kept.

24. For these two points, see Eve Tavor, *Scepticism, Society and the 18th Century Novel*, 1987: 150–8, 194–200, and 221ff. For the postmodern critiques of historical narrative, see the works of Haydn White, and Lyotard's *The Postmodern Condition*.

25. See 'Accessible Worlds', in Chapter 5.

26. Another way of explaining Derrida's intertranslation would be to say that it takes advantage of the interface of chance and necessity. Intertranslation could be said to ride on the chance overlapping and coincidence of sound in different languages, multiplying its chances by multiplying languages and by introducing deviations of its own – 'the mere difference of a letter introduces a clinamen' (1984b: 7) – and turning this into a new kind of sense or necessity.

27. One of the issues which I have not seen raised by anyone and which I am not competent to discuss myself is the extent to which chaos theory only plays out the assumptions already built into the computer programs which it uses to produce its 'results', and what the implications are if that is indeed 'all' that it is doing.

28. For instance: There can be more than one stable solution hiding within a particular system, so that while it might manifest one kind of behaviour over a very long time, another kind can be just as natural to it. Some systems display one sort of behaviour for a long time, fluctuating within certain bounds, and then shift to another sort or reverse themselves. Some shifts show regularities – Mandelbrot called this the Joseph effect (7 years of plenty, 7 years of drought) – and some shifts show instantaneous jumps. Windows of order can appear in chaotic flows, and chaos can unmake order. Systems can be stable and still chaotic; and systems can be stably chaotic for long periods. In fractals, self-identical repetitions can also produce phenomena far exceeding themselves. See Gleich, 1987.

Bibliography

ABT, Clark C. 1970. *Serious Games.* New York: Viking.
ADORNO, T. W. 1984a. *Aesthetic Theory.* London: Routledge.
——, 1984b. *Negativische Dialektik: Jargon der Eigentlichkeit.* Frankfurt: Suhrkamp.
AGACINSKI, Sylviane *et al.* 1975. *Mimesis desarticulations.* Paris: Flammarion.
ALCOFF, Linda. 1988. 'Cultural Feminism vs. Poststructuralism: the identity crisis in feminist theory', *Signs*, Vol. 13, No. 3 (Spring).
ALLISON, David B. 1990. 'The Différance of Translation', in Hugh Silverman & Gary Aylesworth (eds), *The Textual Sublime.*
ALTHUSSER, Louis. 1959. *Montesquieu: Le Politique et L'Histoire.* Paris: P.U.F.
——, 1969. *Lire le Capital.* Paris: Maspéro.
——, 1971. *Pour Marx.* Paris: Maspéro.
AQUINAS, St. Thomas. 1959. *Commentary on De Anima.* London: Routledge.
ARAC, Jonathan (ed.). 1986. *Postmodernism and Politics.* Minneapolis: University of Minnesota Press.
ARISTOTLE. 1959. *De Anima.* London: Routledge.
ARMSTRONG, Paul B. 1988. 'History and Epistemology: the example of *The Turn of the Screw*', *New Literary History*, Vol. 19, No. 3 (Spring).
ARONOWITZ, Stanley. 1981. *The Crisis in Historical Marxism: Class, Politics and Culture in Marxist Theory.* New York: Praeger.
ATTRIDGE, Derek, Bennington, Geoff, & Young, Robert (eds). 1987. *Poststructuralism and the Question of History.* Cambridge: Cambridge University Press.
BANKS, Jerry & Carson, John S. 1984. *Discrete-Event System Simulation.* New Jersey: Prentice Hall.
BAKUNIN, Michael. MCML. *Marxism, Freedom and the State.* London: Freedom Press.
BAL, Mieke. 1985. *Narratology.* Toronto: University of Toronto Press.
BALIBAR, Etienne & MACHEREY, Pierre. 1981. 'On Literature as an Ideological Form', in Robert Young (ed.), *Untying the Text.* London: Routledge.
BANNET, Eve Tavor. 1989a. *Structuralism and the Logic of Dissent: Barthes, Derrida, Foucault, Lacan.* London & Urbana: Macmillan & University of Illinois Press.
——, 1989b. 'Pluralist Theory-Fictions and Fictional Politics', *Philosophy and Literature*, Vol. 13, No. 1 (April).
BARNEY, Stephen A. 1979. *Allegories of History, Allegories of Love.* Connecticut: Archon Press.
BARTHES, Roland. 1975. *The Pleasure of the Text.* tr. R. Miller. New York: Noonday Press.
——, 1977. *Image-Text-Music.* Tr. S. Heath. London: Fontana.

——, 1982. 'Leçon' in Susan Sonntag (ed.). *A Barthes Reader*. London: Jonathan Cape.

BASS, Alan. 1985. 'On the History of a Mistranslation and the Psychoanalytic movement', in Joseph Graham (ed.), *Difference in Translation*.

BASSNETT, Susan & LEFEVERE, André. 1990. *Translation, History, Culture*. London: Pinter.

BATSLEER, Janet et al. 1985. *Re-writing English: Cultural Politics of Gender and Class*. London: Methuen.

BAUDRILLARD, Jean. 1975. *The Mirror of Production*. tr. Mark Poster. St. Louis: Telos Press.

——, 1977. *Oublier Foucault*. Paris: Galilée.

——, 1981. *Simulacres et Simulations*. Paris: Galilée.

——, 1988. *Selected Writings*. ed. Mark Poster. Stanford: Stanford University Press.

BAUMAN, Zygmunt. 1987. *Legislators and Interpreters: on modernity, postmodernity, and intellectuals*. Cambridge: Polity Press.

BENJAMIN, Andrew. 1989. *Translation and the Nature of Philosophy*. London: Routledge.

BENJAMIN, Walter. 1955. *Illuminations*. New York: Harcourt, Brace & World.

——, 1979. *One Way Street and other Writings*. tr. E. Jephcolt & K. Shorter. London: New Left Books.

BENNETT, Tony. 1979. *Formalism and Marxism*. London: Methuen.

——, & WOOLLACOTT, Janet. 1987. *Bond and Beyond*. London: Macmillan.

BENNINGTON, Geoffrey. 1988. *Lyotard, Writing the Event*. New York: Columbia University Press.

BENTON, Ted. 1984. *The Rise and Fall of Structural Marxism: Althusser and his Influence*. New York: St. Martin's Press.

BERMAN, Antoine. 1985. 'La traduction comme épreuve de l'étranger'. *Texte* 4.

BERNASCONI, Robert. 1985. 'The trace of Levinas in Derrida', in David Wood & Robert Bernasconi (eds). *Derrida and Différance*.

BLOCH, Ernst. 1988. *The Utopian Function of Art: Selected Essays*. Cambridge, Mass.: The MIT Press.

BORCH-JAKOBSEN, Mikkel. 1982. *Le Sujet freudien*. Paris: Flammarion.

BOLTER, J. David. 1984. *Turing's Man: Western Culture in the Computer Age*. Chapel Hill: University of North Carolina Press.

——, 1991. *Writing Space: the Computer, Hypertext and the History of Writing*. New Jersey: Lawrence Erlbaum.

BOURDIEU, Pierre. 1977. *Outline of a Theory of Practice*. Cambridge: Cambridge University Press.

——, 1988. *Homo Academicus*. Stanford: Stanford University Press.

BRISSET, Annie. 1985. 'La traduction comme transformation para-doxale'. *Texte*, 4.

BROWER, Reuben. 1974. *Mirror on Mirror: Translation, Imitation, Parody*. Cambridge, Mass.: Harvard University Press.

BURKE, Peter (ed.). 1973. *A New Kind of History: from the writings of Lucien Febvre*. London: Routledge.

BURNEY, Fanny. 1986. *Evalina*. Oxford: Oxford University Press.
BRADLEY, Raymond & SCHWARZ, Norman. 1979. *Possible Worlds: An Introduction to Logic and its Philosophy*. Indianapolis: Hackett.
BRUNTON, Mary. 1986. *Self-Control*. London: Pandora.
CHARTIER, Roger. 1988. *Cultural History: Between Practices and Representations*. Ithaca: Cornell University Press.
CHRISTIAN, Barbara. 1988. 'The Race for Theory'. *Feminist Studies*, Vol. 14, No. 1 (Spring).
CIXOUS, Hélène. 1975. 'Sorties' in Clement & Cixous below.
CLEMENT, Catherine & CIXOUS, Hélène. 1975. *La Jeune Née*. Paris: Union Générale d'Editions.
——, 1980. 'Enclave Esclave' in Elaine Marks & Isabelle de Courtivron (eds). *New French Feminisms: An Anthology*.
COHEN, Ralph. 1989. *Future Literary Theory*. London: Routledge.
COLELLA, A. M. O'SULLIVAN, M. J. & CARLINO, D. J. 1974. *Systems Simulation*. Massachusetts: D. C. Heath.
CONLEY, Tom. 1986. 'Institutionalizing Translation: on Florio's Montaigne'. in *Glyph Textual Studies I: Demarcating the Disciplines*.
CORNFORTH, Maurice. 1954. *Historical Materialism*. New York: International Publishers.
CULLER, Jonathan. 1975. *Structuralist Poetics*. London: Routledge.
DARNTON, Robert. 1982. *The Literary Underground of the Old Regime*. Cambridge, Mass.: Harvard University Press.
DELABASTITA, Dirk. 1990. 'Translation and the Mass Media', in Bassnett & Lefevere (eds), *Translation, History, Culture*.
DE LATTES, Recchini and WEINERMAN, Catalina. 1986. 'Unreliable accounts of women's work: evidence from Latin American statistics'. *Signs*. Vol. 11, No. 4 (Summer).
DE MAN, Paul. 1983. *Blindness and Insight*. London: Methuen.
DEMETZ, Peter. 1967. *Marx, Engels and the Poets*. Chicago: University of Chicago Press.
DENNING, Michael. 1987. *Cover Stories: Narrative and Ideology in the British Spy Thriller*. London: Routledge.
DERRIDA, Jacques. 1972. *Marges de la Philosophie*. Paris: Minuit.
——, 1975. 'Economimesis' in Agacinsky et al., *Mimesis desarticulations*.
——, 1976a. 'Fors'. in N. Abraham & M. Torok, *Le Verbier de l'homme aux loups*. Paris: Flammarion.
——, 1976b. 'Entre Crochets (interview)'. *Digraphe*, No. 8.
——, 1976c. *Of Grammatology*. Baltimore: Johns Hopkins University Press.
——, 1978. *La Vérité en Peinture*. Paris: Flammarion.
——, 1979. *Eperons/Spurs*. Chicago: University of Chicago Press.
——, 1980. *La Carte Postale de Socrates à Freud et au-delà*. Paris: Flammarion.
——, 1981a. *Glas*. Paris: Gonthier.
——, 1981b. *Dissemination*. Chicago: University of Chicago Press.
——, 1982a. *The Ear of the Other: Otobiography, Transference, Translation*. New York: Schocken.
——, 1982b. 'Choreographies'. *Diacritics*, Vol. 12 (Summer).
——, 1983a. 'The Principle of Reason: the University in the eyes of its pupils'. *Diacritics*, Vol. 13, No. 3 (Fall).

———, 1983b. 'Interview with Catherine David'. In Wood & Bernasconi, *Derrida and Différance*.
———, 1984a. *Signéponge*. New York: Columbia University Press.
———, 1984b. 'My Chances/Mes Chances: A rendez-vous with some Epicurean stereophonies' in Joseph Smith & William Kerrigan (eds), *Taking Chances*.
———, 1985a. 'Les languages and les institutions de la philosophie'. *Texte* 4
———, 1985b. Introduction. *Les Sauvages dans la Cité*. Seyssel: Champ Vallon.
———, et al. 1985c. *La Faculté de Juger*. Paris: Minuit.
———, 1986a. *Schibboleth*. Paris: Galilée.
———, 1986b. *Parages*. Paris: Galilée.
———, 1986c. 'The Age of Hegel' in *Glyph Textual Studies I: Demarcating the Disciplines*.
———, 1986d. 'Proverb: He that would pun'. in John P. Leavey, Jr. *Glassary*.
———, 1987a. *Ulysses Gramophone*. Paris: Galilée.
———, 1987b. *De l'Esprit: Heidegger et la question*. Paris: Galilée.
———, 1987c. *Psyché. Invention de l'autre*. Paris: Galilée.
———, 1987d. *feu la cendre*. Paris: des femmes.
———, 1988. 'An Interview with Jacques Derrida' in Easthope, *British Poststructuralism since 1968*.
———, 1989. 'Biodegradables: Seven Diary Fragments' *Critical Inquiry*. 15: 4 (Summer).
DeWITT, Bryce & GRAHAM, Neill. 1973. *The Many-Worlds Interpretation of Quantum Mechanics*. New Jersey: Princeton University Press.
DIACRITICS. 1985. *Marx after Derrida*. Vol. 15, No. 4 (Winter).
DOLEZEL, Lubomír. 1988. 'Mimesis and Possible Worlds'. *Poetics Today*. Vol. 9, No. 3.
DONCHIN, Ann. 1986. 'The future of mothering: reproductive technology and feminist theory'. *Hypatia*, Vol. 1, No. 2 (Fall).
DURING, Simon. 1989. 'After death: Raymond Williams in the modern era'. *Critical Inquiry*. 15: 4 (Summer).
EAGLETON, Terry. 1976a. *Criticism and Ideology: A Study in Marxist Literary Theory*. London: New Left Books.
———, 1976b. *Marxism and Literary Criticism*. London: Methuen.
———, 1985. 'Marxism, Structuralism and Poststructuralism'. *Diacritics*. Vol. 15, No. 4 (Winter).
———, 1986. *Against the Grain: Essays 1975–1985*. London: Verso.
EASTHOPE, Anthony. 1988. *British Poststructuralism since 1968*. London: Routledge.
ECO, Umberto. 1990. *The Limits of Interpretation*. Bloomington: Indiana University Press.
ECOLE Pratique des Hautes Etudes. 1972. *L'Historien entre l'ethnologue et le futurologue*. Paris: Mouton.
EISENSTEIN, Zillah R. 1984. *Feminism and Sexual Equality: Crisis in Liberal Equality*. New York: Monthly Review Press.
EHRLICH, Victor. 1955. *Russian Formalism: History-Doctrine*. The Hague: Mouton.
ELSHTAIN, Jean Bethke. 1981. *Public Man, Private Woman: women in social and political thought*. New Jersey: Princeton University Press.

——, 1986. *Mediations on Modern Political Thought: Masculine/Feminine themes from Luther to Arendt*. New York: Praeger.
FEBVRE, Lucien. 1962. *Pour une histoire à part entière*. Paris: Sevpen.
——, 1973. *Combats pour l'histoire* in Burke, *A New Kind of History*.
——, & Martin, Henri-Jean. 1976. *The Coming of the Book: The Impact of Printing 1450–1800*. London: New Left Books.
——, 1977. *Life in Renaissance France*. Cambridge, Mass.: Harvard University Press.
——, 1982. *The Problem of Unbelief in the 16th Century: the religion of Rabelais*. Cambridge, Mass.: Harvard University Press.
——, undated. *Martin Luther: a Destiny*. New York: Dutton.
FELDMAN, Yael S. 1985. 'Poetics and Politics: Israeli literary criticism beween East and West'. *Proceedings of the American Academy for Jewish Research*, Vol. 52.
FERGUSON, Ann. 1986. 'Motherhood and Sexuality: some feminist questions'. *Hypatia*, Vol. 1, No. 2 (Fall)
FISH, Stanley. 1980. 'Interpreting the Variorum' in Jane P. Tompkins (ed.) *Reader-Response Criticism: from Formalism to Poststructuralism*. Baltimore: Johns Hopkins University Press.
FITCH, Brian T. 1985. 'The Status of Self-Translation'. *Texte* 4.
FOUCAULT, Michel et al. 1968. *Théorie d'ensemble*. Paris: Seuil.
——, 1973. *The Order of Things*. New York: Random House.
——, 1977a. 'The Political Function of the Intellectual'. *Radical Philosophy* 17.
——, 1977b. *Language, Counter-Memory, Practice: Selected Essays and Interviews*. ed. D. F. Bouchard. Oxford: Blackwell.
——, 1979. *Discipline and Punish*. New York: Random House.
——, 1980. *Power/Knowledge: Selected Interviews and other writings*, ed. C. Gordon. Brighton, England: Harvester Press.
——, 1982. 'Afterword' in Hubert L. Dreyfus & Paul Rabinow, *Michel Foucault: Beyond Structuralism and Hermeneutics*. Brighton: Harvester Press.
FREELAND, Cynthia. 1986. 'Woman: Revealed or Reveiled? *Hypatia*. Vol. 1, No. 1 (Fall).
FRIEDLANDER, Judith. 1990. *Vilna on the Seine: Jewish Intellectuals in France since 1968*. New Haven: Yale University Press.
FROW, John. 1986. *Marxism and Literary History*. Cambridge, Mass.: Harvard University Press.
FUSS, Diana J. 1989. 'Essentially speaking: Luce Irigaray's language of essence'. *Hypatia*, Vol. 3, No. 3 (Winter).
GALAN, F. W. 1985. *Historical Structures: The Prague School Project 1928–46*. Austin, Texas: University of Texas Press.
GARNER, Shirley Nelson et al. 1985. *The (M)other Tongue: Essays in Psychoanalytic Interpretation*. Ithaca: Cornell University Press.
GAUTHIER, Xavière. 1976. 'Pourquoi sorcières?' in Marks and Courtivron, *New French Feminisms*.
GEERTZ, Clifford. 1973. *The Interpretation of Cultures*. New York: Basic Books.
GILBERT, Allan H. (ed.) 1962. *Literary Criticism from Plato to Dryden*.

Detroit: Wayne State University Press.
GILLIGAN, C. 1982. *In a Different Voice*. Cambridge, Mass.: Harvard University Press.
GLEICK, James. 1987. *Chaos: Making a New Science*. New York: Viking.
GLYPH Textual Studies I. 1986. *Demarcating the Disciplines. Philosophy. Literature. Art.* Minneapolis: University of Minnesota Press.
GOODMAN, Nelson. 1976. *Languages of Art*. Indianapolis: Hackett.
——, 1978. *Ways of World-Making*. Indianapolis: Hackett.
——, 1984. *Of Mind and other Matters*. Cambridge, Mass.: Harvard University Press.
GORBACHEV, Mikhail. 1987. *Perestroika: New Thinking for our Country and the World*. New York: Harper & Row.
GOULDNER, Alvin. 1980. *The Two Marxisms: Contradictions and Anomalies in the development of Theory*. New York: Oxford University Press.
GRAFF, Gerald. 1987. *Professing Literature: An Institutional History*. Chicago: University of Chicago Press.
GRAHAM, Joseph (ed.). 1985. *Difference in Translation*. Ithaca: Cornell University Press.
——, 1990. 'Around and About Babel'. in Silverman and Aylesworth, *The Textual Sublime*.
GRAMSCI, Antonio. 1968. *The Modern Prince and Other Essays*. New York: International Publishers.
——, 1971. *Prison Notebooks: Selections*. New York: International Publishers.
GREENBLATT, Stephen. 1973. *Sir Walter Raleigh: The Renaissance Man and his Roles*. New Haven: Yale University Press.
——, 1980. *Renaissance Self-Fashioning from More to Shakespeare*. Chicago: University of Chicago Press.
——, 1988. *Shakespearean Negotiations: the circulation of social energy in Renaissance England*. Berkeley: University of California Press.
——. 1989. 'Towards a Poetics of Culture' in Veeser (ed.) *The New Historicism*.
GREENE, Gayle and KAHN, Coppelia. 1985. *Making a difference: Feminist Literary Criticism*. London: Methuen.
——, 1989. 'The Uses of Quarrelling' in Linda Kauffman (ed.) *Feminism and Institutions*. Cambridge: Blackwell.
GROSS, Elisabeth. 1987. 'Philosophy, Subjectivity and the Body: Kristeva and Irigaray', in Elizabeth Gross (ed.), *Feminist Challenges: Social and Political Theory*. Boston: Northeastern University Press.
GUTHKE, Karl S. 1990. *The Last Frontier: Imagining Other Worlds from the Copernican Revolution to Modern Science Fiction*. tr. H. Atkins. Ithaca: Cornell University Press.
HALL, Nor. 1980. *The Moon and the Virgin: reflections on the archetypal feminine*. New York: Harper & Row.
HALL, Stuart. 1988. 'The Toad in the Garden: Thatcherism among the Theorists', in Nelson & Grossberg, *Marxism and the Interpretation of Culture*.
HARDING, Sandra. 1986. 'The instability of the analytical categories of feminist theory'. *Signs*, Vol. 11, No. 4 (Summer).

———, 1987. *Feminism and Methodology*. Milton Keynes: Open University Press.
HAYLES, N. Katherine. 1990. *Chaos Bound: Orderly Disorder in Contemporary Literature and Science*. Ithaca: Cornell University Press.
HAWKESWORTH, Mary E. 1989. 'Knowers, Knowing, Known: feminist theory and claims of truth'. *Signs*, Vol. 14, No. 3 (Spring).
HELLER, Thomas C. *et al*. 1986. *Reconstructing Individualism: Autonomy, Individuality and the Self in Western Thought*. Stanford: Stanford University Press.
HERMANN, Claudine. 1976. *Les Voleuses de la langue*. Paris: des femmes.
HERMANS, Theo. 1985. *The Manipulation of Literature: Studies in Literary Translation*. New York: St. Martin's Press.
HOBSBAWM, Eric & Ranger, Terence (ed.). 1983 *The Invention of Tradition*. Cambridge: Cambridge University Press.
HOLSTEIN, Hans Jürgen. 1974. *Homo Cyberneticus*. Uppsala: Sociografica.
HORKHEIMER, Max. 1972. *Critical Theory: Selected Essays*. New York: Herder & Herder.
———, 1974. *The Eclipse of Reason*. New York: Seabury Press.
———, & Adorno, T.W. *Dialectics of the Enlightenment*.
HOWARD, Jean E. 1986. 'The New Historicism in Renaissance Studies'. *English Literary Renaissance*, 16 (Winter).
HUMM, Peter *et al*. 1986. *Popular Fictions: Essays in Literature and History*. London: Methuen.
IRIGARAY, Luce. 1980. *Amante Marine de Friedrich Nietzsche*. Paris: Minuit.
———, 1981. *Le corps-à-corps avec la mère*. Montreal: Éditions de la pleine lune.
———, 1982. *Passions Élémentaires*. Paris: Minuit.
———, 1983. *La Croyance Même*. Paris: Galilée.
———, 1984. *Éthique de la différence sexuelle*. Paris: Minuit.
———, 1985a. *That Sex which is not One*. New York: Cornell University Press.
———, 1985b. *Parler n'est jamais neutre*. Paris: Minuit.
———, 1987. *Sexes et Parentés*. Paris: Minuit.
———, 1989. 'Sorcerer Love'. *Hypatia*, Vol. 3, No. 3 (Winter).
JACOB, François. 1982. *The Possible and the Actual*. Seattle: University of Washington Press.
JAKOBSON, Roman. 1963. *Essais de Linguistique Générale. I. Les fondations du langage*. Paris: Minuit.
———, 1973. *Essais de linguistique Générale. II. Rapports internes et externes de la langue*. Paris: Minuit.
———, 1978. *Six Lectures on Sound and Meaning*. tr. J. Mepham. Brighton: Harvester.
JAMESON, Frederic. 1981. *The Political Unsconscious*. Ithaca: Cornell University Press.
JARDINE, Alice A. 1985. *Gynesis: Configurations of Women and Modernity*. Ithaca: Cornell University Press.
———, & MENKE, Anne M. 1991. *Shifting Scenes: Interviews on Women, Writing and Politics in Post-68 France*. New York: Columbia University Press.

JAY, Gregory S. 1987. 'Values and Deconstructions: Derrida, Saussure, Marx'. *Cultural Critique* (Winter).

——, 1990. *America the Scrivener: Deconstruction and the Subject of Literary History*. Ithaca: Cornell University Press.

JOHNSON, Barbara. 1985. 'Taking Fidelity Philosophically' in Graham (ed.) *Difference In Translation*.

JONES, Gareth Stedman (ed.). 1982. *Culture, Ideology and Politics*. London: Routledge.

KAUFFMAN, Linda (ed.). 1989. *Feminism and Institutions: Dialogues in Feminist Theory*. Cambridge: Blackwell.

KAVANAGH, James A. 1982. 'Marxism's Althusser: Towards a Politics of Literary Theory'. *Diacritics* (Spring).

KERKHOFF, Manfred. 1985. 'Timeliness and Translation'. *Texte* 4.

KING, Deborah. 1988. 'Multiple Jeopardy, Multiple Consciousness: the context of Black Feminist Ideology'. *Signs*, Vol. 14. No. 1 (Autumn).

KOELB, Clayton & LOKKE, Virgil. 1987. *The Current in Criticism: Essays on the Present and Future of Literary Theory*. Indiana: Purdue University Press.

KUHIWCZAK, Piotr. 1990. 'Translation as Appropriation: the case of Milan Kundera's *The Joke*', in Bassnett & Lefevere (eds), *Translation, History, Culture*.

KUYKENDALL, Eleonor. 1983. 'Towards an ethic of nurturance: Luce Irigaray on mothering and power', in Trebilcot (ed.), *Mothering: Essays in Feminist Theory*.

LACAN, Jacques. 1978. *Le Seminaire II: Le Moi dans la théorie de Freud et dans la technique de la psychanalyse*. Paris: Seuil.

LACAPRA, Dominick & KAPLAN, Steven L. (eds). 1982. *Modern European Intellectual History: Reappraisals and New Perspectives*. Ithaca: Cornell University Press.

——, (eds). 1983. *Rethinking Intellectual History*. Ithaca: Cornell University Press.

——, 1987. *History, Politics, and the Novel*. Ithaca: Cornell University Press.

LACLAU, Ernesto & MOUFFE, Chantal. 1985. *Hegemony and Socialist Strategy. Towards a Radical Democratic Politics*. London: Verso.

LACOUE-LABARTHE, Philippe & NANCY, Jean-Luc. 1973. *Le titre de la lettre. (une lecture de Lacan)*. Paris: Galilée.

——, (eds). 1981a. *Les Fins de l'Homme: à partir de Jacques Derrida*. Paris: Galilée.

——, 1981b. 'Le peuple juif ne rêve pas'. in Rassial, *La Psychanalyse est-elle une histoire juive?*

LACOUE-LABARTHE, Philippe. 1975. 'Typographies'. in Agacinski *et al*. *Mimesis desarticulations*.

——, 1978a. 'La Césure du Speculatif' in Hölderlin. *L'Antigone de Sophocle*. Paris: Christan Bourgois.

——, 1978b. *L'absolu Littéraire*. Paris: Seuil.

——, 1979. *Le Sujet de la Philosophie (Typographies I)*. Paris: Flammarion.

——, 1986. *L'imitation des Modernes (Typographies II)*. Paris: Flammarion.

LAMBERTON, Robert. 1986. *Homer the Theologian: NeoPlatonic Allegorical*

Reading and the Growth of the Epic Tradition. Berkeley: University of California Press.
LARUELLE, François. 1980. *Textes pour Emmanuel Levinas.* Paris: Jean-Michel Place.
LEAVEY, John P. Jr. 1986. *Glassary.* Lincoln. University of Nebraska Press.
——, 1990. 'Lations, Cor, Trans, Re, etc' in Silverman & Aylesworth (eds). *The Textual Sublime.*
LE DOEUF, Michelle. 1980. In *Moi* (ed.), *French Feminist Thought.*
LEFEBVRE, Henri. 1968. *La Vie Quotidienne dans le Monde Moderne.* Paris: Gallimard.
LEFEVERE, André. 1977. *Translating Literature: the German Tradition from Luther to Rosenzweig.* Amsterdam: Van Gorcum.
——, 1990. 'Translation its genealogy in the West' in Bassnett & Lefevere (eds), *Translation, History, Culture.*
LENIN, 1961. *State and Revolution.* in Arthur P. Mendel (ed.), *Essential Works of Marxism.* New York: Bantam.
——, 1971. *What is to be done?* New York: International Publishers.
LEVINAS, Emmanuel. 1965. *Totalité et Infini.* La Haye: Martinus Nijhoff.
——, 1974. *Autrement Qu'être ou au-delà de l'essence.* La Hague: Martinus Nijhoff.
——, 1982. *De Dieu Qui Vient à l'Idée.* Paris: Vrin.
LEWIS, David. 1986. *On the Plurality of Worlds.* Oxford: Blackwell.
LEWIS, Philip E. 1985. 'The measure of translation effects' in Graham (ed.), *Difference in Translation.*
LOCKE, John. 1976. *The Second Treatise on Government.* Oxford: Blackwell.
LOUX, Michael J. 1979. *The Possible and the Actual.* Ithaca: Cornell University Press.
LUKÁCS, Georg. 1964. *Studies in European Realism.* New York: Grosset & Dunlap.
——, 1970. 'Entwicklungsgeschichte des modernen Dramas', in Peter Ludz (ed.), *Literatursoziologie.* Neuwied: Luchterhand.
——, 1971a. *History and Class Consciousness.* Cambridge, Mass.: The MIT Press.
——, 1971b. *Probleme des Realismus I, Werke, Vol. IV.* Neuwied: Luchterhand.
LYOTARD, Jean-François. 1973. *Dérive à partir de Marx et Freud.* Paris: Union Générale d'Editions.
——, 1984. *The Postmodern Condition.* Minneapolis: University of Minnesota Press.
——, 1988. *Peregrinations: Law, Form, Event.* New York: Columbia University Press.
MACHEREY, Pierre. 1978. *A Theory of Literary Production.* London: Routledge.
——, 'The Problem of Reflection'. *Substance* 15.
MACURA, Vladimír. 1990. 'Culture as Translation'. in Bassnett & Lefevere (eds), *Translation, History, Culture.*
MACKINNON, Catherine A. 1988. 'Desire and Power: A Feminist Perspective', in Nelson & Grossberg, *Marxism and the Interpretation of*

Culture.
MAIDMENT, Robert & BRONSTEIN, Russell. 1973. *Simulation Games: Design and Implementation*. Ohio: Merrill.
MAITRE, Doreen. 1983. *Literature and Possible Worlds*. London: Pembridge Press.
MARKS, Elaine & DE CORTIVRON, Isabelle (eds). 1980. *New French Feminisms: An Anthology*. Mass.: University of Massachusetts Press.
MARX, Karl. 1970a. *Preface to the Critique of Political Economy*. New York: International Publishers.
———, 1970b. *The German Ideology*. New York: International Publishers.
———, 1971. *The Poverty of Philosophy*. New York: International Publishers.
MASCIA-LEES, Frances E et al. 1989. 'The Postmodern Turn in Anthropology: cautions from a feminist perspective'. *Signs*, Vol. 15, No. 1 (Autumn).
MELAND, Bernard E. 1976. *Fallible Forms and Symbols*. Philadelphia: Fortress Press.
MERRELL, Floyd. 1983. *Pararealities: the Nature of our Fictions and How we know them*. Amsterdam: John Benjamins.
———, 1985. *Deconstruction Reframed*. Indiana: Purdue University Press.
MESCHONNIC, Henri. 1973. *Pour la Poétique II. Epistémologie de l'écriture. Poétique de la traduction*. Paris: Gallimard.
MILLER, J. Hillis. 1984. 'Thomas Hardy, Jacques Derrida and the Dislocation of Souls' in Smith & Kerrigan (eds), *Taking Chances*.
MOI, Toril. 1987. *French Feminist Thought: A Reader*. Oxford: Blackwell.
MONDADORI, Fabrizio & MORTON, Adam. 1979. 'Modal Realism: the Poisoned Pawn' in Loux (ed.), *The Possible and the Actual*.
MONTROSE, Louis. 1986. 'Renaissance Literary Studies'. In *English Literary Renaissance*, 16:1 (Winter).
———, 1989. 'Professing the Renaissance: Studies in Marxist Dialectics'. In Veeser (ed.), *The New Historicism*.
MOORE, A. W. 1990. *The Infinite*. London: Routledge.
MOUFFE, Chantal. 1988. 'Hegemony and New Political Subjects: Towards a New Concept of Democracy' in Nelson & Grossberg, *Marxism and the Interpretation of Culture*.
MOYAL, Gabriel. 1985. 'La traduction et ses interprétations: les songes de Descartes'. *Texte* 4
MUNITZ, Milton K. 1990. *The Question of Reality*. New Jersey: Princeton University Press.
MURRIN, Michael. 1969. *The Veil of Allegory: some notes towards a theory of allegorical rhetoric in the Renaissance*. Chicago: University of Chicago Press.
NANCY, Jean-Luc. 1973. *La Remarque Spéculative: un bon mot de Hegel*. Paris: Galilée.
———, 1976. *Le Discours de la Syncope. 1. Logodaedalus*. Paris: Flammarion.
———, 1979. *Ego Sum*. Paris: Flammarion.
———, 1982. *Le Partage des Voix*. Paris: Galilée.
———, 1983. *L'Impératif Catégorique*. Paris: Flammarion.
———, 1986. *La Communauté desoeuvrée*. Paris: Christan Bourgois.
———, 1987. *Des lieux divins*. Mauvezin: Trans-Europ-Repress.

Bibliography

NEELY, Carol Thomas. 1988. 'Constructing the Subject: Feminist Practice and the New Renaissance Discourse'. *English Literary Renaissance* (Spring).
NELSON, Cary & GROSSBERG, Lawrence (eds). 1988. *Marxism and the Interpretation of Culture*. Urbana: University of Illinois Press.
NEUMANN, Erich. 1955. *The Great Mother: An analysis of the Archetype*. New York: Pantheon.
NORRIS, Christopher. 1985. *The Contest of Faculties: Philosophy and Theory After Deconstruction*. London: Methuen.
NYE, Andrea. 1989. 'The Hidden Host: Irigaray and Diotima at Plato's Symposium'. *Hypatia*, Vol. 3, No. 3 (Winter).
O'BRIEN, Mary. 1989. *Reproducing the World: Essays in Feminist Thought*. Boulder: Westview Press.
OFFEN, Karen. 1988. 'Defining Feminisms: A Comparative Historical Approach'. *Signs*, Vol. 14, No. 1 (Autumn).
PAGELS, Elaine. 1979. *The Gnostic Gospels*. New York: Random House.
PARRINDER, Patrick. 1987. *The Failure of Theory: Essays on Criticism and Contemporary Fiction*. Brighton: Harvester.
PATAI, Raphael. 1967. *The Hebrew Goddess*. New York: Ktav.
PAULSON, William R. 1988. *The Noise of Culture: Literary Texts in a World of Information*. Ithaca: Cornell University Press.
PAVEL, Thomas. 1986. *Fictional Worlds*. Cambridge, Mass.: Harvard University Press.
PÊCHEUX, Michel. 1988. 'Discourse: Structure or event?' in Nelson & Grossberg (eds), *Marxism and the Interpretation of Culture*.
PICO DELLA MIRANDOLA. 1977. *On the Dignity of Man*. Indianapolis: Bobbs Merrill.
POSTER, Mark. 1990. *The Mode of Information: Poststructuralism and Social Context*. Chicago: University of Chicago Press.
QUILLIGAN, Maureen. 1979. *The Language of Allegory*. Ithaca: Cornell University Press.
RABINE, Leslie Wahl. 1988. 'A feminist politics of non-identity'. *Feminist Studies*, Vol. 14, No. 1 (Spring).
RABUZZI, Kathryn Allen. 1988. *Motherself: a mythic analysis of motherhood*. Bloomington: Indiana University Press.
RAE, Alistair I. M. 1986. *Quantum Physics: Illusion or Reality?* Cambrige: Cambridge University Press.
RASSIAL, Adélie & Jean-Jacques (eds). 1981. *La Psychanalyse est-elle une histoire juive?* Paris: Seuil.
RAY, William. 1984. *Literary Meaning from Phenomenology to Deconstruction*. Oxford: Blackwell.
RESCHER, Nicholas. 1969. *Essays in Philosophical Analysis*. Pittsburgh: University of Pittsburgh Press.
——, 1975. *A Theory of Possibility*. Oxford: Blackwell.
——, 1979. 'The Ontology of the Possible'. In Loux (ed.) *The Possible and the Actual*.
RICH, Adrienne. 1976. *Of Woman Born: motherhood as experience and institution*. New York: Norton.
RICHARDSON, Samuel. 1962. *Clarissa*. London: Everyman, 4 vols.

RIFATERRE, Michael. 1990. *Fictional Truth*. Baltimore: Johns Hopkins Press.
ROBINSON, Douglas. 1991. *The Translator's Turn*. Baltimore: Johns Hopkins Press.
ROSS, Andrew (ed.). 1988. *Universal Abandon? The Politics of Postmodernism*. Minneapolis: University of Minnesota Press.
RYAN, Michael. 1982. *Marxism and Deconstruction: A Critical Articulation*. Baltimore: Johns Hopkins Press.
SAMUEL, Raphael & JONES, Gareth Stedman (eds). 1982. *Culture, Ideology and Politics: Essays for Eric Hobsbawm*. London: Routledge.
SAWICKI, Jana. 1986. 'Foucault and Feminism: Towards a Politics of Difference'. *Hypatia*, Vol. 1, No. 2 (Fall).
SCHNEIDER, Michel. 1985. *Voleurs de mots: essai sur le plagiat, la psychanalyse et la pensée*. Paris: Gallimard.
SCOTT, Joan W. 1988. 'Deconstructing Equality-vs-Difference: or, the uses of poststructuralist theory for feminism'. *Feminist Studies*, Vol. 14, No. 1 (Spring).
SCHOR, Naomi. 1985. *Breaking the Chain: Women, Theory and French Realist Fiction*. New York: Columbia University Press.
SHANNON, Robert E. 1975. *Systems Simulation: the art and science*. New Jersey: Prentice Hall.
SILVERMAN, Hugh J. & AYLESWORTH, Gary E. (eds). 1990. *The Textual Sublime. Deconstruction and its Differences*. Albany: State University of New York Press.
SILVERMAN, Hugh J. & IHDE, Don (eds). 1985. *Hermeneutics and Deconstruction*. Albany: State University of New York Press.
SILVERMAN, Kaja. 1983. *The Subject of Semiotics*. New York: Oxford University Press.
SIMPSON, David. 1988. 'Literary Criticism and the Return to "History"', *Critical Inquiry* 14 (Summer).
SLAWINSKI, Janusz. 1988. 'Reading and Reader in the Literary Historical Process'. *New Literary History*, Vol. 19, No. 3 (Spring).
SMITH, Adam. 1979. *The Theory of Moral Sentiments*. ed. D. D. Raphael & A. L. Macfie. Oxford: Clarendon Press.
SMITH, Charlotte. 1971. *Emmeline*. London: Oxford University Press.
SMITH, Dorothy E. 1987. 'Women's perspective as a radical critique of sociology'. In Harding (ed.), *Feminism and Methodology*.
SMITH, Janet Farrell. 1986. 'Possessive Power'. *Hypatia*, Vol. 1, No. 2 (Fall).
SMITH, Joseph & KERRIGAN, William (eds). 1984. *Taking Chances: Derrida, Psychoanalysis and Literature*. Baltimore: Johns Hopkins University Press.
SMITH, Ruth L. & VALENZE, Deborah M. 1988. 'Mutuality and Marginality: Liberal Moral Theory and Working Class Women in 19th Century England'. *Signs*, Vol. 13, No. 2 (Winter).
SONNTAG, Susan. 1989. 'Against Interpretation'. Reprinted in David H. Richter (ed.). *The Critical Tradition*. New York: St. Martin's Press.
SOSNOSKI, James J. 1989. 'A Mindless Man-Driven Theory Machine: Intellectuality, Sexuality and the Institution of Criticism'. In Linda Kauffman (ed.) *Feminism and Institutions*.

SPIVAK, Gayatri. 1977. 'Glass Pieces'. *Diacritics* 7 (Fall).
——, 1988. *In Other Worlds: Essays in Cultural Politics*. New York: Routledge.
STEINER, George. 1975. *After Babel: Aspects of Language and Translation*. London: Oxford University Press.
STOCK, Brian. 1990. *Listening for the Text: on the uses of the past*. Baltimore: Johns Hopkins University Press.
TAVOR, Eve. 1982. 'Art and Alienation: Lukács' Late Aesthetic'. *Orbis Litterarum* (Winter).
——, 1987. *Scepticism, Society and the 18th Century Novel*. London: Macmillan.
TERDIMAN, Richard. 1985. 'Deconstructing Memory: on representing the past and theorizing culture in France since the Revolution'. *Diacritics* Vol. 15, No. 4 (Winter).
TODD, Janet. 1988. *Feminist Literary Theory*. London: Routledge.
TONG, Rosemarie. 1989. *Feminist Thought*. London: Westview Press.
TREBILCOT, Joyce (ed.). 1983. *Mothering: Essays in Feminist Theory*. New Jersey: Rowman & Allanheld.
ULMER, Gregory. 1986. 'Sounding the Unconscious' in Leavey (ed.) *Glassary*.
VAIHINGER, H. 1968. *The Philosophy of As If*. London: Routledge.
VAINA, Lucia. 1977. 'Introduction: les mondes possibles du texte' and 'Un modèle du mythe du 'grand passage' chez les Roumains', both in *Versus, Théorie des mondes possibles et sémiotique textuelle*, Vol. 17.
VALVERDE, Mariana. 1989. 'Beyond Gender Dangers and Private Pleasures: theory and ethics in the sex debates'. *Feminist Studies* Vol. 15, No. 2 (Summer).
VAN BUREN, Jane Silverman. 1989. *The Modernist Madonna: Semiotics of the Maternal Metaphor*. Bloomington: Indiana Press.
VAN DYKE, Carolynn. 1985. *The Fiction of Truth: Structures of Meaning in Narrative and Dramatic Allegory*. Ithaca: Cornell University Press.
VEESER, H. Aram (ed.). 1989. *The New Historicism*. London: Routledge.
VETTERLIN-BRAGIN, Mary (ed.). 1982. *Femininity, Masculinity and Androgyny: A modern philosophical discussion*. New Jersey: Rowman & Allanheld.
WEBER, Samuel. 1984. 'The debts of deconstruction and other related assumptions'. In Smith & Kerrigan (eds), *Taking Chances*.
——, 1986. 'Caught in the act of reading'. In *Glyph Textual Studies I, Demarcating the Disciplines*.
——, 1987. *Institution and Interpretation*. Minneapolis: University of Minnesota Press.
WHITE, Hayden. 1978. *Tropics of Discourse: Essays in Cultural Criticism*. Baltimore: Johns Hopkins Press.
——, 1987. *The Content of the Form: Narrative Discourse and Historical Representation*. Baltimore: Johns Hopkins University Press.
——, 1989. '"Figuring the nature of the times deceased", Literary Theory and Historical Writing'. In Cohen (ed.), *The Future of Literary Theory*.
WILLIAMS, Raymond. 1977. *Marxism and Literature*. Oxford: Oxford University Press.
——, 1980. *Problems in Materialism and Culture: Selected Essays*. London:

Verso.
WIMSATT, James I. 1970. *Allegory and Mirror: Tradition and Structure in Middle English Literature*. New York: Pegasus.
WOLF, Fred Alan. 1981. *Taking the Quantum Leap*. San Francisco: Harper & Row.
——, 1988. *Parallel Universes: the search for other worlds*. New York: Simon & Schuster.
WOOD, David. 1989. *The Deconstruction of Time*. New Jersey: Humanities Press International.
WOOD, David & BERNASCONI, Robert (eds). 1985. *Derrida and Différance*. Coventry: Parousia Press.
WOODS, John. 1974. *The Logic of Fiction*. The Hague: Mouton.
ZAGARELL, Sandra A. 1988. 'Narrative Community: the identification of a Genre'. *Signs*, Vol. 13, No. 3 (Spring).
ZIGFELD, Richard. 1989. 'Interactive Fiction: a new literary genre?' *New Literary History*. Vol. 20, 341-372.

Index

Abraham, Nicolas, 70
Abt, Clark, 142, 148, 149
Adorno. T. W., 15, 16, 19, 22.
Allegory, theories of, 65–6, 125, 132–140
Althusser, Louis, 5, 6, 7, 8, 13, 17, 41, 177
Annales School, 1, 2, 8, 27
Aquinas, St. Thomas, 46–8
Aristotle, 46–8, 116
Atomists, 116
Aylesworth, Gary, 165

Bakhtin, 11, 22
Bal, Mieke, 155
Balibar, Etienne, 15
Bayle, 190
Banks, Jerry, 147
Barney, Stephen, 136
Barthes, Roland, 15, 30, 158–9
Bassnett, Susan, 165, 168, 169
Baudrillard, Jean, 142, 162
Bauman, Zygmnt, 179, 180, 183
Beauvoir, Simone de, 88
Beckett, 182
Benjamin, Walter, 176, 178, 184–5
Bentham, Jeremy, 115
Black Studies, 27, 39
Blanchot, 61, 83
Bloch, Ernst, 1
Bloomfield, Morton, 135
Bohr, 109
Bolingbroke, 189
Bolter, J., 143
Borch-Jakobsen, Mikkel, 71–2
Bourdieu, Pierre, 159–161, 162, 173
Bradley, Raymond, 118
Brower, Reuben, 164
Brunton, Mary, 125, 126–7, 128, 129
Burney, Fanny, 125–6, 128, 129

Carson, John, 147
Cauldwell, Christopher, 4

Charlemagne, 136
Chartier, Roger, 25
Chaucer, 136
Christian, Barbara, 88
Clarissa, 127, 153–6
Clement of Alexandria, 124
Cixous, Helene, 93
Colella, 141
Cornforth, Maurice, 23
Cresswell, M. J., 116, 151
Cultural Materialism, ix, 1, 2, 8, 10, 14, 29

Dante, 133–5, 136
Darnton, Robert, 8
Deconstruction, ix, 13, 14, 16, 50–3, 85, 101, 104, 138, 139–40, 159, 163, 165
(De)construction, ix, 50–87, 95, 104, 140, 193
Delabastita, Dirk, 180
De Man, Paul, 15, 135, 136, 138
Demetz, Peter, 1
Derrida, Jacques, 6, 14, 15, 27, 50, 52, 53, 58, 59–68, 69, 74, 75, 76, 80–7, 90, 95, 96, 140, 158, 165, 166–7, 168, 169, 171, 172, 173, 174, 175, 176, 177, 178, 183, 184–9, 191–2
Donchin, Ann, 92
Dryden, 164
Dungeons and Dragons, 143, 144, 145–6, 147–50

Eagleton, Terry, 15
Eco, Umberto, 117, 152
Elshtain, Jean Bethke, 92
Emmeline, 125–30
Engels, 2
Evalina, 125–30

Faerie Queene, The, 136

223

Index

Febvre, Lucien, 7, 16, 22, 33–7, 38, 40, 41
Feminist Theory, ix, 27, 39, 88–112, 160, 183
Feuerbach, 72
Fielding, Henry, 115
Fitch, Brian, 182, 183
Foucault, Michel, 6, 8, 13, 33, 37–41, 42, 44, 45, 52, 193
Frank, R. W. Jr, 135
Frankfurt School, 1, 2, 8, 11, 16
Freud, 53, 54, 69, 72
Frye, Northrop, 138

Galileo, 124
Gauthier, Xaviere, 94
Geertz, Clifford, 43, 107
Gellner, Ernest, 190, 191
Genet, 187, 189
Gleick, James, 193
Godard, Barbara, 166
Goethe, 172
Goldmann, Lucien, 5, 8
Goodman, Nelson, 114–15, 140, 151
Gorbachev, Mikhail, 24–6
Gouldner, Alvin, 9
Graf, Gerald, 161–2
Gramsci, 26
Greenblatt, Stephen, 6, 15, 33, 41–4, 45
Grossberg, Louis, 21

Hall, Nor, 92
Hall, Stuart, 24
Harding, Sandra, 89, 94
Hayles, Katherine, 192, 193
Hegel, 3, 44, 69, 105, 176, 177, 187, 188
Heidegger, 51, 57, 61, 83, 176, 177, 178, 183
Hermann, Claudine, 94
Hessiod, 193
Hillis Miller, 168
Hintikka, Jaakko, 116
History, theories of, 1, 3–4, 18–26, 29–44, 52, 58–9, 79, 100, 121–5, 177, 188–194
Holstein, 142
Horkheimer, 6, 16, 22, 114

Hugo, Victor, 181
Humanism, 9–11, 31–33, 34
Hume, 115

Irigaray, Luce, 78, 90, 95–100, 101, 102, 103, 104, 105, 106, 107, 109, 110, 183

Jacob, Francois, 122–3
Jakobson, 158, 164, 166–7, 170, 185–6, 187
Jameson, Frederic, 168
Jardine, Alice, 80, 172
Jerussaleme Liberata, 136
Johnson, Samuel, 164, 190
Joyce, 83, 178

King Lear, 137–8
Kripke, Saul, 116
Kristeva, 89
Kuhiwczak, Piotr, 182

Lacan, 10, 27, 43, 53, 54, 68, 69, 71, 72, 82, 109
Laclau, Ernesto, 7, 20
Lacoue-Labarthe, Philippe, 50, 54–8, 60, 61, 68, 69, 71, 72, 73, 75, 76, 77, 82, 177
Lazaro, Rayes, 92
Le Doeuff, Michelle, 88, 94
Lefevere, Henri, 165, 168, 169, 181
Leibnitz, 116
Lenin, 3, 4, 11, 19, 24, 26–28
Levinas, 50, 51, 58, 63, 64, 68–9, 76, 77, 78, 79, 80–1, 86, 171
Lewis, David, 116
Lewis, Philip, 174
Locke, 125
Lotman, Yuri, 5
Lukacs, Georg, 5, 8, 13, 14, 15, 20, 22, 26
Luther, 35–6, 40
Luxemburg, Rosa, 11
Lyotard, 20, 28, 158

Macherey, Pierre, 15,
MacKinnon, Catherine, 24
Mackenzie, Henry, 129
Macura, Vladimir, 181–2

Index

Maidment, Robert, 141
Maitre, Doreen, 117, 119, 120, 121, 151, 157
Mandadori, Fabrizio, 118
Marini, Marcelle, 172
Marx, 1, 3, 5, 6, 9, 10, 11, 12, 13, 17, 18, 19, 21, 31, 44, 46, 52, 58, 72, 79, 176, 177
Marxism, 1, 2, 4, 10, 14, 16, 19, 21, 23, 25, 34–5, 38, 52, 58, 79, 89, 162, 177
Marxist Paradigm, 1, 3–4, 5–28, 29–44, 46–9, 53, 85, 108, 111, 122, 162–3, 169, 181
Meland, Bernard, 135
Menke, Ann, 172
Merrell, Floyd, 117, 118, 119, 120, 121, 140, 151
Meschonnic, Henri, 166, 167–8
Montrose, Louis, 8, 45
More, Hanna, 128
More, Thomas, 42
Morton, Adam, 118
Mouffe, Chantal, 7, 20, 25
Moyal, Gabriel, 171
Murrin, Michael, 124, 135, 137

Nancy, Jean-Luc, 7, 29, 33, 50, 51–2, 58, 62, 68, 69, 71, 72–3, 76, 82, 85, 177
Nelson, Cary, 21
Newmann, Eric, 90–1
New Criticism, 2, 104, 162, 169
New Historicism, ix, 1, 2, 8, 10, 14, 16, 17, 23, 29, 41, 107–8
  see also History, theories of
Newton, 114
Nietzsche, x, 39, 41, 83, 176, 177

O'Brien, Mary, 92
Origen, 124
Orlando Furioso, 136

Parmenides, 116
Pavel, Thomas, 113, 117, 119, 120, 151, 152, 153
Pecheux, Michel, 25
Pico della Mirandola, 31, 32
Piers Ploughman, 136

Plantinga, Alvin, 116
Plato, 46, 55–58, 83, 167, 175
Plekhanov, 4
Ponge, 83, 178
Postmarxism, 1, 7, 10, 11, 17, 19, 21, 23, 24, 58, 78, 101, 104, 111, 180
Poststructuralism, ix, xi, 1, 2, 4, 7, 8, 10, 11, 13, 14, 15, 16, 17, 19, 27, 29, 30, 32, 36, 41, 48–9, 101, 104, 107, 108, 111, 113, 114, 117, 159, 169, 180, 190
Psyche, theories of, 34, 35, 36, 53, 54, 56–7, 68–73, 74–5, 77, 78, 115

Quilligan, Maureen, 124–5, 134, 135, 136

Rabelais, 36, 40
Rabbuzi, Kathryn Allen, 92
Rabine, Lesley Wahl, 94
Reader Reception Theory, 1, 2, 10, 14, 156–7
Rescher, Nicholas, 116–17, 118
Rich, Adrienne, 91
Richardson, Samuel, 127, 153
Riffaterre, Michel, 119, 153
Robinson, Douglas, 168, 171, 174
Rose, Hilary, 92
Roussel, Raymond, 39

Said, Edward, 27
Saussure, Ferdinand de, 170, 187, 189
Sawicki, Jana, 94
Scott, Joan, 91
Schneider, Michel, 86
Schwartz, Norman, 118
Scramble Books, 144–5
Shakespeare, 137–8, 139
Shannon, Robert, 141, 146, 150
Sheridan, 127
Self-Control, 125–30
Semiology, 17, 107
Smith, Adam, 129
Smith, Charlotte, 125, 126, 127, 128, 129
Smith, Dorothy, 107, 108
Smith, Ruth, 93

Socrates, 56, 124, 167, 175
Sonntag, Susan, 139
Spenser, 137
Spivak, Gayatri, 13, 27
Steiner, George, 163, 169, 170, 171
Structuralism, xi, 1, 5, 10, 11, 14, 117, 123, 192

Trotsky, 3, 124

Vaihinger, Hans, 114
Valenze, Deborah, 93
Van Dyke, Carolynn, 132, 133, 136

Van Gogh, 59, 140
Vaina, Lucia, 151
Voltaire, 116

Walton, Kendall, 119
Weber, Samuel, 85
Williams, Raymond, 17, 22
Wimsatt, James, 133, 135
Wittgenstein, 2
Wolf, Fred Alan, 133
Wollstonecraft, Mary, 154
Woods, John, 119, 152

Zhdanov, Andrei A., 4, 12
Zigfeld, Richard, 149